Wyoming:
The Paradox of Plenty

Wyoming:
The Paradox of Plenty

THE ALLURE AND RISK OF A MINERAL ECONOMY

David Freudenthal

WordsWorth ✳ *Cody, Wyoming*

ACKNOWLEDGEMENTS

My thanks to the Good Lord for the time he allows me on this earth.

My heartfelt gratitude to Nancy my life partner for more than 40 years, Hillary, Bret, and Katie for making life a wonderful, ever-changing adventure!

I am grateful to the many people who have helped find data and documents. Most particularly the Wyoming Division of Research and Statistics, ably led by Wenlin Liu, Administrator and Chief Economist and Don Richards, Budget and Fiscal Administrator with the Legislative Service Office. Everyone at the Wyoming State Library went above and beyond in guiding me through the maze and finding obscure documents.

Included in this note of thanks are my friends Paul Lang, Jack Speight, Rob Hurless, and Chris Boswell. They were incredibly patient as I worked through various drafts and ideas. Our modern Wyoming historian, Phil Roberts provided kind encouragement to risk looking at history through an economic/tax policy lens.

Renée Tafoya was a dedicated editor with a keen eye for detail. She gracefully reviewed and edited poorly typed, painfully long, lawyer paragraphs.

Readers will no doubt find mistakes and perceived errors of judgment. All of which are my responsibility.

ISBN 978-1-7334897-0-6
Library of Congress Control Number: 2022921565
First edition paperback

Editor: Renée C. Tafoya

Cover photo: Drew Halverson
Douglas, Wyoming / United States - September 30, 2017: A BNSF Railway loaded coal train climbs out of the Powder River Basin in Wyoming.

Author photo: Wyoming State Archives

Published by WordsWorth
Cody, Wyoming
www.wordsworthpublishing.com

Printed in the United States of America

CONTENTS

INTRODUCTION

*"Our children and grandchildren leave to
find a job and build their future elsewhere."*

In commodity dependent regions of the United States, it's a common complaint. Whether the commodity is agricultural or mineral, the complaint is eventually voiced by the residents who remain when the economy no longer attaches significant value to the region's production. Similar voices have been heard in areas dependent on a manufacturing economy, such as textiles or furniture. Common to all these is a deep—often historical—over dependence on a single industry or industrial sector for jobs, economic activity, and tax revenues to support public services. Wyoming may be foremost among a handful of states wherein the complaint has been virtually statewide for nearly half a century. Wyoming's economy is consistently ranked among the least diversified in the United States. Originally based on agriculture, the state soon transformed into a minerals-based economy—largely energy minerals. Buffeted by the ups and downs of commodity markets, citizens either leave or adopt a stoic attitude. "It is what it is" summarizes an attitude of accepting the future will be like the past. Ultimately the future does not replicate the past. Mark Twain observed, "History does not repeat itself, but it often rhymes."

People are smart and they know in their gut that history does not repeat and sometimes doesn't even rhyme. Nearly every gathering of any size in Wyoming eventually turns to a discussion of the need to create jobs, diversify the tax base, and grow alternative economic sectors. Inevitably someone brings up Wyoming's singular dependence on the mineral industry for employment and tax revenues. "How did this happen," they ask. After some wringing of hands and gnashing of teeth, the discussion dies, and everyone returns to daily life. But the discussion shouldn't end. After one such discussion, my friend Butch, a successful Cheyenne businessman, asked how Wyoming became so dependent on mineral taxes. Having been honored to serve as Wyoming's governor, I felt obligated to answer. "It was the passage of the first mineral severance tax in 1969, which coincidentally was the year I graduated from high school."

Upon reflection, my response seemed too glib and hollow. A substantive reply needed research. Sadly, the answer is contrary to Wyoming's aspirational attachment to the Cowboy Ethic—the ruggedly independent, self-made, carry-your-own-weight Westerner. Wyoming's reliance, some would argue addiction, to mineral revenues is not the consequence of a single action. A series of decisions and non-decisions over more than 100 years cemented this reliance. Wyoming's experience is not necessarily applicable to every state in America, but it certainly echoes within regions of a given state.

Wyoming's history and economy present an object lesson in, or a striking example of, *the Paradox of Plenty* (also known as the "commodity curse") with an important exception. *The Paradox of Plenty* is an economic theory advanced in the mid to late 1900s to assess development in third-world countries. *The Paradox of Plenty* as an economic theory has been criticized as painting with too broad a brush. However, it remains among the basic constructs for examining the evolution of commodity economies.

No American likes comparisons to third-world economies. Those of us who love Wyoming and are proud of its history are no different. Truthfully, Wyoming began as a commodity state and remains one today. Not all the development characteristics within *the Paradox of Plenty* fit Wyoming's history, but many do.

Analytically, *the Paradox of Plenty* begins with a massive influx of outside capital to extract and export a resource for processing and sale elsewhere. Generally, the producers within the region are "price takers" not "price makers." Commodity prices, particularly for energy commodities, can shift quickly and dramatically. Wyoming can check this box.

Classically the region focuses, almost exclusively, on the extractive industry. Significant investment in alternative economic sectors to supplement or eventually replace the mineral economy does not occur. Wyoming can check this box.

Adherents to this economic theory contend the affected regions generally have lower growth rates than the surrounding regions or states. Critics of the theory argue factors other than focused emphasis on the minerals economy contribute to the slow growth rate. Wyoming can check this box.

Wyoming's slow growth rate compared to surrounding states was dubbed "the hole in the doughnut of Mountain State prosperity" by a Cheyenne businessman at a 1999 University of Wyoming forum titled "Leadership and the Future of Wyoming." A column by David Broder of the *Washington Post* further quoted an articulate student of the class of 2000:

> But this is a time when we need visionary leaders. Wyoming has been a boom and bust state, its fortunes tied to the markets for oil and gas coal, and cattle. We need leaders ready to take a risk and bring Wyoming into the next millennium." And finally, the student concluded: "I don't see the opportunities for myself in Wyoming. I am looking outside.[1]

The young woman no longer resides in Wyoming.

Columnist and politico, Bill Sniffin, has resurrected the "doughnut hole" reference at various times in his statewide commentary.[2]

A common characteristic of commodity economies is expanded political and governmental influence exercised by the dominant industries. Wyoming can check this box.

Eventually external market conditions, political forces, or exhaustion of the resource reduce demand for the regional resource, a circumstance beyond the control of the resident population. In response, the region attempts to create barriers to corporate exit and offer incentives to retain the industry. Wyoming can check this box. Various severance tax reductions and modifications of environmental protections have been provided. Under the mantel of economic development, millions have been spent on research and projects to improve the prospects for the commodity economy. Legislators and governors have funded litigation and adopted statutes intended to force utilities to extend the life of fossil fuel power plants in Wyoming and around the United States. These efforts, while politically useful, have failed to offset the larger economic and political forces at play.

Further, the theory holds, the incumbent population gains little or no economic benefit from the extractive industry. On this point, Wyoming breaks the mold. Wyoming citizens have enjoyed significant economic gains from the extractive industries. Ownership of mineral lands and surface ownership of lands underlain by minerals have netted considerable wealth for Wyoming citizens. Ancillary and support industries have fueled wealth and well-paid employment for individuals and families. One hundred and five years after Wyoming became a Territory, a permanent savings fund was created and supported by mineral tax revenues. Collectively, Wyoming enjoys remarkable levels of public services and educational opportunities while consistently paying among the lowest personal taxes in America. An analysis by the Wyoming Economic Analysis Division and the Wyoming Taxpayers Association proves the point: a family of three with a modest income and a home utilizes $28,280 in public services and pays $3,770 in personal taxes. The difference or "gap" is $24,512.[3] As will be discussed later, this developed because of nearly 80 years of tax relief (some of it legal and some illegal) and increased energy mineral production. The gap is filled mainly by mineral tax revenues, federal funds, and investment earnings. The investment earnings are rooted in prior mineral revenues placed in investment accounts. Wyoming's minimal personal taxes, grand public services, and major employers are dependent on the mineral industry, mineral taxes, and federal largesse. The economy lacks the diversity to support the gap; a worrisome dependency for anyone concerned about Wyoming's people and future.

For multiple decades, people have wondered how long this convenient dependency would last. Formulating an answer has generally been deferred by an influx of federal money or simple endurance of the pain until external events change the price and/or demand for Wyoming's mineral resources. "Oh Lord, grant me another boom, I promise not to screw it up this time" is a common bumper sticker during the downturns. The notable exception to the "do nothing policy" was in 1993 when Governor Sullivan and the legislators courageously increased the sales tax from 3 to 4%.

Wyoming's experience beginning in 2020 is illustrative. Oil prices dropped precipitously as Saudi Arabia and Russia engaged in a price war. COVID-19 was first identified in the United States that January. Economic consequences for the world economy were immediate and dramatic. Wyoming's public revenue projections crashed as oil prices briefly entered negative territory and the American economy faltered. As the private economy contracted, Wyoming followed suit. Projected governmental revenues were upside down at all levels. Serious budget cuts were proposed as the consequences of Wyoming's singular tax base were exposed. Muted discussions of tax increases surfaced but quickly disappeared. Real decisions were on the table.

Alas, federal aid came to the rescue. According to the Wyoming Legislative Service Office, the estimated federal COVID-19 related aid for Wyoming governments, businesses and citizens totaled $8,020,000,000.[4] Roughly half of the aid went directly to various levels of government. As a frame of reference, the Federal Reserve estimates the entire Gross State Product for Wyoming in 2020 was $36.3 Billion. The Peter G. Peterson Foundation's summary of spending for the 22 major COVID federal funding programs lists the per capita federal spending in Wyoming as $14,569.[5] Wyoming received more than any other state, except perhaps Vermont.

An unexpected bonus was a rebound in energy markets. Coal prices exceeded pre-pandemic levels. For a variety of reasons, oil and gas prices rose dramatically. Public revenues from traditional sources (non-COVID-19 aid) were more than adequate to fund state and local budgets. With the combination of traditional revenue sources and COVID aid, governments were awash in funding. Hard decisions disappeared. The political drama focused on what to do with the extra public funds.

While the public and political relief was palpable, most people recognized Wyoming still confronted a daunting economic, employment, and public revenue future. Coal production remains on a long-term decline. Oil and gas remain relatively healthy but less attractive compared to other parts of the nation. History will not repeat itself. Implementing a workable future requires an understanding of the past. This book applies the basic construct of *the Paradox of Plenty* to the history of Wyoming with an emphasis on the period between 1966 and 1986. During these 20 years, underlying historical trends were accelerated by American energy, economic, and environmental policies to define much of Wyoming's predicament today.

ORGANIZATION OF THE TEXT

The text is organized into six main sections. The first, comprising Chapter 1 contains a brief sketch of Wyoming and the path to statehood. It reviews the decision to rely on ad valorem (in proportion to value) property taxes on real and personal property; tax rates would be applied to 100% of the property's fair market value. This chapter recounts the debate surrounding the unsuccessful effort to impose a special per unit of production tax on coal—in effect the first severance tax debate— and traces the beginning of illegal tax breaks given to all property except mineral production.

Chapter 2 outlines the economic difficulties of the 1920s and 1930s that resulted in the state's first sales tax. Wyoming's core tax base of agriculture and minerals industries was hit hard during the Depression. In addition, the federal government was placing increasing expectations on the states to participate financially in the federal assistance programs. The economic crisis made it clear the tax base needed to be diversified.

Chapter 3 focuses on the 1966 election of Republican governor Stan Hathaway, the onset of the mineral boom, enactment of the first severance tax, and the creation of a state permanent saving/investment fund. Severance tax revenues supported tax relief for individuals and the entire agricultural sector. State-level environmental protection was begun in response to emerging federal interest in energy independence and emerging state and national concern for environmental protection.

Chapter 4 discusses Wyoming's response to the major evolutions of American energy and environmental policy during the late 1960s and early 1980s. Emblematic of those changes are the adoption of National Energy Independence/Energy Security goals and the creation of federal statutes regulating environmental degradation. Key events are highlighted with no attempt to replicate the detailed analysis undertaken by others.

Chapter 5 covers the boom from 1974 to 1982. Evolving attitudes towards the energy boom and protection of "Wyoming's Way of Life" aided in the election of Democratic Governor Ed Herschler in a predominately Republican state. Governor Herschler would serve 12 years spanning turbulent energy development, a discouraging downturn and the onset of an economic bust. The first eight years would see significant population growth, increased severance taxes, additional tax relief for citizens, greatly expanded aid to local governments and environmental protection.

Chapter 6 encompasses the accelerating economic downturn and the onset of the "bust," roughly from 1983 through the election of 1986. Wyoming suffered severe economic setbacks, prompting attempts to reduce severance taxes and environmental protections. Recognizing Wyoming's distinct lack of economic sectors beyond minerals, political actors would undertake a series of lackluster efforts to diversify the economy. The primary emphasis would be on Wyoming's low tax environment as an economic development tool. Litigation originated during this period challenging the constitutionality of Wyoming's de facto tax preferences and tax relief system. The Wyoming Supreme Court declared the nearly 90-year-old system unconstitutional. Our response was to promptly amend the Constitution to enshrine our tax preferences.

The Epilogue recognizes that the only real statewide boom occurred between the late 1960s and early 1980s. Greater state population growth occurred in the single decade between 1970 and 1980 than during the four subsequent decades combined. Despite Wyoming's current economic and public revenue circumstances, the cycles inherent in *the Paradox of Plenty* are not inescapable. It will require a difficult self-assessment and active pursuit of economic diversification. Such diversification will require sustained, meaningful investment of public and private dollars. Perhaps most difficult, will be the acceptance of increased taxes borne by individuals and non-mineral taxpayers to bridge the gap between the appetite for public service and available revenues. For some, it may be equally difficult to accept an increased population with increased diversity.

CHAPTER 1
RELIANCE ON PROPERTY TAXES

Wyoming is in 1976, as it was in 1776, too high, dry, and cold for the needs and tastes of most people. Also, much of the soil is rocky, sandy, shallow, alkaline, or otherwise unsatisfactory. The Indians did not disrupt the soil, nor have the White men plowed more than 7 or 8 percent of it.[1]

These words, penned by Wyoming historian T.A. Larson as part of America's Bicentennial Celebration, are bittersweet for those of us who love Wyoming and its people. With its nearly 100,000 square miles, Wyoming is America's tenth largest and least populated state. (2021 Population: 578,803 according to the Census Bureau) Wyoming's economy has never supported a large population. This circumstance is only partly due to geography, climate, and geology.

Wyoming is landlocked near the mid-point of the Continental United States. The landscape is primarily mountains and high plains desert. The mean elevation is approximately 7,000 feet, with the tallest peak being 13,804 feet and limited areas with elevations below 4,000 feet.

Wyoming's climate is described as primarily semi-arid. Variations in elevation create wide temperature ranges throughout the state. Summers are mild to warm with generally cold winters, although temperatures have been warming. According to the National Oceanic and Atmospheric Administration's National Center for Environmental Information, "Temperatures in Wyoming have risen 2.5 degrees Fahrenheit since the beginning of the 20th century, and nearly every year of this century has been above the long-term average."[2] Precipitation is limited except for the snowpack in the high mountains. This lack of rainfall, along with soil conditions and relatively short growing seasons, explain Wyoming's non-participation in the great agriculture cropland expansion in the settling of the West.

Sitting atop the Continental Divide, Wyoming contributes to four major river systems: the Missouri-Mississippi, Green-Colorado, Snake-Columbia, and the Great Salt Lake. Geologic evolution and the various tributaries to these rivers created magnificent vistas of mountains, valleys, and streams dear to the hearts of citizens and visitors alike.[3] The plains primarily support livestock grazing and wildlife. While the foliage is rich in protein, it is relatively sparse; thus, considerable range acreage is required to support livestock.

Railroads, coal mining, and livestock were the seminal economies of early Wyoming. But minerals, not agriculture, have been the primary driver of Wyoming's wealth. Geologic time created reservoirs of oil and gas, extensive coal beds amenable to underground and surface mining, and the largest uranium reserves in the United States. Bentonite and trona development contribute significantly to the state's economy, while iron ore, gold, copper, and other minerals have also played a part.

Scenic vistas, mountains, expansive plains, and seven National Parks draw millions of tourists and recreationists to Wyoming every year. This pilgrimage has made tourism and recreation Wyoming's second largest industry.

Agriculture, which once dominated Wyoming's economy, is the 3rd largest economic sector. Primarily a livestock producer, Wyoming is home to more cattle and sheep than people. While agriculture generally accounts for around 5% of the gross state product, it remains a significant part of Wyoming's self-definition as the "Cowboy State."

WYOMING BECOMES A STATE

The Territory of Wyoming was organized by Congressional action in July of 1868. Citizens of the newly minted Territory desired to quickly join the

Union, confident that statehood would bring order, protection, status, and federal resources to an emerging area. As a Territory, Wyoming's citizens felt unrepresented in the nation's capital, particularly after Washington politicians selected a series of appointed governors and officials to oversee territorial affairs. After less than 15 years, Wyoming's citizens began, in earnest, the drive for statehood. Wyoming was admitted to the Union on July 10, 1890, as the 44th state.

The potential for mineral development was an integral part of Wyoming's plea for statehood. In a document entitled *Memorial Praying for the Admission of Wyoming into the Union of States*, Wyoming offered an account of agriculture claiming 3,000,000 head of livestock and a glowing prospect for mineral production to show "...a sufficient material foundation upon which to build a state." The *Memorial* continues as follows:

> ### The Material Foundation is Vast and Substantial.
> On this head, there is but little need of enlargement, since the resources of Wyoming are already known to the world as being unsurpassed, either in variety or extent, by those of any equal area. Of the whole area, the greater portion offers as good grazing for stock as can be found in the world, some ten million acres (15% of land mass) are irrigable and fertile valley lands, irrigable by means of numerous streams, no less remarkable for the permanence of water supply than for their wide and equal distribution over the whole Territory; while the eccentric chains and spurs of mountains, much broken up broad stretches of valleys and plain, besides many of them being clothed with forests of timber are great storehouses of mineral wealth containing not only gold and silver, copper and tin, but an almost unexampled supply of other minerals such as iron, asbestos, mica, plumbago, sulfur, mineral paint, kaolin, fire clay, and gypsum; also granites, sandstones, limestones and marbles in great variety. Moreover, outside of the mountain ranges, some twenty thousand square miles of broken and basin lands are underlain with coal of excellent quality in veins of extraordinary thickness. Vast deposits of soda and magnesia in many localities, while the oil basins are so many and

so extensive as to indicate that Wyoming may become one of the
most important oil districts in the world.[4]

This same *Memorial* to Congress referenced an 1880 Census count of
20,000 people but claimed the population was much greater in 1889. In
advancing the cause of statehood, Wyoming's Territorial Representative
to Congress, Joseph P. Carey, asserted that the Territory had more than
enough population to be granted statehood compared to other statehood grants. He did not choose to own a particular number but relied
on the optimism of others. According to Carey, "a Governor who was
much opposed to State government estimated the Territory's population
in 1887 to be 85,000." Exuberant, rather than optimistic, seems to be
the polite way to describe this estimate since the U.S. Census Bureau's
historical records show a Wyoming population of 62,555 in 1890, the
year statehood was granted. On the positive side, there were likely more
than 3,000,000 head of livestock in Wyoming. The *Memorial's* represen-
tations about banking infrastructure and finances were similarly ambitious
compared to reality. A fascinating study of early banking in Wyoming by
L.M. Woods forces the conclusion that "banking" at the time was divided
between a shopkeeper's safe and a few brave souls opening banks, largely
reliant on outside capital. A shortage of indigenous capital would remain
a persistent problem in Wyoming.

Fortunately, Washington politicians did not look closely at the numbers offered by the Territory, and Wyoming became a state. The cause was
aided by the policies of President Harrison and Congressional interest in
the admission of additional states.

Perhaps the complicated settlement patterns of the American West
simply necessitated the creation of a new state. T.A. Larsen described
Wyoming as a "pass-through state" — pioneers moved through in search
of gold or more promising land for agriculture development.[5] Settlement
was primarily driven by the railroads and the hearty souls who decided to
make a life in Wyoming.

Creating boundaries for Wyoming was a complicated jigsaw puzzle
that took nearly 100 years to sort. Wyoming sits atop the Continental
Divide with a series of mountain ranges directing the water from melting

snowpack to other parts of America via four major river basins. Original European claims to land in the New World were vast and uncharted, with the claimed lands often defined by major river drainages or mountain ranges. Britain, Spain, and France claimed portions of what is now Wyoming, with a substantial part of Wyoming within the Louisiana Purchase. The Republics of Mexico and Texas variously claimed portions of Wyoming.

The United States eventually gained control of the lands which became Wyoming. Between 1821 and the organization of the Wyoming Territory in 1868, various lands were designated as Indian Country, Nebraska Territory, Dakota Territory, Oregon Country, Oregon Territory, Washington Territory, Idaho Territory, Republic of Texas lands, and Utah Territory. Wyoming's capitol city of Cheyenne, located in the state's southeast corner, was originally platted and named by the Union Pacific Railroad. It was incorporated on August 8, 1867, as the "Town of Cheyenne, Dakota Territory." As Congress admitted other states and defined territories, the portions of what became Wyoming were excluded for various reasons. Some cynical observers have suggested that Wyoming is an area not sought by other states and territories. It is, however, hard to explain the poor judgment of other states and territories.

While a bit flowery and overblown, the state's founding fathers' sense of Wyoming's potential was not misplaced. Not anticipated was the extent to which Wyoming's resources would be processed beyond the state's borders. Our economy for 130 years of statehood has been primarily characterized by the export of minerals and livestock for processing and sale elsewhere. The secondary export has been young men and women.

WYOMING'S EARLY TAX STRUCTURE

Fundamental to any government is the ability to impose taxes securing revenue to support its citizens' services and infrastructure expectations. The creation of a taxing authority, along with restrictions on that authority, were part of the original discussions in the 1889 Wyoming Constitutional Convention. General reliance on property taxes was the established order for emerging states in the late 1800s. Ad valorem property taxes were applied to both real and personal property.*

Wyoming's Constitutional Convention did consider a per unit coal tonnage tax (effectively a privilege or severance tax) to be applied to every ton of coal shipped out of the state. The context of the discussion is important. Wyoming's Territorial tax scheme rested entirely on real and personal property taxes. Of the property taxes collected, 75–80% remained in the county, and the rest supported the Territorial government. The debate reflected in the *Journal and Debates of the Constitutional Convention of the State of Wyoming*[6] (hereinafter "Debates") makes clear the problem was valuing coal lands for purposes of ad valorem property taxes. In 1889, it was nearly impossible to accurately determine the value of property underlain by a mineral resource. Estimating the extent of the resource underground was more art than accuracy. People watched the Union Pacific Railroad accumulate great wealth from coal and understood coal lands were more valuable than farmland or grazing ground.

Meanwhile, land on which coal was mined was more than likely being taxed the same as grazing ground. In some corners, there was a sense that the problem related to maladministration or failure of the tax assessor to perform the assigned duties. The original proposal to correct this perceived inequity was not a property tax; it was a per-ton privilege tax to be paid on each ton of coal regardless of its value. The proposal was to divide ⅓ of the proceeds of the tax to the county and ⅔ to the state. Convention Delegate Melville C. Brown was the leading proponent.

Melville C. Brown, a prominent Republican from Laramie, was President of the 1889 Constitutional Convention. Born in Maine, Brown moved to Laramie in 1867 and became a member of the legal bar in 1868. Brown's truly remarkable legal career included a stint as United States Attorney for the Territory of Wyoming and lead counsel in several significant Wyoming cases.[7] His business acumen did not match his legal prowess, as most of his business ventures failed. His rhetorical skills seem unmatched by any of the other delegates. Brown proved to be a forceful and determined supporter of the constitutional coal tonnage tax applicable to coal shipped out of state.

---

* "Ad valorem" means taxing an item based on its value rather than a flat tax per unit.

Extensive debate ensued when Henry G. Hay, a successful Cheyenne Republican businessman with extensive banking and real estate holdings, including mining properties, offered an amendment taken from the Colorado Constitution, which effectively left mining lands untaxed. Hay's essential argument was that Colorado had prospered by virtue of this policy.

Brown rose in opposition:

> The mines have been mined out...the wealth has been carried
> from the state and is in the hands of non-residents...and not one
> cent tribute has been paid to the government. Colorado is just
> so much poorer today than when she adopted her constitution....
> (DEBATES, P. 638)

Brown, warming to his topic, transitioned to Wyoming's circumstance as he saw it:

> The coal business in Wyoming today is the largest industry in the
> Territory and pays the slightest possible percentum [sic] towards
> the support of the territory... (DEBATES, P. 639)

> ...in Wyoming this year nearly two-thirds of the whole amount
> (coal production) will be used and shipped out of the limits of
> the territory. A tax of this kind comes out of the consumer. Is
> there any reason why the people who have the benefit of the coal
> should not pay something to support the government of the
> state? (DEBATES, P. 638)

> ...the Union Pacific on all its coal lands, and it owns many
> thousands of acres, pays but the smallest possible trifle in the way
> of taxation to support the government, and other companies can
> be expected to do the same thing. (DEBATES, P. 641)

> I tell you, gentlemen, this tax will be the lifeblood of the state,
> will keep it up and help support it and save the people of the state
> from burdensome taxation. (DEBATES, PP. 642–643)

Hay's initial response was rather tepid. He argued that in the future, not all mines would be owned by Union Pacific. He would gladly see Wyoming enjoy the prosperity Colorado had enjoyed from mineral development. (DEBATES, PP. 640–643) Hay concludes his argument:

> It is said that we don't get anything like what we ought from
> those mines, that is not the fault of our present laws, it is the
> fault of our assessors and the people who own the mines. But
> as I said…I don't like to see a special tax of that kind in the
> constitution…. (DEBATES, P. 644)

Clarence D. Clark from Uinta County took up the laboring oar in opposition to the tonnage tax. Clark was originally from New York state. He arrived in Uinta County to work in the Union Pacific Railroad's legal department. Clark's Republican political career began in 1882 as a county attorney and eventually led to the United States Senate.[8]

Clark began his response to Brown by reminding the assembly of the unique and unprecedented nature of a direct tax not based on the article's value subject to taxation. "I believe it to be the first time anything of the kind has been sought to be put in a constitution." Clark further asserted that the coal industry was not as profitable as Brown represented and should not be singled out for a special tax. He suggested the tax would create a wasteful surplus for the state government to spend. Further, it was unfair and inappropriate for the state to suddenly take the lion's share of the proceeds of this tax at the expense of county governments. (DEBATES, P. 648)

Clark recognized his personal conflict due to his own efforts to open a coal mine. He cited the competition coal faces from Iowa, Colorado, Washington, and Australia. His passion flared as he approached the injustice of taxing coal and not any other minerals:

> I feel the injustice more perhaps because I have personally
> invested and become interested in this coal matter. (DEBATES, P.
> 650)

> …I simply ask for justice, and if any man in this convention can
> rise to his feet when called on to vote upon the proposition and

say it is just to tax me because I own a coal mine, and at the same
time it is just to allow my neighbor to go Scott free because he
owns a silver mine. (DEBATES, P. 653)

Laramie County delegate H.E. Teschemacher joined the fray by suggesting other states might impose a similar tax on their significant products, such as wheat in South Dakota or cotton in Georgia. Republican
Teschemacher was a financier and cattleman who would later be involved
in the Johnson County cattle war. A moderating voice came from Charles
N. Potter, a Republican lawyer from Michigan who relocated to Cheyenne
in 1876. Potter proclaimed he had no financial interests in this dispute.
Potter rejected the original special tax and the substitute amendment. He
supported an ad valorem tax applicable to all mines. Further, he asserted
that the matter should not be addressed in the constitution but left to
future legislatures:

> I am willing to give to the Legislature the power, if they deem it
> wise, to tax these mines, all mines alike, on the gross product....
> (DEBATES, P. 657)

Sheridan County Delegate H.A. Coffeen brought the agricultural perspective to the floor. Democrat Coffeen was born in Ohio, educated in
the sciences, and made a living as a college professor and lecturer for a
time. He arrived in Sheridan in 1884 to open a grocery store.[9] Coffeen
supported taxing the coal lands:

> ...these coal lands, instead of paying taxes on a valuation of
> twenty dollars an acre, we are told by those best informed that
> they pay taxes on the basis of something less than one dollar per
> acre...these coal lands are not paying their just share of taxes of
> this territory, as the farmlands and other lands of this territory.
> (DEBATES, P. 658)

Coffeen articulated the perceived disparity between coal being taxed once
(when produced and immediately sold). At the same time, a rancher pays
tax on cattle for three years as the livestock is raised and finally brought
to market.

The debate continued for days. Eventually, a compromise was reached—the special tax and the tax holiday were both rejected. All mines would be taxed based upon the ad valorem value of its gross product plus surface improvements—such tax to be in lieu of taxes on the land. In effect, the production of the mine would be subject to property tax at the same rate as other properties based on its fair market value. The revenue split between county and state remained the same. The question of a special tax was left to the wisdom of future legislatures.

This approach produced one of the most colorful phrases from the Convention, Delegate Brown observed:

> If there is anything an honest man abhors, it is to see a monied
> corporation in politics, and if you say that this matter shall be
> by the Legislature, you are saying when you do it, every monied
> corporation in Wyoming engaged in coal mining will come into
> your Legislature as a politician and seek to have that tax put down
> to the lowest possible point. You force them to do it, and I don't
> blame them any, you and I would do the same…. It is forced
> into politics, forced into the lists of these men that go into your
> Legislatures wearing brass collars. As you have seen in the past
> men elected to our Legislatures wearing the brass collars of the
> great railroad corporation, you will see just such men wear the
> brass collar of the great monied mining corporations. (DEBATES,
> P. 668)

The phrase "brass collar" is a not-so-flattering reference to the permanent brass collar placed on men forced to labor in the coal mines of Scotland during the 1700s. This brass collar reference could be heard occasionally in the Wyoming legislative lobbies during the 1970s and 1980s.

Arguments offered by proponents and opponents of the tax during the Constitutional Convention would echo over the decades every time mineral taxation issues arose. Future debates would not always be along strictly partisan lines; however, a significant Republican anti-mineral tax orthodoxy emerged rather quickly.

While it was not referenced in the Constitutional debates, taxing minerals in place would not have been a workable policy in Wyoming. Nearly 75% of the minerals in place are owned by the federal government and are not legally subject to state taxation. Once the mineral is produced, it becomes the private property of the miner and is subject to taxation. Livestock was to be taxed as personal property for similar reasons. Stockgrowers owned far more livestock than could be supported on their privately owned lands. The federal government owned most of the land used to support the livestock industry. And like federally owned minerals, the federal surface is not legally subject to taxation. Capturing taxable value from agriculture required taxation of livestock.

Reliance upon ad valorem taxation of real and personal property would remain the support for the provision of state and local government services, including education, until the 1930s.

The Constitution of 1889 reflected the dominant view that government taxing authority and ability to incur debt needed to be strictly controlled. Article 15 created taxing authority within limited parameters with greater flexibility in funding education:

> STATE GOVERNMENT — [T]here shall be levied annually a tax not to exceed four mills on the dollar of the assessed valuation of the property in the state except for the support of state educational and charitable institutions, the payment of state debt and the interest thereon.

> COUNTY GOVERNMENT — There shall be levied annually a tax not to exceed twelve mills on the dollar for all purposes including school tax, exclusive of state revenue, except for the payment of public debt and the interest thereon. An additional tax of two dollars per person between the ages of twenty-one and fifty years shall be levied for county school purposes.

> CITY LEVY — No incorporated city or town shall levy a tax exceeding 8 mills on the dollar in any year, except for the payment of its public debt and interest thereon. (DEBATES P. 44-46)

Article 16 of the Wyoming Constitution tied public indebtedness to the assessed (taxable) value of the jurisdiction. State indebtedness could not exceed 1% of the previous year's assessed valuation. And such indebtedness had to be approved by a vote of the people. The state could not engage in any work of internal improvement unless approved by a two-thirds vote of the citizens. County and municipal debt was limited to 2% of assessed valuation, also subject to a vote of the citizens. (DEBATES P. 46–47)

EROSION OF THE WYOMING TAX BASE

Measured against current tax policies, Wyoming's early taxation and indebtedness standards appear unduly restrictive. Such judgment is unfair to the founding fathers. The assumption underlying the constitutional provisions was that taxable value would be equivalent to the fair market value of the personal and real property subject to taxation. None of the Convention participants could have envisioned Wyoming abandoning the fair value of a property for purposes of taxation and assessed value determination. Nevertheless, contrary to the newly adopted Constitution and within the lifetime of the Convention's members, Wyoming—through administrative fiat—would abandon fair value tax assessment of non-mineral production property. Tax relief, be it legal or illegal, is politically popular.

By the time the severance tax was adopted in 1969, Wyoming's political leadership had informally adopted a policy of assessing non-mineral property at far less than its fair market value. The actual value subject to taxation was likely 75% less than the fair market value envisioned by our founding fathers. The only exception was mineral production which was assessed at 100%.

It is important to understand the role this administrative erosion of the broader tax base played in encouraging direct reliance on mineral taxes, specifically the severance tax. Under the Wyoming founding father's theory determining tax revenues was the simple equation of fair market value times tax rate equals revenue. A property with a fair market value of $100,000 would have a taxable value of $100,000. A county imposing the maximum 12 mill levy tax rate (1.2%) would receive $1,200. At some point, without statutory or constitutional support, Wyoming added a debasement factor or assessment ratio to the equation. The equation became fair market value times an assessment ratio to determine assessed (taxable) value. This adjusted taxable value multiplied by the tax rate equals revenue. A $100,000 fair market value times an assessment ratio of 30% equals a taxable value of $30,000. Taxable value ($30,000) times tax rate 12 mill maximum (1.2%) equals $360—less than a third of the revenue envisioned by the founding fathers.

Exactly when this informal, illegal tax relief originated remains unclear. But it was real. A 1981 Management Audit of the Ad Valorem Tax Division[10] documents the tax relief progression. In 1900, non-mineral property was assessed at 100%. By 1938 the debasement number or assessment ratio applied to fair market value was 60%, leaving 40% untaxed. In 1965 it was 17%, leaving 83% of the fair market value untaxed. This informal tax relief could be tolerated because mineral production, assessed at 100%, had increased significantly since 1900.

A secondary effect of the erosion of the tax base was to limit the government's ability to raise funds to build public facilities through the issuance of bonded indebtedness. Constitutional provisions limit indebtedness to a certain percentage of the assessed value of the jurisdiction. Reducing taxable value by 70% reduces the ability to raise funds through the issuance of bonded indebtedness by 70%.

With the traditional tax base eroded by administrative fiat, governments had little recourse but to look elsewhere for funding. Citizens looked to local governments, local governments looked to the state, and the state looked to minerals.

A 1988 study highlighted the second result of tax base erosion by administrative order—the creation of additional levels of government:

> Wyoming's ratio of assessed valuation to the fair or true market value of non-mineral property was at or near 100% at the turn of the century. By 1980, the assessment ratio of residential properties was estimated to be near 10%. Due to this erosion, property tax has lost its effective revenue-raising capacities in municipalities and counties with little mineral valuation. One of the reactions to this problem was to skirt the Constitutional mill levy limits by creating a multitude of special districts with

their own taxing powers. The state now has more than 15 types of special districts, which can levy taxes of as much or more than cities and counties, 'layering' taxing authorities into a maze. It is estimated that more than 380 districts are currently operating in Wyoming.[11]

CHAPTER 2

Necessity Forces a Sales Tax

In the 1930s, Wyoming was forced to diversify its tax base. Agriculture and other property interests' complaints about the unfair burden they shouldered became common under the property-based tax system. These complaints, combined with the state's economic decline and loss of property tax base,* the public's expectation of assistance, and the desire to gain federal Depression-era aid, made expansion of the tax base in the mid-1930s a necessity. The decision to institute a sales tax is thoughtfully and thoroughly discussed in more detail by Wyoming historian Phil Roberts.[1]

Wyoming was hit hard shortly after WWI. Long before the stock market crash of 1929, Wyoming's predominantly agricultural economy was in desperate shape, confronting low prices, drought, and agricultural surpluses. The 1926 Wyoming State Board of Equalization *Biennial Report* catalogs the drastic decline in agriculture between 1919 and 1926:

> We believe values of livestock of all kinds and lands reached their
> peak in the year 1919. Cattle in numbers decreased 461,737,
> or approximately 45%; decreased in value $30,422,863.00, or

---

*   The loss of tax base in the 1930s was partially due to assessment ratios reducing the taxable value of non-mineral properties by approximately 40%.

approximately 71%. Sheep decreased in number 736,284 and
in value $6,926,437.00. The number of acres of taxable lands
increased 7,906,608, while the total lands show an increase
of only $8,739,454.00. The average value of per acre having
decreased from $7.71 in 1919 to $5.13 in 1926. [2]

Statements by the State Board of Equalization were taken seriously as it was charged with overall responsibility for implementing, policing, and accounting for tax policy within the state.

The one bright spot for Wyoming was the added revenue from new federal royalty payments under the federal Mineral Leasing Act of 1920. Prior to the Act, oil was treated as a "locatable" mineral. Individuals or companies would file a "placer claim" on federal minerals, which could mature into ownership of the minerals and the surface land. Even Buffalo Bill Cody speculated for oil using placer claims in the early 1900s.[3] In this way, title to the land and minerals moved from the hands of the federal government to private ownership without royalties or other payments due to the federal government. The transfer of non-taxable federal property into taxable private property significantly benefited the states and counties.

In the early 1900s government officials, particularly east of the Mississippi, began to assert that federal minerals belonged to all Americans and should not be transferred to private parties. World War I had heightened concerns about oil supplies for the American economy and military. A series of scandals, a Presidential withdrawal of oil-bearing federal lands from private development, and concentrated oil development by a few corporations led to proposals to retain federal ownership of the minerals. This was not to the liking of Congressional representatives from the public land states (mainly in the Rocky Mountains).

Colorado Congressman Taylor offered full-throated opposition to a leasing system:

> ...it would result in the development of a huge bureaucracy which
> would absorb the royalties in expensive administration, and would
> create a host of government employees who could never be pried

from their jobs; that the leasing system involved a heavy loss
of taxes to the states and counties of the West; that it deprived
western people of their freedom, compelling them to surrender
the sovereign right of American citizens to local self-government
and become permanently helpless, if not servile, tenants under
federal tyrants and autocratic predatory bureaucrats,…an outrage
upon a free people.[4]

It became clear that the eastern establishment would succeed in creating a system whereby ownership of the minerals remained with the federal government, which would grant leases for private development and require payment of royalties.

Arguments quickly moved to who gets the royalty dollars. Lamentations of the lost tax base for state and local governments carried the day. Only 10% of the revenue would go to the federal treasury, 37½% went to the state where the lease was located, and 52½% was dedicated to the Reclamation Fund for the development of water projects, primarily in the West. Federal mineral royalties would eventually become a significant source of funds for Wyoming. FMRs peaked in 1924 at $4,223,298 (67.6 million in 2021 dollars), then declined quickly and remained modest until after WWII.[5]

Mirroring the decline in agriculture, coal production fell in the 1920s. Coal employment fell from 8,166 in 1920 to 5,639 in 1928.[6] Anyone who has done land title work in Wyoming has seen the tangible demonstration of the general economic decline as evidenced by the significant number of tax foreclosures during the twenties and thirties. Wyoming faced a financial and fiscal crisis.[7]

Politics in the late twenties was dominated by the notion that cutting government spending was the answer. Overpaid public employees and wasteful spending were cited as the root of the problem. Most Wyoming politicians manfully opposed accepting aid from the federal government. The economy continued to falter, and the financial crisis deepened. Among the hardest hit were local jurisdictions, who, at the time, were responsible for public education, welfare programs, and care of the indigent. Confronting declining revenue, local governments dealt with real poverty and displacement among their citizens.

Wyoming's 1932 gubernatorial race pitted Democrat Leslie Miller against Republican Harry Weston. Both candidates bemoaned the state of affairs, gingerly avoiding any discussion of tax increases. Democrat Miller won, having promised a 25% reduction in government expenditures, reducing taxes and the cost of gasoline. He also promised Wyoming would not accept federal assistance. (He wisely abandoned this position rather quickly.)

With the convening of the 1933 Legislature, the new governor proposed deep cuts in government spending. The Legislative body adopted his recommendations and cut even deeper. The new administration and legislature were under significant pressure to address the state's problems. The greatest pressure seemed to come from agricultural interests complaining about the unfairness of a system forcing them to bear the lion's share of the tax burden.

Standard fare in the discussions of needed revenue was a variation of today's call to "...diversify the tax base and lower my taxes." Legislative discussions were far-reaching and often far afield—proposals included an income tax, a sales tax, liquor taxes, legalization and taxing of gambling,

Governor Leslie A. Miller 1933–1939

Miller found success in the field of oil exploration and production and became president of Aero Oil Company. He served two terms in the state legislature and was elected to the state senate but resigned his seat to undertake an unsuccessful campaign for governor. However, he won election to the governorship upon the death of Frank Emerson, and was elected to a second full term in 1934. During Miller's service as governor, Wyoming initiated it's first sales tax. After being defeated for reelection in 1938, he served as a Democratic National Committeeman.

Photo: National Governor's Association.

etc. But progress was non-existent, and the default was to create a committee. Legislators agreed to create a bicameral, bi-partisan committee to study the issues and recommend a special session of the Legislature, if appropriate. In 1933, the relief rolls included one out of every five Wyoming citizens. The pressure was on.

The Legislative Committee on Taxation immediately became embroiled in controversy when it retained the Chicago-based Griffenhagen consulting firm for the sum of $10,000 (205,331 in 2021 dollars). Griffenhagen's report was controversial from the outset. While arguably logical on efficiency grounds, items such as a statewide police force, consolidation of nearly 400 schools into a single statewide school district, a unicameral legislature, and a reduction in the number of counties fell on angry ears. The report's serious criticism of Wyoming's tax system and a buffet of improvement recommendations were rejected.

The Tax Committee, having ignored most of Griffenhagen's suggestions, recommended a property tax reduction of 50% and removing personal property held for personal use from the assessment rolls. Income would be generated by a "net income tax" on businesses and individuals.

Governor Miller convened a Special Legislative Session in November of 1933. Proponents of the sales tax, the income tax, the privilege tax, and the gambling tax returned to their respective corners. One area of agreement was the view that outside experts from Chicago were seeking to centralize too much power in Cheyenne.

The regionalism visibly present during the original Constitutional Convention remained alive and well. Among the most vocal critics of the Griffenhagen report were the agricultural interests, whose anger focused not only on what was recommended but something not recommended: the proposals did not include livestock in the list of personal property to be removed from the tax rolls. A tumultuous session produced action on a gas tax, a liquor tax, and legislative approval to accept federal funds.

The election of 1934 saw Miller resoundingly re-elected. All candidates generally avoided taxation issues. Miller's campaign was "promises made, promises kept." He had reduced the cost of state government 25–30%, but the deteriorating condition of the economy and citizen demands made it clear that revenue was needed beyond the federal aid and work programs. In addition, the federal government was placing increased expectations on the states to participate financially in the federal assistance programs. Throughout 1934, support for a sales tax seemed to be growing.

Wyoming's State Board of Equalization *Biennial Report* for 1933–1934 demonstrated the state's desperate straits by highlighting the decline in property valuations. According to the report:

> Valuations have been reduced since 1929 to the amount of $140,799,156, or more than 31%.

> The total value of property assessed by the State Board in 1934 was $119,685,315, which was a decrease from 1933 of $4,179,270, of which oil constituted the major portion. [8]

Wyoming's method of valuation of property for taxation purposes divides the process between state assessed property (primarily minerals and select industrial) and locally assessed property (mostly real and personal property). The Board's report showed similar decreases for locally assessed property. It also documented the flash point of tax lien foreclosures.

When property taxes are delinquent, the government places a lien on the property. If taxes remain unpaid, the government eventually forecloses and holds title until the land is sold to a private party. Property owned by the government based on foreclosure of a tax lien is not assessed for taxation. The 1934 report chose to demonstrate the impact of tax lien foreclosures empirically:

> There were 151,304 fewer acres assessed in 1934 than in 1933 on account of so much real estate having been transferred to the County roll.

The Board of Equalization's parting shot was advice for the 1935 Legislative Session:

Suggestions for Legislation

> It is apparent that some form of taxation in which all have some share should be had in order to relieve to some extent the present

excessive burden on owners of real and personal property. This could be a general sales tax, an income tax, or some combination of the two. After making careful study of the tax laws in effect in various States and the results obtained therefrom and endeavoring to apply them to conditions existing in Wyoming, the Board has arrived at the following conclusion which is somewhat different than any plan now in use, but which meets the conditions in Wyoming better than any other plan.

That all State and school revenues shall be raised through a combination of Sales and Income Tax, neither of which need be sufficiently high to cause great hardships upon any class of citizens.

This would leave only the Counties levies to be raised from the property tax outside of incorporated towns, while within the towns the city levy would be added. This would not in any way be an additional tax but would be a more equal distribution of the tax burden.

This would relieve tangible property of from 15% to 59% of its present tax burden, depending on the location as regards the different school districts or municipalities. [9]

The first Legislative Session of Governor Miller's second term was different in tone. The need for added revenue was accepted by most of the legislative body. It was also different in make-up as many of the strident voices for and against the various proposals were gone. Income taxes enjoyed limited support, but the combination of sales and income taxes offered by the Board of Equalization gained no traction. Eventually, the body would settle on a temporary sales tax measure, which was regressive as it taxed food and drugs. Sales tax proponents acknowledged this fact but were largely indifferent to the consequences. Arguments to justify the regressive effect included the rationalization that taxing food was fine because low-income people did not pay property taxes. To assure passage, other powerful interests such as services and agricultural products were excluded from the tax. When there is tough medicine to be delivered to the citizenry, politics dictate that the medicinal treatment first be temporary—even though everyone knows, or least suspects, it is permanent. The sales tax was designated as an "Emergency," and the legislation included a termination date. Passage was assured. Interestingly, the illegal property tax relief given to citizens through administrative fiat appears to have never been publicly discussed in the 1930s. A 1981 report from the Wyoming Legislative Service Office found that assessments of non-mineral property were only 60% of fair market value.

The emergency sales tax measure was not the only revenue-raising measure passed. Gambling advocates promoted gaming as an answer to the financial crisis. Following a contentious and uncertain path, the gambling legalization, licensing, and taxing measures arrived on the governor's desk. Notwithstanding objections from the religious community and others, the 1935 Legislature chose to legalize and tax most forms of gambling, even though Governor Miller had spoken out against the legalization of gambling. While some claimed he might sign the bill, Governor Miller was true to his convictions and vetoed the measure. The basic combination of property tax and sales tax remained the primary generators of government revenues for the next 34 years. Sales tax revenues flowing into the state coffers facilitated additional relief to property taxpayers. In the 10 years preceding the sales tax, the statewide property tax rate expressed in mills varied between 3.5 and 5.0. For the next 34 years, the statewide mill levy exceeded 2.0 only once and remained below 2.0 mills for 22 years.[10] Approximately a 50% property tax rate reduction following the passage of the sales tax.

Governor Miller is seldom recognized for his courage and strategic thought in guiding Wyoming through incredibly difficult and contentious times. Imposition of new taxes is never easy. It is hard to imagine the courage, effort and strategic thought it took in the middle of an economic depression.

CHAPTER 3
ADOPTION OF THE SEVERANCE TAX:

The Hathaway Years

The imposition of a severance tax was seriously considered three times before the 1966 election. In addition to the Constitutional Convention, a second attempt to constitutionalize a severance tax occurred in 1924. Democratic Governor Ross succeeded in getting a constitutional proposal for a severance tax on the November ballot. Governor Ross, a popular candidate for re-election, promoted the proposal throughout his campaign. However, Ross died in early October. The primary voice for the constitutional severance tax amendment was lost.

The Rocky Mountain Oil & Gas Producers aggressively campaigned against a severance tax. Typical of their efforts was a full-page advertisement in the *Casper Daily Tribune* on November 3, 1924, calling for tax reductions, not tax increases. The ad pointed out, "… the oil industry is already bearing its just share and more than its share of the taxes of the state." More people voted for the amendment on election day than against it. Nonetheless, the amendment failed. Wyoming law requires a majority of all people voting on election day to vote favorably on the amendment for it to become law. In effect, a failure to vote *for* the amendment counts as a "no" vote. Many people who voted that day simply did not vote on the amendment at all. Thus, it failed.

Wyoming's third significant discussion of severance taxes came in the gubernatorial election of 1950. A legislative proposal for a severance tax was defeated in 1949, but the issue rolled into the 1950 governor's race. Democrat J.J. McIntyre supported a severance tax. Republican Frank Barrett was opposed. According to Larsen's *History of Wyoming*, the oil industry, particularly the Rocky Mountain Oil and Gas Association, smote "McIntyre hip and thigh." This election saw the emergence of the alliance between oil and gas and the stock-raising industry. According to Larsen:

> J. Elmer Brock, prominent cattlemen, helped out by asserting that the consumer would pay the tax and that a severance, once applied to oil, would soon be applied to cattle, sheep, and grain not processed in the state. More and more ranchers were sharing in oil-lease and oil-royalty income, which may have made them more sympathetic to the oil and gas industry than they had been in the 1920s.[1]

McIntyre lost the election.

It would be 16 years before severance taxes would again be a significant electoral issue. Until then, the primary political campaign fodder was lack of population growth, unfair tax burdens, economic diversification, and government spending. Any minor movements on taxes and revenues were within the bounds of the status quo—that is, until the election of 1966. Tax discussions during the 1966 election rehashed some of the old arguments, but they were conducted against the backdrop of a Wyoming economy quite different than 1924 and 1950.

Wyoming's pre-WWII economy followed the national economy's path at a somewhat slower pace. With the advent of WWII in 1939, America's wartime production demands turned the corner for Wyoming's economy. Oil production grew from approximately 21 million barrels in 1939 to about 39 million in 1946. Agricultural products and fossil fuel resources were in great demand, and Wyoming was glad to contribute more than its share.

Wyoming joined the other states in lobbying to offer locations for

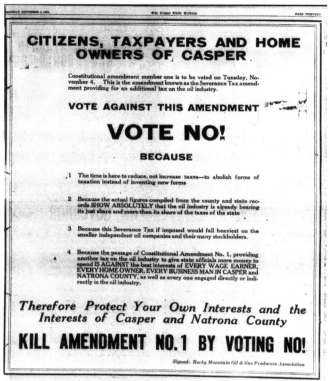

Photo: *Casper Star Tribune* Archives

military facilities. The efforts produced a new army air base in Casper, a Japanese internment camp near Cody (not something everyone supported), a prisoner of war camp in Douglas, and the expansion of the military facilities in Cheyenne. However, these were largely temporary and failed to fundamentally change Wyoming's economy.

While much of America became industrialized during WWII, Wyoming remained a source of raw materials exported beyond its borders. There were some small refineries in Wyoming and some industrial activity, but again, the products were shipped out of state. Jobs were plentiful, and wages were up. Personal income rose, as did bank deposits and wealth. Other than the strain of rationing,* life was good for the people of Wyoming. The essential nature of

---

* As World War II came to a close in 1945, so did the government's rationing program. By the end of that year, sugar was the only commodity still being rationed. That restriction finally ended in June 1947. Plenty of other goods remained in short supply for months after the war, thanks to years of pent-up demand.

Wyoming's economy did not change, though our population declined between 1940 and 1950. During this period, America saw people leaving agriculture and moving to the cities and towns. Wyoming followed the pattern.

America was the only industrial power left intact after WWII. America's productive and industrial might transformed from a war economy into an economy driven to produce goods and services to accommodate returning soldiers, growing families, and general prosperity. America converted its industrial "Arsenal of Democracy"[*] to creating and exporting materials for a world needing rebuilding. Larsen refers to the postwar period as "Twenty Years of Abundance in Wyoming."[2] The mineral resources of Wyoming were in great demand. In short order, mineral production firmly established itself as the state's most important industry. Agriculture fell behind tourism which became a substantial contributor to the economy. The total population grew slightly, but there remained a net out-migration of young people.

In 1966, thirty years after the adoption of the sales tax, Wyoming's economy was not "your grandfather's economy." The state's mineral industry grew with new team members in the mineral sectors: uranium, trona, iron ore, and bentonite. Tourism and recreation became even more important to Wyoming's economy, growing at a faster rate than oil and gas.

URANIUM

Securing uranium supplies for the WWII Manhattan project was a critical but silent priority. Uranium for the two atomic bombs dropped by the United States came not from America but from the Democratic Republic of the Congo. After the War, tensions escalated with Russia, and the Cold War commenced. National defense planners recognized the rapid emergence of the Soviet Union's atomic bomb program. Creating a larger, sustained supply of domestic uranium was a fundamental national defense priority.

---

[*] "Arsenal of Democracy" was the phrase used by U.S. President Franklin D. Roosevelt in a radio broadcast on the threat to national security, delivered on December 29, 1940—nearly a year before the United States entered the Second World War (1939–1945). "Arsenal of democracy" refers to the collective efforts of American industry in supporting the Allies.

Creating this supply became the task of the Atomic Energy Commission (AEC) established by the Atomic Energy Act of 1946. The 5,000 employees and the various federally owned research, design, and production facilities tied to the Manhattan project were transferred to the AEC Uranium concentrate would be developed under federal auspices through a program of guaranteed price and quantity purchases. AEC also included funding for road and infrastructure construction because so many of the uranium reserves were in remote areas. While recognized as a direct subsidization of an industry, the program was a national necessity for the Cold War struggle. Expectations around the Atomic Energy Act of 1946 and subsequent amendments in 1954 were to supply adequate uranium concentrate for national defense as well as develop peaceful uses for atomic energy.

Peaceful use development was known as the Plowshare Program. Plowshare's biggest push was the development of nuclear-powered electric generation plants.

While Wyoming was never seriously considered as a site for a nuclear power plant, Plowshare did include a proposal for developing Wyoming's natural gas reserves. In the late 1960s, the AEC and Texas El Paso Gas Company announced plans to detonate five 100-kiloton devices, approximately 10,000 feet below ground to fracture a tight gas formation for future commercial development of a natural gas field. Project Wagon Wheel[3] was the name attached to the effort, and Sublette County was the proposed site for the detonations. County and area residents were unpersuaded by the AEC and El Paso assurances that the project presented no risk to residents or the environment. Particularly troubling was the AEC's acknowledgement that three billion cubic feet of radioactive natural gas would be produced and flared. Radioactive elements are not entirely destroyed by flaring and would eventually be deposited in and around the area. Despite assurances of "no harm" provided by the AEC, residents voted more than three to one against the proposal in a straw vote. Eventually, political pressure and dismal economics forced the abandonment of the project.

Uranium had been identified in Wyoming in the early part of the

20th Century. While Wyoming lagged in the exploitation of the uranium resource, its abundance and quality were soon demonstrated. As with most things in our nation's capital, uranium development had a political component. Wyoming's political leaders actively pressed the AEC to include Wyoming in its uranium development program. These efforts and the quality of the reserves persuaded the AEC to open the door to Wyoming, and several facilities began operation in the 1950s. Encouraged by the guarantee of price and quantity purchase, at least five uranium mining and milling operations existed in Wyoming in 1966. Under the original contracts, uranium production could only be sold to the federal government.

Uranium development in Wyoming was limited to mining the ore and reducing it to "yellowcake," a concentrate generally exceeding 70% U3O8, the first step in reducing uranium ore to nuclear energy. Uranium ore must be finely crushed and treated to remove the uranium from the host rock. The volume of ore needed to create a modest amount of yellowcake is relatively massive. To generate 2,238 tons of U3O8 in 1967, Wyoming mined 1,238,000 tons of uranium ore.[4] The ability to strip mine most of Wyoming's uranium reserves moderated production costs, yet Wyoming was unsuccessful in attracting facilities to process uranium beyond the yellowcake. The small volume of usable material, post milling, and initial processing made it attractive to ship the yellowcake elsewhere for additional processing into fuel rods. The AEC subsidies were intended to terminate in 1966 but were extended to 1970. This AEC "stretch out" proposal was necessary as national defense needs were being met faster than expected. During the "stretch out," uranium began transitioning its sales to private industry. The operative assumption was that a viable commercial market would emerge for peaceful uses of uranium. Nuclear power plants were under construction, with many more on the drawing boards throughout the United States. Optimistic predictions surrounded the evolution of the domestic, peaceful-use uranium market; it was thought that uranium prices and markets would skyrocket. In 1966, Wyoming looked forward to significant future economic contributions from the uranium industry. However, uranium production would eventually plummet due to power plant safety concerns (Three Mile Island), cancellation of power plant plans due to high cost, and competition from international sources.

TRONA

Trona is a little recognized but important mineral in America. The same is true in Wyoming. Trona is a sodium bicarbonate ore created by the deposition of sodium, alkaline, and bicarbonate in a 15,000-square-mile lake that once covered southwestern Wyoming. Lying deep underground, the multiple seams of Wyoming trona constitute the largest deposit in the world. Following extraction, the ore is processed into soda ash. Soda ash has a vast array of uses, from the bicarbonate soda found in every kitchen to the manufacture of glass.

Surface deposits of the alkaline substance were used by early settlers and wagon trains passing through the area for cleaning and medicinal purposes in the 1800s. In the early to mid-1900s, oil and gas exploration documented the existence of massive underground trona deposits. These seams stretched for miles and miles. Mining and processing at scale began in the early 1950s when Westvaco (now Genesis Alkali) built a plant to produce commercial-quality soda ash. In 1962, Stauffer Chemical built a second plant. By 1966, plans were underway for Allied Chemical Company to complete the construction of a third plant by 1968. Prospects for further expansion were bright. Trona continues to be a mainstay of the economy in southwest Wyoming.

IRON ORE

For decades people understood Wyoming's landscape included significant deposits of iron. Successful, small-scale mining and milling operations had existed in Wyoming, supporting local economies, but significant growth commenced in 1960 when US Steel broke ground on an open pit mining operation near Atlantic City, Wyoming. A nearly 100-mile rail spur connected the mine with the Union Pacific mainline in Rock Springs. The ore was processed into pellets for shipment to Utah via Rock Springs. This large-scale operation became the lifeblood of Lander, Wyoming. Iron ore production was 2,066,000 tons in 1967.[5] In 1966, America's steel industry was prospering and there was every reason to believe the mine and mill would be part of Fremont County for decades to come. Iron ore production in Fremont County ended in 1983.

BENTONITE

Formed from volcanic ash immersed in seawater over millions of years, Bentonite is a fine clay with amazing sealing, absorbent, and expansion properties. Wyoming has significant reserves of bentonite, often referred to as the clay of a thousand uses—ranging from drilling mud to cat litter and cosmetics. Mining and production of bentonite accounted for 55,090 tons in 1936. Other than limited local impacts, it was an unseen part of the Wyoming economy when the sales tax was adopted. In the mid to late forties, Bentonite production accelerated rapidly largely tied to oil and gas production in America. By 1966 bentonite production was nearly 2 million tons.

TOURISM

The majesty of Wyoming's mountains, the great plains, the natural wonders of Yellowstone, and the grandeur of the Tetons had long attracted visitors from Theodore Roosevelt to wealthy Americans seeking outdoor adventures. Sporadic efforts to promote Wyoming as a place to visit, or perhaps settle, were a part of Wyoming since statehood. After World War II, slightly more serious efforts were adopted by Wyoming Commerce and Industry Commission. Eventually, a separate Wyoming Travel Commission was created in 1955. Most marketing efforts were focused on selling Yellowstone National Park and Wyoming's cowboy heritage.

In 1962, Wyoming's new Governor Cliff Hansen decided Wyoming needed a more aggressive approach to tourism. Frank Norris, a Greybull hotelier, was selected to lead the renewed effort in Cheyenne. It was a timely effort as America's economy was growing, people had money to spend and long family vacations by automobile were the new 'normal'. Tourism's contribution to Wyoming's economy had grown significantly since WWII. Quantification of the growth and impact of tourism from

WWII to 1966 is difficult because of limited data and the lack of a statistical definition of tourism during those years. A 2002 University of Wyoming study entitled, *Economic Trends in Wyoming's Travel and Tourism,* recognized this problem and suggested visitation to Yellowstone Park as representative:

> Yellowstone Park is the world's first national park created on
> March 1, 1872. Its opening also arguably marks the beginning of
> Wyoming's tourist industry and can be looked at as a proxy for
> growth.[6]

In 1935 when the Selective Sales Tax Act was adopted, visitation to Yellowstone was less than half a million people per year. In 1965, visitations exceeded 1.5 million people per year. Other Wyoming activities such as Cheyenne Frontier Days, skiing in Jackson, fishing, and hunting were also drawing visitors to Wyoming.

ELECTION OF 1966

Wyoming's post-WWII prosperity was unevenly distributed within the state. Geologic distribution of mineral deposits tended to determine the areas of economic activity, jobs, and wealth. Nine refineries were located in Wyoming, refining nearly ⅓ of the oil produced in the state. Coal production had not recovered from the railroad's transition from coal to diesel power. Uranium, trona, and iron ore reserves continued to be developed. Trona and iron ore contributed to Wyoming's reputation as a mineral storehouse. In aggregate, revenue from minerals made up an increasing share of state and local government revenues, although tourism, hunting and fishing may well have been Wyoming's fastest-growing industry during this period. Agriculture remained strong but declined in the number of farms, ranches, and employees.

These encouraging economic times were not accompanied by commensurate population growth. Wyoming's population growth rate remained lower than the national growth rate. The decade between 1950 and 1960 produced a net out-migration from Wyoming. Public and political discussions echoed the long-standing complaint against the exodus of young people and the lack of economic diversification. While Wyoming citizens were generally content, economic development would again be the backdrop of the 1966 election. Political parties and candidates dedicated significant energy and many words to the topic.

The Democrats were particularly optimistic about the 1966 election because of their amazing performance in the 1964 election. The aftermath of President Kennedy's assassination and the discomfort presented by Senator Goldwater as the Republican nominee for President led Wyoming to cast its electoral votes for Lyndon Johnson. The Wyoming House of Representatives had a Democratic majority for the first time in 30 years and the Senate was 13 Republicans and 12 Democrats. Improved prospects accompanied the decision by the popular incumbent Governor Cliff Hansen to run for Senate rather than seek a second term as governor.

Both political parties were strong enough to field several solid candidates for governor in their respective primaries. The Democrats fielded five candidates including two Casper attorneys, Ray Whitaker and Ernest Wilkerson, former legislator Howard Burke, former governor Jack Gage, and Cheyenne mayor Bill Nation. The winner was Ernest Wilkerson with only 31% of the vote, Nation and Gage capturing more than 20% each. Wilkerson had his work cut out for him to simply solidify his support among the Democrats. The smaller Republican field included three candidates: millionaire and stalwart of the old guard, Joe Burke, Arthur E. Linde, and Stanley K. Hathaway. Hathaway garnered 55% while Burke received 42%. Hathaway had been Goshen County Attorney in the 1950s and served as Republican Party Chairman from 1964 until announcing his candidacy for governor in 1966. Hathaway not only secured a much larger primary vote percentage than Wilkerson, but his time as Party Chairman had connected him with Republicans throughout the state.

Severance tax policy would again take center stage in the 1966 race for governor. The general orthodoxy within the dominant Republican Party was simple—leave minerals alone and rely on sales tax revenues, property taxes, and federal mineral royalties distributed back to the state.

Wilkerson forced the severance tax issue with the campaign slogan, "Wyoming Wealth for Wyoming's People." He proposed a 3% severance tax with half to fund current expenses and half dedicated to a permanent fund. Wilkerson further suggested some form of tax relief be provided to mineral producers creating Wyoming jobs by processing minerals within Wyoming.

Hathaway ridiculed the severance tax and suggested it may well be unconstitutional or, alternatively, perhaps a study was in order. Hathaway was aided by the usual industry groups and the "Committee to Save Jobs in Wyoming." The committee, akin to a modern-day dark money group, was funded by unknown persons and entities with no apparent evidence of links to the Hathaway campaign, although the ads encouraged voters to elect Hathaway. The Committee ran ads against the severance tax proposal claiming lost jobs and economic development. Hathaway won the election with 54% of the nearly 121,000 votes cast.

Clearly, the disagreement over severance taxes played a part in Wilkerson's defeat. But simple stylistic and personal differences between the two men also played a part. Wyoming voters could easily identify with Hathaway, a smart young attorney, practical, and without pretense. Wilkerson was less relatable. Neil Pierce in his 1972 book, *The Mountain States of America*, described Wilkerson:

> Refined, silver-haired, and a bit fastidious, Wilkerson was the most un-Wyoming-like candidate that one could imagine—which may account, in part, for his loss.[7]

Wilkerson's campaign reflected his personality. Campaign materials included long single-spaced advertisements, pamphlets, and issue papers. His answers to questions were erudite and lengthy. A bit shy and standoffish, Wilkerson simply lacked the common touch.

Wilkerson lost the election battle but won the war for a severance tax. Wilkerson would be vindicated when his anti-severance tax opponent requested a severance tax for government operating expenses in his second Legislative Session in 1969—followed in 1974 by Hathaway's endorsement of a permanent wealth trust fund supported by a 1½% severance tax.

HATHAWAY'S FIRST TERM

Newly elected Governor Stan Hathaway's Inaugural Address on January 2, 1967, called for a commitment to the high ideals of government service. A few days later, he would deliver his Message to the Wyoming Legislature, which was again solidly Republican.

HATHAWAY'S FIRST LEGISLATIVE SESSION

Hathaway's Message to the Wyoming Legislature was ambitious, positive, and progressive. It followed a pattern set by Governor Cliff Hansen's 1965 seven-thousand-word address. Wyoming historian Larsen judged Hansen's address as "...the most progressive gubernatorial address in the state's history since Joseph M. Carey emptied his cornucopia of reform proposals in 1911."[8] Of course, Larsen rendered this judgment before Hathaway's election. Which of the two governor's messages was the more progressive is left to individual judgment. The key attribute both governors shared is a clear expression of purpose and change being essential for Wyoming to achieve its potential and aspirations. A second attribute of the two messages was the courage to ask for tax increases on the citizens to fulfill the governor's vision of Wyoming's promise. In fact, Governor Hansen's proposed Executive Budget asked for many of the tax measures eventually promoted by Hathaway. Hansen's budget message contained a simple truth: "A Governor does his job only if he offers a method financing for all the recommended and potential appropriations likely to come before you."[9]

Hathaway's 1967 Legislative Message began by citing a list of challenges: the challenge of state equality and assistance to those in need, the challenge to "pursue evolution of our thinking," an understanding that problems do not go away. In Hathaway's words, "[t]hey are solved or they worsen." Hathaway also made clear his belief that Wyoming citizens would have to adapt to an uncertain future and be responsible for building the state. Finally, Hathaway advanced a balanced characterization of Wyoming's split personality relative to the federal government. In his words:

The federal government is our government. Many federal
activities are essential, constructive, desirable, and beneficial. But
the over balance of federal activity in a state will ultimately destroy
that state's government.[10]

A governor's address to the legislature is in part a pep rally, but always
includes a list of recommended actions. Hathaway's list was ambitious
and extended.

Hathaway called for an increase in the minimum wage, the creation
of an arts council, air pollution control, educational television, increased
educational funding, emphasis on vocational education, support for a new
community college in Fremont County, a constitutional amendment to
allow Initiative and Referendum, state participation in Medicaid, creation
of an Industrial Development Corporation to take advantage of federal
Small Business Administration funding, and several labor bills. While the
list is extensive, the underlying emphasis was on economic development
and education. No reference was made to tax increases or the funding
necessary to support this activist agenda. The only reference to taxes was
a suggestion to either correct the problems with the Inventory Tax or
phase it out. The less-than-smooth operation of the Inventory Tax was
the hook for those long opposed to its existence. Tax increases would be
tucked away in his proposed budget.

Hathaway's Biennial Budget reflected the spending priorities of his
Message to the Legislature. He made clear that funding Wyoming's
priorities reflected in his Budget would require additional revenue. He
did not leave a leadership vacuum, but recommended tax increases in his
transmittal letter for the proposed Executive Budget for the 1967–1969
Biennium:

The following are suggested possibilities for providing increased
revenue to the General Fund:

– An increase in the tax on cigarettes from 4 cents a package to
7 cents per package

– An increase in the excise tax on beer from 2 cents a gallon to
6 cents a gallon

– An increase in the excise tax on liquor from 10 cents per pint or fraction thereof to 20 cents per pint or fraction thereof, and an increase in the excise tax on wine from 3 cents per pint or fraction thereof to 6 cents per pint or fraction thereof

– An increase in the use tax from 2½ percent to 3 percent to complement a uniform 3 percent sales tax

– An increase in the State property tax of 1¾ mill (Can be done by the State Board of Equalization upon recommendation of the Governor.)[11]

According to the budget document the additional revenue would amount to $8,168,828, (67,964,649 in 2021 dollars).

By end of the Session, the Republican-controlled legislature implemented most of the recommended tax increases. Action was taken to reduce taxes by gradually shrinking the inventory tax through the year 1971 and to exempt inventories entirely after January 1, 1972.

Newspapers of the day reflect individual legislators' objections to certain tax increases. Such objections were not particularly along partisan lines. Nor were the objections based on an across-the-board "No New Taxes" mantra. There was a general recognition that added revenue was needed to fulfill the promise of Wyoming. The dominant view was the revenue should be raised by taxes on the activities of Wyoming citizens. A majority of Wyoming citizens were apparently comfortable footing the bill for Wyoming to be part of a growing and changing America. There is no evidence of a voter uprising against incumbents running for re-election in 1968.

1969: THE SEVERANCE TAX SESSION

In 1969, The State Senate was controlled by the Republicans (18/11) and Republicans controlled the House (42/13). Governor Hathaway's 1969 Message to the Legislature was again a progressive document. Entitled *Preparing Wyoming for Quality Growth in the Seventies*, the governor's speech renewed several requests from 1967. It focused on economic development, mined land reclamation, air quality protection, education, and governmental action. Notably, the message was much more optimistic about national interest in energy minerals fueling growth in Wyoming:

> But yesterday is not today—nor will today be the same as tomorrow. Each day, each new month, each new year bring new challenges, new problems and change. Change is inconvenient and calls for personal adjustment—but should not be feared.
>
> You have heard me say many times that Wyoming is at a crossroads in her history. I say today Wyoming is standing on the threshold of tremendous development.
>
> Recognition of Wyoming's importance not only to the Rocky Mountain region but to the nation is now a reality. The state is becoming more important as a source of energy fuels and other minerals; as a site in which modern technological and scientific industry can grow and prosper in a quality environment; and as a retreat offering a few days, weeks or months of healthful relaxation and recreation for millions of Americans not endowed as we are with clear air, pure water, open and beautiful skies.
>
> Impressive indeed has been the upsurge in oil and gas and uranium exploration and production, and the new interest in coal and other minerals portend a tremendous growth for Wyoming.
>
> I can tell you unequivocally that the great majority of Wyoming's people want their state to grow. [12]

This expectation of growth and change may account for the—not so subtle—shift from a simple call for growth to preparing for "quality growth."

As in 1967, taxes are barely referenced except for a 43-word-statement under the heading *Budget Financing*:

> The executive budget that I will present to you later this week is realistic and responsible. It cannot be totally financed from existing revenue sources. My budget message, therefore, will suggest to the legislature an additional tax upon the extracted minerals of Wyoming.

The Message to the Legislature did not specify the amount or type of mineral tax, but the subtext was a "severance tax." Hathaway, having campaigned against the "severance tax" chose not to employ the phrase. Apparently, the proposed budget was 8 million dollars underwater (64 million in 2021 dollars). The 1969-1971 Biennial Budget made the request much clearer. Under the heading "Suggested New Revenue" was the following language:

> When appropriations for the School Foundation Program,
> community colleges and other special appropriations are added to
> the Departmental budgets, it is obvious that a new revenue source
> will be required. I suggest to the legislature a mineral extraction
> tax in amount equal to 1% of the value of the gross product
> extracted.[13]

At that time, the state property tax was ½ mil. The fiscal profile included increasing the mil levy to 1½ mils producing $3.6 million. The mill levy increase would have generated twice that amount had the tax base not been reduced to less than 75% of its Constitutionally-mandated fair value. (A severance tax may not have been needed if property were taxed at 100% of value and the full 4 mil property tax base applied.) The remaining budget shortfall would be covered by a 1% mineral extraction tax producing an additional $7.6 million. These additions left a balanced budget and protected the auditors required cash balance.

Once introduced, the severance tax of 1% easily passed the Senate and the House in 1969. Revenue-raising bills must originate in the House. The Bill to enact the severance tax was introduced by C.H. Davis, Harold Hellbaum, and Leon Keith. Due to differences between the individual bills passed by the Senate and the House, a Conference Committee was appointed to iron out the differences. The final vote on a bill is the vote to accept the Conference Committee report. The final Senate tally was 20 ayes, 7 noes and 3 excused. The tally in the House was even more lop-sided with 54 ayes, 2 noes, and 5 absent. Two names that would become household names in Wyoming politics, Al Simpson and Ed Herschler, voted "aye" on the final vote.

Strategic legislative assistance came from an unlikely source — Representative Warren Morton (R-Natrona). Representative Morton was an extremely intelligent, articulate, Yale-educated, successful, independent oil man from Casper. Morton, who would later run for governor, was a staunch supporter of free enterprise and the oil and gas industry. In later years he would oppose what he considered unjustified increases in severance taxes. But in the effort to pass the original severance task, his actions personified the best of Alexis de Tocqueville's 1835 assessment of the American's understanding of "enlightened self-interest." The notion being, sometimes it is appropriate to compromise one's immediate self-interest for the advancement of the common good, particularly when one realizes they too would benefit from the advancement of the common good.

Hathaway succeeded in securing the exact tax he had opposed and criticized in his election three years before. The reality is Hathaway made a pragmatic and logical decision in the best interest of his state. Perhaps he simply understood the phrase from Lincoln's 1862 Message to Congress: "The dogmas of the quiet past are inadequate to the stormy present."

Governor Hathaway and the Republican legislators supporting the severance tax were subjected to considerable criticism by industry and their own party. Even the early meetings with the Republican legislative caucus were hostile. According to Jack Speight (Chief of Staff to the governor), Hathaway was booed during an early Republican legislative caucus when explaining the proposed "...tax on extractive minerals." Hathaway had anticipated a less-than-warm response, nonetheless, he remained confident his decision was correct. In an observation to Speight as they left the meeting, Hathaway remarked, "that went well, didn't it?" There were also supportive members of the caucus, most notably Representative Warren Morton.

A certain folklore exists in Wyoming suggesting the state was forced to pass the severance tax because the government coffers were empty. State financial documents for the time do not support such a claim. There may have been cash flow problems due to the annual payment of property taxes, but Wyoming certainly was not financially impoverished.

The Wyoming Department of Revenue and State Treasurer Reports for the time show a consistent, healthy five million dollars surplus in the

General Fund (40 million in 2021 dollars). The General Fund is the account from which most government expenditures are drawn. This five-million-dollar figure is in the context of a general fund budget of around thirty million dollars. Clearly, Wyoming's government was not broke. The books were balanced and then some. Further, the state had unused taxing authority within the 4-mil levy state property tax allowed under the Constitution.

A severance tax made sense for two practical political reasons. First, the public was unlikely to welcome more fees or taxes in 1969 given the increases from 1967. Wyoming's complicated real and personal property tax structure and the sales tax meant everyone personally felt changes in tax rates. Revenue was generated largely through taxation of real and personal property, cigarettes, gasoline, insurance, inheritance, and various vehicle-related fees. Managing assessments and taxes were divided between state and local governments. The state handled minerals, select industrial properties, and sales tax. The individual county assessor's task was more granular. Ten or more classifications of land plus improvements had to be identified and valued for assessment purposes. Livestock categorized as cattle, horses, mules and asses, sheep, swine, and goats were subject to tax. Dogs, fur-bearing animals, poultry, and bee colonies were counted and assessed separately. Personal property had more than 25 categories including equipment, tractors and threshing machines, household furniture, musical instruments, televisions, radios, private libraries, household electrical and gas appliances, merchandise inventories, etc. A separate category was established for "Stock and Shares in Banks, etc."

Further complications arose from the number of taxes and taxing districts. There were twelve different taxes levied: state and county general fund levies, two educational levies, levies for county fairs, hospitals, and libraries, some levies for debt retirement and interest, and two county levies for welfare and health. Plus, there were fees for predatory animal control, livestock inspection, and sheep inspection.

Given the number of items subject to tax and the division of tasks combined with a complicated system of levies and fees, one can understand the political reluctance to tackle restructuring this system and/or increasing rates. The search for other revenue sources became inevitable. Pragmatic state leadership may have concluded the future of Wyoming's tax base rested with extractive minerals.

A second practical political reason was simply an understanding of human nature. The long-standing citizens' position on taxation articulated by Senator Russell Long of Louisiana (Chairman of the Senate Finance Committee) seemed quite appealing. Senator Long's summary is quite straightforward — "Don't tax me, Don't tax thee, Tax that fellow behind the tree."

In Wyoming's case "that fellow behind the tree" was the mineral industry. And the mineral industry simply passed the tax on to the out-of-state consumer.

The expectation of "tremendous growth" announced by Hathaway in his 1969 address to the Legislature was not political hyperbole. Forces outside Wyoming and beyond our control were dictating the future. America's appetite for electricity derived from fossil fuels and nuclear power continued the dramatic increase in demand inaugurated by the end of WWII. In the context of *the Paradox of Plenty*, a massive influx of outside capital was on the horizon. Wyoming wisely decided to enhance its wealth as the resources were extracted and sold elsewhere. In fact, it may have been the only logical decision available. The unfortunate result was two traps: a singular focus on the mineral economy and tax reductions for our citizens.

LOGIC BEHIND TYING WYOMING'S ECONOMIC AND REVENUE FUTURE TO MINERALS

Recognition of Wyoming's mineral future was not a fanciful proposition. A report released in 1969 detailed the expectations of Wyoming's mineral future. The report drew upon an understanding of the changing status of energy minerals in the United States and abroad.

An extensive, 4-volume report entitled *Review and Forecast, Wyoming Mineral Industries* by Cameron Engineers was commissioned by the Wyoming Natural Resource Board and the State Water Planning Program.[14] Cameron examined various sectors "...in depth to determine its development and importance as of 1967 and to project expected development to years 1972, 1980, 2000, and 2020."[15] The report assumed the then-present political policies would prevail into the future. An assumption that would prove inaccurate. Similarly, Cameron inaccurately assumed availability of water would not limit mineral development and industrialization.

"No consideration was given to the lack of water in any given area. For example, if resources and other conditions indicated the need for creation of a new industry or expansions of an existing industry, our forecast was not to be affected by the possibility of a lack of necessary water. Apparent lack of water was to be no constraining factor."[16]

Cameron noted Wyoming's encouraging growth in mineral production and related employment. It also provides a blunt summary of Wyoming's "exporter status."

> Wyoming's mineral industries are not generally interrelated. Most of Wyoming's production of crude oil, for example, is exported to other states. Most of Wyoming's production of trona, iron ore, uranium, phosphate rock, etc., also are exported for use as raw material in the production of higher-value products.
>
> The small population of the state, the correspondingly small local markets for products, and the great distances to the major population (market) centers presently serve as obstacles to the development of integrated industrial developments within the state. A feature of Wyoming's economy has been the lack of manufacturing industries.
>
> The present economy of the state is greatly dependent upon the mineral industries, and the mineral industries are dependent upon the production of usable raw materials that can bear the cost of transport to distant market centers.[17]

Our circumstance has not changed substantially since this was written in the late sixties.

The following charts reflect the magnitude of projected mineral development in Cameron's *Review and Forecast: Volume I.*

PETROLEUM

Consistent with the accepted wisdom of the time, Cameron anticipated a steep decline in conventional oil production in the United States. Wyoming was no exception. Similarly, Cameron was bullish on the prospects for oil shale development. The report did note the Wyoming oil shale reserves were not among the best reserves in America.

WYOMING PETROLEUM INDUSTRY FORECAST				
	1972	1980	2000	2020
Crude Oil (1000 BBL)				
Forecast	140,000	75,000	30,000	30,000
Actual	125,222,375	114,143,544	58,020,990	88,507,057
Natural Gas (Million Cu. Ft.)				
Forecast	250,000	250,000	100,000	100,000
Actual	285,426,141	349,518,516	1,294,152,091	1,327,105,636

SOURCES: Cameron p. 81, Wyoming Department of Revenue Annual Reports for 1973, 1981, 2001, 2021.

WYOMING SHALE OIL PRODUCTION FORECAST				
	1972	1980	2000	2020
Forecast				
FACILITY: Open Pit Mining Barrels Oil/Day	None	50,000	50,000	50,000
FACILITY: In-Situ Reporting Barrels Oil/Day	None	50,000	100,000	150,000
Forecast State Total	None	100,000	150,000	200,000
Actual (Shale Oil was never produced in WY)				
	0	0	0	0

SOURCES: Cameron p. 95, Wyoming Department of Revenue Annual Reports for 1973, 1981, 2001, 2021.

COAL

The discussion begins with an assessment of Wyoming's vast coal resources and the shift from underground to surface mining. It then summarizes the basis for the new coal demand. "The major part of the new coal requirement will be to supply raw material for production of 'synthetic' liquid and gaseous fuels to supply fuel to large-capacity coal-fueled electric generators." (CAMERON P. 106) The summary of 130 expected coal mines and processing facilities in Wyoming by 2020 reflected the dominant view that coal was to be a major fuel source for meeting national demand for electricity and petroleum substitutes.

WYOMING FACILITIES OPERATIONAL IN 2020	FORECAST NUMBER	ACTUAL NUMBER
Coal Mines	69	16
Steam-Electric Power Plants	34	11
Synthetic Liquid Fuel Plants	10	0
Gasification Plants	10	0
Coal Carbonizers	7	0

SOURCES: Cameron p. 107, Wyoming Department of Revenue Annual Reports for 1973, 1981, 2001, 2021.

COAL PRODUCTION PROJECTIONS

Coal production was 3.6 million tons in 1967. Most of the new coal production was to be used in electric power plants, coal liquefaction plants, and coal gasification plants—all located in Wyoming. Only a small fraction of the coal production was expected to be exported beyond our borders.

WYOMING COAL PRODUCTION FORECAST (million tons)						
	1972	1980	1990	2000	2010	2020
Forecast	7.3	38.7	97.2	167.7	275.0	360.9
Actual	11	95	184	339	442	219

SOURCES: Cameron p. 113, Wyoming Department of Revenue Annual Reports for 1973, 1981, 2001, 2021.

URANIUM

The Cameron report notes Wyoming uranium reserves represented 38.9 percent of the nation's known reserves of U3O8. There were 5 operating uranium mills at the time of the Cameron report. The report adds: "Although Wyoming produces about 20 percent of the nation's yellowcake product, none of the subsequent enrichment, reactor fuel fabrication, or re-processing operations are performed within the state."[18]

WYOMING URANIUM INDUSTRY FORECAST U3O8 Yellowcake (annual tons)					
	1967	1972	1980	2000	2020
Forecast		6,000	16,000	25,000	5,000
Actual	2,328	4,216	6,036	1,037	23

SOURCES: Cameron p. 127, Wyoming Department of Revenue Annual Reports for 1973, 1981, 2001, 2021.

BENTONITE

The Cameron report summarizes their findings as follows: "Eleven bentonite processing plants operated in Wyoming in 1967. About 1.5 million tons of bentonite were produced in the state, valued at about $14.3 million." (CAMERON P. 132)

The Cameron Report projected that 4 more plants will be in operation by 2020: "Wyoming's bentonite industry comprises 75 percent of the total U.S. bentonite industry. The consuming industries, in order of tonnage demands for bentonite, are iron ore pelletizing, foundries, and the oil well drilling industry."[19]

WYOMING BENTONITE PRODUCTION FORECAST Tons of Dried Bentonite (millions)				
	1972	1980	2000	2020
Forecast	1.8	2.1	2.5	2.5
Actual	2.0	3.6	4.2	4.5

SOURCES: Cameron p. 136, Wyoming Department of Revenue Annual Reports for 1973, 1981, 2001, 2021.

IRON ORE

Cameron discusses industry status, reserves, different types of ore available in Wyoming, processing facilities, etc.

WYOMING MINE-RUN ORE PRODUCTION FORECAST Mine Run Ore Production (millions of short tons)					
	1967	1972	1980	2000	2020
Forecast		4.85	5.55	7.9	10.05
Actual	4.75	4.5	4.6	0	0

SOURCES: Cameron p. 161, Wyoming Department of Revenue Annual Reports for 1973, 1981, 2001, 2021.

SODIUM/TRONA

The report catalogs Wyoming's massive trona deposits and recognizes the current operations. It further estimates rapid expansion and stiff competition from other sources in later years.

WYOMING TRONA PRODUCTION FORECAST (millions of tons)				
	1972	1980	2000	2020
Forecast	5.3	7.4	9.0	10.0
Actual	4.8	12.2	17.8	17.6

SOURCES: Cameron p. 93, Wyoming Department of Revenue Annual Reports for 1973, 1981, 2001, 2021.

Cameron was not alone in projecting projected significant mineral production expansion. Through the early and mid-sixties, momentum had been building for a shift to coal-based generation to meet America's thirst for electricity. A bit late to act, the Department of Interior initiated the North Central Power Study Report of Phase I (NCPS) in 1970. The study design was to evaluate a coordinated mobilization of resources to meet the expanding American demand for electricity. Undertaken later than the Cameron report, the NCPS captured the same national energy expectations.

The NCPS encompassed 13 Midwestern and Rocky Mountain states.

The premise was for mine-mouth power generation and the construction of a massive system of power lines to distribute the energy throughout the region. The plan envisioned 10 one-thousand-megawatt mine-mouth coal-fired electric generating stations in the Wyoming Powder River Basin coal fields. Water would be moved from various reservoirs in Wyoming and Montana to meet the water demands of the plants.

Even if the various projections were only 50% correct, minerals were going to boom in Wyoming. Some in Wyoming were tempted to revisit a song popular in 1929 and adopted by the Roosevelt Administration in 1932 — "Happy Days are Here Again." Not everyone joined in the songfest.

Political and civic figures often assert ownership of an economic boom, essentially mimicking the rooster who crows in the morning taking credit for the rising of the sun. At the time, Governor Hathaway did not claim credit for the mineral boom. Hathaway and most of the legislators had lived long enough to know commodity demand and price were beyond the control of the state. Experience sometimes leads to wisdom—leading the state to implement measures to capture a portion of the commodity revenue stream and to protect Wyoming's heritage and environment. (*See Chapter 4 for a brief discussion of the American Energy and Environmental Policy Shaping Wyoming.*)

Hathaway, the 1966 simple "growth and no taxes" candidate became the "quality growth and severance tax governor." A portion of Wyoming voters would eventually come to view Hathaway as tilting towards growth at the expense of environmental and lifestyle concerns.

1970: HATHAWAY'S RE-ELECTION

To no one's surprise, Governor Hathaway decided to seek re-election. Hathaway had a positive record of activity in state government and was well-liked. The Wyoming economy was doing well. Annual mineral production had increased during Hathaway's first term. According to a 1988 Joint Legislative Executive Study of Revenue and Expenditures, the increases from 1966 to 1970 were substantial:

– Coal production had increased from 3.7 million tons to 7.4 million tons.

– Oil production had increased from 134.5 million barrels to 155.8 million barrels.

– Natural Gas production increased from 267 million mcf to 318 million mcf.

– Uranium production has increased from 916,415 tons to 2,042,074 million tons.

– Trona production had increased from 2.1 million tons to 4.0 million tons.[20]

The outcome of the election was never really in doubt. Hathaway defeated Cheyenne attorney John Rooney, 63% to 37%.

Wyoming's citizens may not have understood the long-term import of tying the state's future to minerals and severance tax revenues, but in 1970 it was judged to be a fine decision.

HATHAWAY'S SECOND TERM: ADJUSTING TO THE ENERGY BOOM

1971 was the first Legislative Session of Hathaway's second term. In his Legislative Message, Hathaway began by restating his inaugural theme: "The challenge for all of us in the 70s is to help Wyoming grow with quality." Our economy "has been steadily growing and Wyoming is slowly growing in population." He was also pleased to submit a state budget that "...does not require new taxes or tax increases." And for the first time, no general government property tax would be imposed. Largely due to severance tax revenues, the general government statewide mill levy (tax) had not been imposed since 1969. Gone was the clarion call for more growth that had dominated the prior 20 years of Wyoming's history.

In addition to the tax relief afforded by eliminating the statewide property tax, Hathaway proposed the gradual reduction and elimination of the property tax mill levy imposed by each county for support of county welfare. Legislation would be offered to gradually reduce and then eliminate the county welfare levy. The tax burden was shifted to the state severance tax. Hathaway supported state participation in the federal Medicaid program created in 1965 with the passage of Title XIX of the Social Security Act. Medicaid provided a 50% federal match for state expenditures to provide healthcare and other services to the poor.

Hathaway pushed for more funding for environmental protection programs and support for local planning legislation. Five bills would be submitted by the Department of Economic Planning and Development as part of Wyoming's quality growth plan "concerning county and city planning and zoning."

Wyoming's lifelong distaste for income taxes found voice in legislation to pre-empt local governmental authorities from imposing any form of taxation linked to income. Nothing had changed since the 1930s.

One legislative action would prove controversial in subsequent years. Under the heading "Conservation of Water Resources," Hathaway invoked the longstanding and factually justified fear that Wyoming would lose its water to downstream states. Hathaway shared this concern, "If Wyoming does not use its unappropriated Green River water before the Central Arizona Project comes on stream in 1980, we stand the real danger of losing it forever."

In arid Wyoming, water was (and remains) a major issue. Wyoming is entitled by interstate compacts and case law to utilize a certain amount of the water originating within the state. The lack of population and economic growth in the state means significant portions of Wyoming's water entitlement remain unused. It simply flows downstream — a circumstance bringing joy to the hearts of the downstream states.

Given the growth scenarios discussed previously, it was clear the Powder River Basin lacked sufficient water resources to support the potential development. The North Central Power Study had mapped a plan to take water from basins in Wyoming and Montana to support a massive coal-fired power generation and coal gasification complex in Campbell County, Wyoming.

For Hathaway and most legislators, moving water out of the Green River Basin to support the development in the Powder River Basin seemed an obvious solution. The argument in favor of the legislation was to at least use the water within Wyoming, even if it meant transferring the water from one river basin to another.

Introduced in 1971 as a State Senate bill, the "Green River Feasibility Study" legislation directed the Department of Economic Development to:

> ...undertake forthwith a feasibility and financing study, which shall include various methods of financing to include funding by issuance of revenue bonds for the development for projects as defined in this act, for the necessary facilities to make maximum, practical, beneficial and multiple use of Wyoming's water in the Green River and Great Divide Basins and to the degree that there is water in excess of present and foreseeable uses in the Green River and Great Divide Basins, for the maximum and multiple use of Wyoming's Green River water in other basins within the state.[21]

Controversy would eventually engulf this trans-basin diversion proposal. Many residents in the Green River Basin viewed the diversion of their water to another basin as paramount to stealing water they would need in the future. Residents in other water basins throughout Wyoming viewed the proposal with alarm, reasoning that if water could be stolen from the Green River Basin they could be the next to lose their water.

1973 WYOMING LEGISLATURE

In October of 1972, the feasibility study authorized in 1971 to evaluate the trans-basin diversion of water from the Green River Basin to northeast Wyoming's coal country was released. The Department of Economic Development and Planning retained the engineering firm of Tipton and Kalmbach located in Denver to perform the study. Under the rather grand title *Engineering Report on the Development of Presently Unused Water Supplies of the Green River Basin in Wyoming: with Particular Reference to the Feasibility of Providing Additional Reservoir Storage* (referred to as the Diversion Report),[22] the report triggered another of Wyoming's periodic water wars. The Diversion Report determined that a combination of reservoir storage with potential aqueducts and pipes could move between 100,000 and 300,000-acre-feet of water over the mountains to partially meet the water needs of coal-fired electric generation plants and synthetic fuel facilities in northeast Wyoming. Southwestern Wyoming viewed the report as supporting the theft of their water by political and industrial interests in other parts of Wyoming. They were ready to prove the saying, "In Wyoming, whiskey's for drinking and water's for fighting."

The federal government had notified Wyoming of inadequacies in its regulatory structure related to land and water environmental protection. Congress was moving legislation to force local and state land use planning across America. The federal Environmental Protection Agency, created in 1970, was coming of age.

Additional actors and organizations emerged in Wyoming as part of the national conservation and environmental movement. According to a March 1974 newsletter from the Wyoming Outdoor Council, "the 1973 Legislative Session marked the beginning of the citizen-environmental lobby in Cheyenne...." Other environmental/conservation groups secured lobbyists and intended to be active in 1973. The Wyoming Chapter of the Sierra Club had been organized in the early 1970s. With two lobbyists in Cheyenne, the group was focused on environmental legislation, particularly state industrial facility siting legislation. In explaining their purpose, executive committee chair Art Fawcett quoted the motto "Not blind opposition to progress, but opposition to blind progress."[23] With more than ten major coal facilities under discussion, concern about dangerous trace elements released in coal combustion and processing led the Audubon Society to call for a study of trace elements in coal.

Hathaway's 1973 Legislative Message followed a now-familiar pattern. It highlighted a healthy and growing state economy along with increased personal income and employment. The growth in solid mineral production was touted as well. Hathaway demonstrated a nuanced understanding of the relationship between oil and gas production and state revenues. Pointing to reduced oil and gas production numbers, Hathaway reminded the Legislature that price increases for oil and gas had still produced increased tax revenues. Wyoming was also receiving more federal dollars by virtue of President Nixon's Revenue Sharing program. The largely unrestricted income to the state added to the already expanded flow of public revenues.

Hathaway's budget asked for increased funding—a 28% increase in general fund expenditures alone. Even with expanded governmental services, plenty of money was left to support expanded tax relief for Wyoming's citizens. High levels of public services combined with tax reductions? Sounds a bit like *the Paradox of Plenty*. Hathaway requested a property tax exemption for the homes of the elderly and disabled, estimating that 8,069 households (in certain categories) would qualify for the program. To offset the loss of property tax revenues to local governments, the Legislature was asked to appropriate $750,000 (4,695,000 in 2021 dollars). This program came to be known as the Homestead Exemption. But wait, there is more tax relief. Hathaway's Message continues:

> The personal property tax upon household furniture and appliances, musical instruments, jewelry and clothing is impossible to assess in an equitable manner and is therefore discriminatory. I propose that it be repealed with a resulting tax saving for nearly every Wyoming taxpayer. Based upon present valuations, the tax savings would be approximately $1,739,000 per year (10,886,140 in 2021 dollars).

An additional tax relief measure that Hathaway did not request in his Message but did support and sign was a change in the method of valuing agricultural lands. Agricultural interests had long complained the "fair market value" system of assessing agricultural lands was burdensome. Fair market value in theory is the price of the land as determined by a transaction between a willing buyer and a willing seller. The agricultural interests contended the lands did not produce enough income to justify the taxes they paid. In other words, the land may sell for the projected "fair market value" but the land did not generate a great deal of income. Agricultural interests were often "land rich and cash poor." The Legislature agreed. Agricultural land would no longer be assessed at its fair market value. Instead, it would be valued based on its capacity to produce agricultural crops or commodities. While not described as an income tax, the valuation of agricultural property would be pegged to agricultural income generated instead of fair market value. The Legislature clearly understood this was a substantial tax break. The legislation included a 5-year hold harmless based on the "...average assessed valuation for 1971 and 1972." It would be nearly 15 years before the Wyoming Supreme Court would strike down this statutory tax preference.

Hathaway also asked for the passage of the Environmental Quality Act (EQA) to consolidate environmental programs in a single agency, like the federal EPA. Passage of the EQA was never in doubt—general agreement existed regarding the need for the consolidation and enhanced air, land, and water regulatory provisions. Equal impetus came from the preference for state rather than federal enforcement of environmental regulation.

However, significant issues arose as to the EQA provisions related to strip mining. Representative Morton (R-Natrona) had introduced a strip-mining regulation bill to update and expand upon the 1969 Open Cut Reclamation Act. Fellow representatives had their own suggestions to strengthen the reclamation provisions, and of course, senators had their own thoughts to offer. A third player in the reclamation drama were environmental/conservation interests. Joining the discussion were groups of county commissioners from the counties most impacted by coal development.

Slightly more than halfway through the session, the tension between Governor Hathaway and environmental spokesman Tom Bell, the editor of *High Country News*, spilled into the media. According to a January 12, 1973, article in the *Casper Star Tribune*, Bell asserted, "The mining interests are in Cheyenne in droves trying to beat down any attempt to strictly regulate their activities. They are finding attentive ears in Governor Hathaway and far too many legislators...." Governor Hathaway was even more direct and somewhat scathing in his reference to Bell when asked about published criticism by the Lander environmentalist. "Mr. Bell speaks so often, and it seems to me out of focus so much." Hathaway told the press conference, "He hasn't had anything good to say about this administration for six years."

Representative Morton pointed out that the final bill had incorporated various proposals from legislators and the public, citing the bill's growth from 18 pages upon introduction to 52 pages as passed.

Among the state senators pushing for stronger reclamation standards were Tom Stroock from Natrona County and Malcolm Wallop from Sheridan County. Both supported and argued for the bill in its final form. This was the beginning of Malcolm Wallop's unsuccessful run for governor and subsequent successful run for the U.S. Senate. While the process was contentious, the final reclamation provisions were much stronger than the original bill offered by Representative Morton. Most of the changes eventually enjoyed reluctant support from Representative Morton.

Of note were two provisions strengthening the power of individual citizens that were inserted in the Environmental Quality Act (EQA) during floor debate. One condition required a mining company applying for a permit to mine include a document showing the surface owner (if different from the mineral owner) had consented to the conduct of the mining operation. If the surface owner withheld consent, the Environmental Quality Council could issue an "order in lieu of consent" after a hearing and public notice. The required findings determined that the mining operation "…does not substantially prohibit the operations of the surface owner.…" This was a significant shift in the power relationship between the mineral estate owner and the surface landowner. Before this amendment, the mineral estate was the dominant estate, which meant that the mining operation could utilize the portion of the surface land needed to develop the minerals. Compensation to the surface owner was generally limited to the value of any surface improvements and loss of productivity. This 1973 amendment strengthened the hand of the surface owner but left the basic dominance of the mineral estate in place. It became more expensive to assert this dominance, but it still existed.

In 1974, the EQA would be modified to fundamentally change the relationship between the mineral owner and the surface owner for a limited class of surface owners. The class consisted of "resident or agricultural landowners" defined primarily as ownership pre-dating January 1, 1970, operating a ranching or agricultural enterprise, or gaining a "significant portion of their income from farming and ranching operations." For this class of surface owners, no mining permit could be granted without their written consent. One commentator correctly observed: "Wyoming's surface owner consent law has the practical effect of reversing the legal position of the surface owner and the mineral estate owner."[24] As to this class of landowner, the coal companies could no longer obtain an order in lieu of consent from the Environmental Quality Council. They either paid whatever the surface owner requested, or mining could not proceed.

A second amendment inserted on the floor created a cause of action allowing any individual whose water well or supply was damaged by a mining operation's disturbance of a water aquifer to proceed against the mining company. Members of the 1974 Legislature were demonstrating an interest in protecting the economic and cultural interests of Wyoming citizens.

Legislation establishing and funding a State Land Use Commission was also passed. For some, the impetus was the need for improved land use planning and zoning within Wyoming to accommodate anticipated growth. For others, the concern was pending federal legislation[25] designed to force states and localities to engage in planning and zoning. However, the federal legislation ultimately failed.

Trans-basin water diversion from the Green River to other parts of Wyoming ignited heated legislative discussion, even though no action was requested. In legislation allowing Wyoming to purchase 60,000 acre-feet of water storage in Fontenelle Reservoir, Senator Robert Johnson (D-Sweetwater County) charged the authors of the Green River Feasibility Study (Tipton and Kalmbach, Inc.) were biased in favor of moving water to coal country in northeast Wyoming. The alleged conflict was Tipton Kalmbach's representation of Reynolds Aluminum. Reynolds was planning a massive coal project near Buffalo. Senator Johnson spoke for many in Wyoming, asserting, "I'm not sure we want to rob one basin for the benefit of another."[26]

Reynolds Aluminum had, for many years—dating back to the 1950s—worked to secure control of coal, water, and land ownership in rural Johnson County, fueling various theories about the intended use of those resources. Speculation ended in 1972 when Reynolds announced plans to construct a $2.2 billion (14.63 billion in 2021 dollars) power plant and gaseous diffusion plant to enrich uranium fuel.

Expectations of booming growth were heightened based on expanded oil and gas activity, expanded trona extraction and processing, development of coal mines throughout the state, power plant construction in Rock Springs, and anticipated uranium development. Various news outlets carried stories about the impact of growth in rural Wyoming. Typical headlines were "Sweetwater County has 'medical crisis' start."[27]

Hathaway was sensitive to the problems of local governments facing "dramatic growth in the next few years whether they want it or not," acknowledging that population growth comes before the tax base. Further, most of the tax base would be in the county and beyond the taxing authority of cities and towns that would host the expanded population. Direct financial assistance from the state was not supported by the Legislature or Hathaway. Instead, the recommended response was for the state to make low-interest loans to impacted municipal areas that would pledge future local revenues for repayment.

A legislative attempt was made to increase the severance tax. House Bill 152, sponsored by ten House members, would have increased the severance tax by 2%, giving half of the increase to the general fund and the remainder to be deposited in the Common School Permanent Land Fund. It died a quick death in committee.

The plethora of development proposals in Wyoming in the early 1970s prompted Representative Meenan (R-Natrona County) to introduce an "Electric Facilities Siting Act." The act would require review, analysis, and regulation of major electric facilities seeking to locate in Wyoming.[28] The legislation arrived too late for consideration in 1973, but it cued the issue for further consideration in 1974 and passage in 1975.

Despite the boom in development and population and the resulting economic strain on government services, legislative distaste for income taxes remained strong. A proposed constitutional amendment offered by Representative Nels Smith, a rancher from Crook County, gained bipartisan support. Smith's proposed amendment would credit all other taxes paid by a taxpayer against any potential tax imposed on income. Voters passed the amendment in November of 1974.

Within weeks following the adjournment of the Legislature, plans for another major power plant (1200 MW) were announced for the same vicinity as the proposed Reynolds Aluminum Project. Growing concern about population and environmental impacts was reflected in a comment by Wyoming's only elected independent member of the Legislature hailing from Johnson County—the site for both proposed facilities. "They waited until the Legislature had gone home," Holland said. "If they'd made the applications earlier, I'll bet the Legislature would have made some changes in the Environmental Quality Act."[29]

1974 WYOMING LEGISLATIVE SESSION:
TAXES AND PERMANENT FUND

Coal continued to boom throughout 1973. For the first time, Wyoming coal sold for $24 a ton (150.24 in 2021 dollars).[30] It was a record price and harbinger of things to come.

Following the 1973 Legislative Session, the Wyoming Outdoor Council released a scoring of Wyoming legislators' performance on critical environmental issues. Only Representative Turner (R-Teton County) received a perfect 100 score. The highest ratings in the Senate went to June Boyle (D-Albany County), Dave Hitchcock (D-Albany County), Tom Stroock (R-Natrona County), and Malcolm Wallop (R-Sheridan County). Three senators received a score of zero, including Dick Jones (R-Park County), who would be the Republican candidate for governor in 1974. The top scores in the House went to Democrats Rodger McDaniel (Laramie County), Dennis Stickley (Albany County), and Walter Urbigkit (Laramie County).[31]

Environmental impact, growth issues, and severance taxes remained major topics in the media throughout 1973. Public attitudes were evolving into a more skeptical and protective approach to the predicted growth boom. An additional conservation/environmental group, the Powder River Basin Resource Council (PRBRC), was incorporated in August 1973. Water quality, freshwater aquifers, and managing the social impacts of development were the moving force behind the group's formation. Sponsors of the 1200 MW power plant in Johnson County had begun drilling exploratory water wells southwest of Buffalo, looking for a water supply. Jack Chase, a PRBRC board member, told the *Casper Star Tribune*, "When they came in here and started monkeying with the water in the mountain, it really got to people. I think water will draw people into a state of arms quicker than anything. I think they are more concerned about water than strip mining."[32]

Governor Hathaway had hinted he might not seek a third term as governor. Quiet and appropriate speculation among potential candidates began, and when Hathaway made it official in December of 1973, ambitions were unveiled.

In January 1974, *High Country News* editor Tom Bell called for increased severance taxes, industrial siting legislation, stronger reclamation standards, etc. Bell acknowledged that the nation needed the coal but called for stricter controls. He referenced various non-Wyoming published sources suggesting "...northeastern Wyoming could become one of the planned 'national sacrifice areas' where the country would be ravaged to provide power to the nation."[33]

Concerns about the environmental and social costs of accelerated growth naturally migrated into a discussion of "Wyoming after the boom." Public service costs related to a booming population would require more money today. But what about tomorrow? Minerals can only be extracted once. How would Wyoming support itself when the minerals were gone, or the extraction companies moved on? Discussions logically turned to increased severance taxes and a Permanent Wealth Fund championed by Ernest Wilkerson in 1966. And these discussions would shape the 1974 Legislative Session.

Competing severance tax increase measures were offered by both Republicans and Democrats. Democrats were particularly aggressive on the issue of increased severance taxes, which had periodically been part of the Democrat agenda since the 1920s. Before the session, United Press International surveyed legislative attitudes on the tax. Not all legislators responded, but seventy-nine percent of respondents favored it.

This confirmed a point made by Senator Leimback (D-Natrona) — "the people are for it."

In January 1974, Hathaway told the Wyoming Press Association that a coal tax bill offered by Senator Harry Leimback (a potential Democratic candidate for governor) was a partial answer,

> But, we should be looking for a 'total bill' ... I believe there is justification for an increase of taxes on fossil fuels."[34]

The Wyoming Mining Association (WMA) did not outright oppose severance tax increases but preferred a study to consider the issue in 1975. "What I object to is the punitive theory of taxation," said Bill Budd, executive secretary of the WMA, "They're saying tax the rascals now."[35]

Legislative proposals during the 1974 session targeted aid to impacted schools, called for a halt to groundwater use transfers until a study could be completed, and required industrial facilities to be analyzed and permitted two years prior to construction. Increasingly, media throughout the state covered the challenges to housing, public infrastructure, medical care, schools, and social services precipitated by the "boom town" growth in southwest Wyoming and Campbell County in northeast Wyoming. United Press International ran a story listing these, and similar items under the headline "Boom reaction may plague session."[36]

Four paragraphs in the staunchly Republican *Casper Star Tribune* editorial published the Sunday before the Legislative Session captured the moment:

> Wyoming is on the brink of massive mineral development and population surge. Witness what is happening around the state, notably in Gillette and Rock Springs. The impact will be felt statewide as Wyoming coal and minerals are mined to meet national needs.
>
> The Democratic Party is aware of this. We hardly have to direct your attention to the groundswell of support Sen. Harry Leimback reports he has received for his coal excise tax.
>
> We hardly have to direct your attention to the chagrin, if not dismay, that Democratic Senator Leimback's bill has wrenched

from some spokesman for the petroleum and minerals industry and some segments of the Republican party.

The Democrats, we believe, have grasped this political moment given impetus by awakened concern about our environment, the present and immediate future of Wyoming. And do not forget Watergate, inflation, and corruption in government.

It will no doubt be an interesting session and could well be one of the most important ones in Wyoming history.[37]

GOVERNOR HATHAWAY'S
1974 MESSAGE TO THE LEGISLATURE

Speaking before a legislative audience with more than a few would-be governors present, Hathaway delivered his final Legislative Message on January 23, 1974. Recognizing Wyoming attitudes had changed, his address was progressive and politically astute.

Hathaway's 1974 budget expansion requests were relatively modest: an increase in the Land Quality budget to handle the expanding volume of mining permit applications, money for Wyoming to participate in the national Bicentennial celebration, and added support for health and social services. His capital construction requests and proposal to expand education funding were significant but well within the available dollars. In the matter of K-12 education, Hathaway renewed his request to make the 12-mil school levy a state tax rather than a county tax in order to equalize school funding statewide. According to Hathaway, "No Wyoming school children should be penalized, now or in the future because they do not happen to live in a county that has a lot of coal, or a lot of oil, or a lot of gas, or a lot of uranium."

Hathaway's legislative proposals and budget sought to strengthen the Department of Environmental Quality to maintain state versus federal management of environmental protection programs.

Just as he had with the Green River Feasibility study for trans-basin diversion, Hathaway waded into the controversy surrounding a proposed coal slurry pipeline from Wyoming to Arkansas. Energy Transportation

Systems, Inc. proposed to build a pipeline from Wyoming to move pulverized coal by water to Arkansas. This proposed coal slurry pipeline would rely on groundwater extracted from formations below a depth of 2,500 feet in Niobrara County. Hathaway noted the absence of any statute prohibiting the export of Wyoming's water without prior legislative approval. He then proposed such a statutory provision. Under Hathaway's plan, the proposed law would also authorize the planned ETSI coal slurry pipeline, subject to certain actions by the State Engineer. Part of the attraction of the slurry pipeline was to create competition for the railroads, which exercised immense power over the coal industry as they were the only way to get coal delivered to power plants around the nation. The railroad interests waged war against the idea of slurry pipelines in Wyoming and other states through which the lines would pass. Hathaway viewed the slurry line as "…most important to the future of the State." Hathaway had previously suggested, "…there was some 'briny' underground water in the state that could be piped out of state in the coal slurry pipelines since it was not fit for other uses."[38] As with any proposal involving water, slurry pipelines would prove controversial.

Hathaway had not abandoned his plan for Joint Powers Boards among local governmental entities to qualify for low-interest loans from the state to build population impact infrastructure. He urged passage of this impact program, telling the Legislature, "The State has an obligation, and that is why we suggest the loaning of permanent funds." Hathaway still did not support direct grants to impacted communities.

Profoundly surprising to some was Hathaway's public endorsement of a severance tax increase to 3%, evenly divided between a newly created, constitutionally protected permanent fund for future generations and increased funding for the state's general fund to support expanded government expenditures and tax relief for the citizens. Hathaway had campaigned against this proposal in 1966 when it was promoted by his Democratic opponent Ernest Wilkerson.

The income generated by the permanent fund "…should be used by this and future generations for impact aid, for water development, for many different things this state does and will need." Hathaway expressed hope for a permanent fund account of 1 to 2 billion dollars by the end of the century. Hathaway correctly believed general fund expenditures would continue to increase as they had doubled during his time in office.

Hathaway had previously remained steadfast in opposition to increases in the severance tax beyond the 1% authorized in 1969, he had retained, since 1966, his opposition to a severance tax supporting a permanent fund. "Stan Drops a Bomb" was the headline in the *Casper Star Tribune* on the day following his address to the Legislature.

Reaction to Hathaway's change of public position was generally positive within the legislative body.

Industry response was generally negative, although several independent oil operators supported the permanent fund. Ed Litman, an executive with Echo Oil, was strident in his opposition. "The current mineral tax proposals stink, and they frankly make me damn mad." He posed seven questions challenging the thinking of Republicans and conservative Democrats. Two of the questions were unnecessarily harsh but undoubtedly prescient. They remain unanswered.

> Since when has Republican and Conservative Democratic thinking embraced a Welfare State philosophy that is bent on removing other forms of tax revenues to be replaced by punitive taxes on one industry?

> Are Wyoming residents suddenly so devoid of personal responsibility that they reject any form of tax on themselves at the expense of someone else? Is this at last to be the promised land where all of life's needs are plucked from trees, and why hasn't consideration been given to other forms of fully participating tax policy such as an income tax, property tax, and other forms of use taxes? [39]

Three days after delivering his Legislative Message, Hathaway would display a similar sentiment, expressing a "hope the rest of us not become so selfish that we think the mineral industry should pay all of it." Nonetheless, Hathaway would use the podium of his Legislative Message to press for more tax relief for Wyoming citizens.

Hathaway's announcement was not a "bomb" for the Republican legislative leadership. Shortly before the session convened, Hathaway was advised there were enough Republicans prepared to vote with the Democrats to pass the proposed legislation. Most of the Democratic legislators had supported the idea for years. Now, there were more than enough Republican legislative votes to assure passage. Like it or not, the idea of increasing the severance tax and a permanent fund was an idea whose time had come.

Under the January 26 *Casper Star Tribune* headline, "Stan explains tax switch," Hathaway insisted, "It was not a change in position at all." A few months earlier, Hathaway suggested the tax discussion should wait until 1975 because "...the industry was in a state of flux." The story summarized Hathaway's adroit response, "the key factor in his decision to propose the measure this session was, he said, the economic change in Wyoming, particularly the past three or four months. 'There isn't any reason it should be a political issue at all,' he said, adding that the 'key' is the permanent fund."

Democrats legitimately felt robbed of their signature issue. Crying foul, the Democrats argued that the Republicans, who had for decades resisted Democratic severance tax efforts, had just hijacked their issue. Since Republicans controlled the Legislature, Republican names would be on the legislation Democrats had pursued for decades. Senator Harry Leimback (D-Natrona County) and State Party Chairman Don Anselmi led the charge. While welcoming the Republican conversion, they resented the Republicans getting credit. Republican Party Chairman Jack Speight, a former Hathaway aid, responded in kind. Two days after Hathaway's speech, on January 25, the *Casper Star Tribune* carried the following account of an interview with Chairman Speight in which he deftly responded:

> Reminded that some Democrats claim the governor and the GOP
> lifted the recommendation from their party platform, Speight
> retorted, "Maybe they're not giving the Republicans enough
> credit for having some common sense also. It's the sense of what
> the people want," he said, adding that giving the people what they

want is what government is all about.

Arguments at the time suggested the Republican leadership understood the increased severance tax arguments were moving from smoldering embers to a flame. Rather than risk a wildfire, they chose to control the blaze by offering a limited increase and a permanent fund.

In his Message, Hathaway proudly reviewed a list of tax relief measures previously provided to taxpayers. No statewide property tax, phased out inventory tax, removal of the county property tax for welfare, and removing personal property tax for individuals were on the list.

Hathaway made a plea for further tax relief. First, property tax relief could be granted by replacing the 6-mil county school property tax levy with general fund money. The added severance taxes had significantly increased general fund revenues. His second priority "...would be an exemption for sales tax on food, which would apply to all Wyoming citizens."

The Legislature chose not to replace property tax support for public schools with general fund revenue. Instead, a Joint Resolution was placed before the voters to authorize up to 12 mills of state property tax to replace the mil levy imposed by counties to support schools. A Casper Democrat, Edness Kimball Wilkins, waited to see if a Republican would introduce a bill implementing Hathaway's request to remove the sales tax on food. When none appeared, she re-introduced her bill from the 1973 session to remove the sales tax on food. It was met with the same indifference from the legislative majority as existed in the 1930s when the sales tax was originally imposed.

Hathaway described the market for coal, oil and gas, and oil shale as fuels "...where the seller's market instead of the buyer's market prevails." Hathaway rightly made no mention of the persistent argument that severance tax increases would kill growth in Wyoming. Adding 3% to Wyoming's severance tax in 1974 did not alter the course of energy development in Wyoming. Whether energy fuels are a buyer or seller's market was not then and is not now determined by Wyoming tax policy. As with nearly all commodities, the buyer's or seller's market is determined by numerous factors, including relative scarcity of the commodity, market demand, currency exchange rates, and governmental policies such as Energy Independence, as discussed in the next chapter.

Republicans were in the majority and controlled which names would be on the severance tax bills. And the names would not be Democrats. Republican representatives Morton and Hellbaum sponsored House Joint Resolution 2, proposing a constitutional amendment to increase the tax to 3% and create a permanent mineral trust fund. Representative Morton was not enthusiastic about the 1½% for operating funds. Citing expected revenue increases from rising prices and production, Morton "...indicated operating funds for operating could be raised in other ways."[40] Final passage in the House was 55 ayes/2 nays, and in the Senate, it was 30 ayes/0 nays. Voters would pass the constitutional amendment in November of 1974 by a wide margin.

Representatives Simpson and Hellbaum undertook a coordinated approach in House Bill 36. As passed, House Bill 36 raised the severance tax to 3% while making a specific provision of 50% or 1½% to be placed in the permanent fund should the constitutional amendment pass in November 1974. While there was a bit more wrangling with HB 36, it ultimately passed with substantial support in the House and the Senate.

Responding to growth and impact was a mixed bag. Authorization for local governments jointly operating joint facilities was granted. Portions of the Wyoming Environmental Quality Act were strengthened. Baby steps were taken towards providing dollars to assist areas impacted by growth. None of the normal funds available for the operation of state government were allocated to impact aid. The source of the funds was to be federal dollars from "bonus bids" for federal coal, oil shale, or geothermal resources. Bonus bids arose as part of the bidding process for federal minerals under the 1920 Minerals Leasing Act. In competing to secure a given tract for development, companies would offer a "bonus bid" over and above the obligation to pay the required royalty to the federal government. At the time, 37½% of the bonus bid was returned to the state where the federal minerals were located. House Bill 8 (Enrolled Act 10), introduced by Representatives Morton and Hellbaum, established an "impact and emergency account" to hold any bonus bid revenues received by the state. The five statewide elected officials, set as the Wyoming Farm Loan Board, could expend or loan funds "...only to assist in the emergency construction or operation of public schools, other public educational institutions, and public roads, or for the construction or operation of such schools, institutions, and roads in impacted areas."

An impacted area was defined as "...a political subdivision or district in which either sudden or prolonged population growth has caused both social and economic stress of such a nature that the total present resources available are not sufficient to resolve them properly and effectively."

Direct dollars for impacted communities were still not on the agenda for Hathaway or the legislative majority.

Legislators put forward other unsuccessful proposals related to taxation, growth management, and assistance. Notable was legislation offered by Representative Rex Arney (R-Sheridan County). In northeastern Wyoming, Sheridan County was one of the eight counties slated for significant growth in the Northern Great Plains Resources study. Arney offered the "Energy Development Information and Siting Act" (House Bill 18)[41] to manage and control growth to minimize adverse impacts on Wyoming's environment and citizens. No attempt was made in the legislation as introduced to stop growth. The policy and purpose section specifically recognized the necessity of additional facilities to meet national energy demands. But it went on to say, "...the Legislature further finds that it is necessary to ensure that the location, construction, and operation of major industrial facilities and energy conversion facilities will produce minimal adverse effects on the environment and upon the citizens of this state." The legislation passed the House with a huge majority and died in a Senate Committee. Management of future impact issues was on the minds of legislators. A Select Committee on Industrial Impact was created in October of 1973. As a result of the 1974 Session, the committee was given new impetus with a charge to present specific impact management recommendations to the 1975 Legislature.

Industrial facility siting and resolving growth impact issues would emerge as significant issues in the 1974 elections, particularly the race for governor.

CHAPTER 4
MAJOR FEDERAL POLICY SHAPES
WYOMING'S ECONOMY

1966 to 1986

While we in Wyoming speak boldly of controlling our own destiny, the reality is much different. External events, markets, technological advances, and national policies related to energy, minerals, and the environment drive change in Wyoming. We have the capability, but not always the will, to craft our response to inevitable change. This section discusses, in broad strokes, the evolution of American energy policy and environmental policy largely defining Wyoming between 1966 to 1986. The forces discussed in this chapter still define Wyoming today.

FEDERAL ENERGY POLICY

Wyoming's energy and mineral economy was initially a modest part of the overall American energy economy. But increased energy demand within the United States and internationally, combined with an unstable and ever-changing world, converted energy, particularly oil, into a global issue. International events, federal government policies, global growth rates, and the relative value of U.S. currency affect the price and production of Wyoming minerals more than anything Wyoming might do.

Volumes have been devoted to analyzing the evolution of American energy policy. Issues of foreign policy and international events are an integral part of those works. Most notably, the price and availability of oil have dominated the motivation of various policy efforts over the last six or seven decades. No attempt is made here to replicate the notable work of others. Still, it is important to show the correlation between policies adopted by the United States and events in Wyoming.

America's energy policy post-WWII through the 1960s was one of benign neglect. United States energy production largely met demand and energy prices were relatively stable. Oil imports were of modest concern, and exporting oil was not uncommon depending on the world economy and international events. Domestic supply and demand were balanced mainly by the Texas Railroad Commission and other state regulatory bodies, which had the power of "proration." Under a proration regime, the Texas Railroad Commission would gauge demand and adjust the amount of oil and gas individual operators could produce. Since Texas was, by far, the most significant oil production region, such action balanced supply and demand, thereby effectively setting oil prices. Wyoming never adopted proration for both political and practical reasons. As a political matter, proration was unacceptable. Proration was seen, particularly by smaller operators, as government interference with free enterprise and the right to develop resources. As a practical matter, Wyoming's production level and resource reserves were relatively small compared to Texas and other regions. Our producers remained subject to the range of prices established by the Texas Railroad Commission. This circumstance remained until three factors shifted America's position from price maker to price taker. Wyoming had been and would remain a price taker.

First, the post-WWII world period saw phenomenal growth in energy demand as the European nations and Japan recovered from wartime destruction. America exported significant amounts of oil to Europe as part of the Marshall Plan to rebuild Europe. Second, Europe shifted from relying on coal to oil as the major energy source. As European demand and refining capacity grew, the Mid-East became Europe's dominant source of oil. The importance of Mid-East oil reserves became evident during WWII. As the War drew to a close in 1945, President Franklin Roosevelt forged a relationship between the United States and Saudi Arabia, based on oil. Third, new sources of oil, particularly in the Mid-East and South America, were discovered and brought into production, often below the cost/prices in America. Even though imports increased, supply and price remained relatively stable as British and American oil interests largely controlled Mid-Eastern oil supplies.

America was a net exporter of oil at the end of WWII. Post-WWII saw a gradually accelerating pace of oil imports. There was little national concern about supply or price since the nominal world price of oil remained relatively constant between 1955 ($2.25) and 1970 ($2.35). Supply disruptions were uncommon and easily managed through alternative sources. Importation of oil into American markets continued to rise and gradually began to be seen as a threat to the domestic energy industry. Portions of the American oil industry sought limitations on imports. At the same time some policymakers viewed reliance on imported oil as a national security issue. A series of studies and committees examined the issue. The initial response to the studies' results was to encourage "voluntary" import reductions. Of course, neither the American companies purchasing the oil, nor the producing countries really cared to comply. After all the proposed limits were "voluntary" and few people volunteered.

In 1959, President Eisenhower issued "Proclamation 3279 — Adjusting Imports of Petroleum and Petroleum Products into the United States." Relying on a determination that "...crude oil and the principal crude oil derivatives and products are being imported in such quantities and under such circumstances as to threaten to impair the national security,"[1] With this, Eisenhower inserted the federal government into the energy marketplace. It was a complicated approach based on demand and dividing the country into producing regions. Generally, the order restricted imports to "...approximately 9% of total demand..." with some areas limited to the level of imports during the 1957 calendar year. Within three years the import quota shifted from the unwieldy demand model to the simple calculation of 12.2% of domestic production. The underlying policy was not limited to national security, it was also an attempt to protect and increase domestic production.

In the background was a "peak oil" discussion initiated by M. King Hubbert who argued in 1956 that American conventional oil production would peak in 1970.[2] Hubbert was a physicist and geologist with Shell petroleum. His work has since been both lauded and criticized. Lauded because his prediction proved accurate and criticized because the 1970 prediction was his secondary scenario and some of the assumptions about available reserves and consumption were less than precise. Nonetheless, the notion of reduced ability to rely on domestic oil production as the major source of supply in an energy-hungry America became part of both public policy and private sector discussions. Ironically, with the advent of unconventional drilling and production techniques, the discussion in 2018/2019 was no longer about peak supply but about predicting the peak demand for oil and gas.

Oil and energy prices were generally stable during most of the 50s and 60s. There were short oil flow disruptions in 1953 with a change of government in Iran and again in 1957 when Egypt nationalized the Suez Canal. However, American policymakers were focused on domestic economic issues, the Cold War, and the threat of spreading communism.

The post-WWII British policy of de-colonization led to a withdrawal of British troops from the Mid-East, leaving American and British oil interests along with the existing power structure in the Mid-East remaining in charge for a while. Little noticed was the formation of OPEC (Organization of Petroleum Exporting Countries) in 1960, with Saudi Arabia, Kuwait, Venezuela, Iran, and Iraq as the original members. They came together over the decline in their oil revenues and a shared view that the oil-producing companies were treating them unfairly. America did not see the giant tree this small grain of mustard seed would become.[3]

Oil prices had begun to rise in the early 1970s as American conventional oil production peaked in 1970 and began to decline. Meanwhile, the oil-exporting countries began to flex their muscle, even though OPEC was not particularly effective or unified in the years preceding 1973.

American energy policy began a transformation as an unintended consequence of a "New Economic Policy" announced by President Richard M. Nixon on August 15, 1971. Part re-election politics and part economic policy—Nixon and his advisors gave little thought to the larger implications of the new Policy. Faced with inflation, a war in Viet Nam, unemployment, the balance of payment issues, and a 1972 re-election campaign—Nixon decided to take bold action, giving little thought to the larger implications and consequences of his plan. Nixon's transmittal letter accompanying the January 1972 *Annual Report of the Council of Economic Advisor* summarized the New Economic Policy:[4]

> The conditions called for decisive action. On August 15, 1971, I announced these actions. First, I imposed a 90-day freeze on prices, wages and rent. Second, I suspended conversions of dollars into gold and other secure assets. Third, I imposed a temporary surcharge on imports, generally at the rate of 10%. Fourth, I proposed a number of tax changes intended to stimulate the economy.

The wage and price controls invoked by Nixon relied on the President's authority under the Economic Stabilization Act of 1970. The report transmitted by President Nixon acknowledged that the 90-day freeze would "...be followed by a more flexible and durable—but still tempo-rary—system of mandatory controls." The general economy suffered from price controls until 1974. The machinations of oil and gas price controls evolved, over the next decade, into complex multi-tiered pricing systems, old versus new oil, and a windfall profits tax. In addition to creat-ing confusion in the price control/pricing system, the process discour-aged significant investment in oil and gas production. The last vestiges of controlled oil prices ended under President Reagan in early 1980. The legal authority for the Act was set to expire in late 1980 and would have been ended by Reagan had the authority not ended by itself. The general 10% import surcharge did not reduce oil imports but did add to the prices paid by consumers.

Abandoning the gold standard was a necessary step since the United States simply could not honor requests to convert dollars to gold and/or hard assets. Too many dollars were afloat in the U.S. and world economy. The effect of surprising the world with an abrupt abandonment of the gold standard was a devaluation of the dollar and an increase in oil import prices. Since oil was priced in dollars worldwide, devaluation meant the producing countries could not purchase as many goods and services per dollar derived from the sale of oil. To offset these losses, the price of imported oil was increased. In the short run, the consequences seemed manageable. In the long run, a new economic force was brought to bear on oil pricing. The price of oil has tended to move inversely to the dollar's valuation against other world currencies. A strong dollar tends to depress oil prices, while a weak dollar tends to increase the price of oil. Wyoming exercises no control over currency valuation but has felt the effect of extended valuation cycles.

As oil and energy consumption continued to grow in the United States and throughout the world, the stage was set for the oil exporting countries to understand and exercise the power inherent in control of oil reserves and production. Rehearsals were over, and Act One of weaponizing oil commenced in 1973.

In early 1973, President Nixon announced the end of the Mandatory Oil Import Quota.[5] At that point, oil imports were 30% of domestic consumption. The original import quotas had been raised by Presidents Kennedy, Johnson, and Nixon. In mid-October of 1973, Syria and Egypt began the Yom Kippur War by assaulting Israel. The Nixon Administration sided with Israel and manifested support through a $2.2 billion military aid package. The Arab states united in suspending oil shipments to the United States and other countries aligned with Israel. The oil embargo seems to have come as a surprise to the Nixon Administration, but the real shock was to America's businesses and consumers. Gasoline prices skyrocketed, supply shortages emerged, and long lines at gasoline stations were seen throughout the urban areas of America. It would be an understatement to suggest the American public was alarmed and demanding action. The embargo was short-lived. Oil deliveries from the Arab world resumed in March of 1974, but the impact on American energy and foreign policy was not short-lived. It is still felt today. America suddenly confronted a world in which our post-WWII hegemony no longer existed.

At the height of the crisis, in November 1973, Nixon spoke to the nation, attempting to prepare people for the supply shortages expected to extend into the winter months. He provided the basic outline of his approach, including energy conservation measures. Most importantly for Wyoming, Nixon's *Address to the Nation About Policies to Deal with the Energy Shortages* emphasized development of domestic energy resources:[6]

> ...I am directing that industries and utilities which use coal—which is our most abundant resource—be prevented from converting from coal to oil. Efforts will also be made to convert power plants from the use of oil to the use of coal.

> ...I am asking the Atomic Energy Commission to speed up the licensing and construction of nuclear plants. We must seek to reduce the time required to bring nuclear plants on-line—nuclear plants can produce power—to bring them line from 10 years to 6 years, reduce that time lag.[7]

In his proposed emergency energy act, Nixon requested additional federal powers from Congress including the imposition of daylight savings time on a year-round basis, mandatory conservation measures to include restrictions on shopping hours for commercial businesses, and mandatory speed limits. He also requested the ability to waive environmental requirements for energy production. In an irony of history, Nixon, the President who signed the National Environmental Policy Act, created the Environmental Protection Agency, signed the Endangered Species Act, the Clean Air Act Extension, and proposed the Safe Drinking Water Act, would ask Congress for:

> ...the necessary authority to relax environmental regulations on a temporary, case-by-case basis, thus permitting an appropriate balancing of our environmental interests, which all of us share, with our energy requirements, which of course, are indispensable.

This request would be repeated over decades in various federal energy plans. Nixon ended his address with a "call to arms":

> Let us unite in committing the resources of this Nation to a

> major endeavor, an endeavor that in this Bicentennial Era we can appropriately call 'Project Independence.'
>
> Let us pledge that by 1980, under Project Independence, we shall meet America's energy needs from America's own energy reserves.

The approach advocated by Nixon was a stark departure from past federal policy. Federal intervention into energy markets had, except during times of war, been relatively modest. There were occasional import and tariff protections plus efforts to resist monopolies or protect consumers from price gouging. The step toward directing which resources to develop, restricting energy utilization, and enforcing conservation during peacetime constituted a major expansion of the federal role in energy. For Wyoming, the implications were clear. Developing domestic energy supplies were a priority and Wyoming was home to all three—coal, oil and gas, and uranium.

Of lasting importance was the establishment of "energy independence" as the standard political position in all future elections. In their own fashion and in the context of their times, American Presidents, regardless of party, would re-state this call to arms. In the end, it would not be political pronouncements but advances in science and technology, driven largely by the private sector, that moved America towards energy sufficiency. Clearly, government policies, including basic research and development funding, tax subsidies, and favorable government policies helped pave the way.

Nixon's expectations of great growth in energy production were shared by the private energy economy. Utilities began working on aggressive plans to build out America's coal and nuclear power fleet.

Due to Nixon's resignation, many of his ideas did not bear fruit, but they did not die. On January 15, 1975, the new President, Gerald R. Ford delivered a State of the Union Address to Congress.[8] He briefly restated the role of the surplus energy capacity in the United States during the 1960s as maintaining stability throughout the world and preventing the development of an effective oil cartel; followed by the recognition that since 1970, America's surplus capacity had been consumed. Rather than invoke energy independence, Ford spoke of restoring "...our country's surplus capacity...to assure ourselves reliable and adequate energy and help foster a new world energy stability for other major consuming nations." All of this was to be accomplished by 1985. Necessary tools in President Ford's estimation included oil import restrictions, fees, taxes, reduction of environmental requirements, expedited siting, state-level Public Utility Commission reform and incentives for energy production, energy conservation, and the ability to override federal and state environmental restrictions. Ford referenced coal as "...our most abundant domestic resource...." Of considerable concern to President Ford was the slowdown in the build-out of power plants:

> In recent months, utilities have cancelled or postponed over 60 percent of planned nuclear expansion and 30 percent of planned additions to non-nuclear capacity. Financing problems for that industry are worsening. I am therefor recommending [tax credits] to specifically speed the construction of powerplants that do not use natural gas or oil.

His goals were clearly set forth:

> I will ask for the funds needed for energy research and development activities. I have established a goal of 1 million barrels of synthetic fuels and shale oil production per day by 1985 together with an incentive program to achieve it.

> I have a very deep belief in America's capabilities. Within the next ten years, my program envisions: 200 major nuclear powerplants; 250 major new coal mines; 150 major coal-fired powerplants; 30 major new oil refineries, 20 major new synthetic fuel plants; the drilling of thousands of new oil wells; the insulation of 18 million homes; and the manufacturing and sale of millions of new automobiles, trucks, and buses that use much less fuel.[9]

Just as Nixon's energy message was very much in Wyoming's mineral storehouse, Ford's message reinforced a focus on domestic oil production, coal production, and nuclear power.

But President Ford's program did not fare well in Congress, although he successfully secured the Energy Policy and Conservation Act of 1975, which set automobile mileage standards and created the Strategic Petroleum Reserve. Otherwise, his experience was similar to Nixon's; Congress became mired in regional differences and ideological struggles about the role of government combined with disputes within and among energy players. Congress had plausible excuses for inaction. Nonetheless, national policy and the private sector continued their focus on coal, oil shale, and nuclear to meet energy demands, most particularly for electric power generation. Major oil companies had traditionally stayed out of the coal industry, but government interference in oil markets and the national push towards coal (which was not subject to price regulation) moved oil companies into the coal business. This would be very evident in the development of Wyoming's Powder River Basin coal reserves.

Governor Jimmy Carter of Georgia defeated Gerald Ford in the 1976 election. A change of Presidents did not change the basic direction of energy policy. President Carter sought to reduce imports, increase domestic production of oil, including synthetic fuels, and reduce reliance on oil by increasing the utilization of coal in the electric power generation sector. Carter remained supportive of nuclear energy, but his concern about the spread of the capacity to create atomic weapons tempered his enthusiasm and he subjected nuclear power policy to an intense review. President Carter was more aggressive than his predecessors about energy conservation.

President Carter was elected in a period of "stagflation." Economic growth was stagnant, and inflation was on the rise. Oil imports from OPEC had risen every year since 1973. President Carter devoted much of his Presidency to energy issues—production and conservation. In his first year in office, Carter submitted an ambitious energy plan to Congress. In June of 1977, the Congressional Budget released an analysis of the plan:

> The energy plan submitted by President Carter to the Congress
> contains more than 100 interdependent proposals aimed at
> reducing consumption of petroleum, converting from oil and
> natural gas to coal as an energy source, and increasing the

domestic supplies of energy.[10]

Carter's plan was not well received by Congress, particularly the Senate. The National Energy Act, signed by President Carter in November 1978, bore a limited resemblance to his original proposal, but portions of natural gas deregulation, energy conservation measures, and renewable energy proposals did survive. In terms of increased reliance on domestic energy sources, the fuel use act was important. Properly known as the Power Plant and Industrial Fuel Use Act of 1978,[11] the act mandated "...that no new baseload electric power plants may be constructed or operated without the capability to use coal or another alternate fuel as a primary energy source."

Carter's predecessors had devoted limited funds and some regulatory policy to conservation and renewable energy development. Carter advanced those efforts with vigor and symbolism. He also sought limitations on imports which proved unpopular.

In the fall of 1978, an Iranian oil workers' strike began a cycle of unrest, eventually overthrowing the Shah of Iran in January 1979. Replacing him was a revolutionary movement openly hostile to America led by Ayatollah Ruhollah Khomeini, who had returned from exile to govern Iran. The strike and revolutionary movement disrupted world oil supplies. The crisis accelerated when 52 Americans were held hostage in the American Embassy. President Carter sought to embargo Iranian oil ports despite the fact that Iran only provided around 5% of world oil supplies. The accumulated loss of production since January of 1979 and the embargo led to the nearly doubling of world oil prices. America faced another oil shock.

Public reaction to the price increases tied to the oil shock was immediate and angry. Action on energy conservation and development of domestic energy resources was demanded. Members of Congress and the Carter administration quickly reacted. On the energy production side, Carter proposed gradual decontrol of domestic oil prices and a windfall profits tax on producers. Gradual decontrol with added taxes sent a mixed message to producers. Carter remained focused on developing oil and gas products from oil shale and coal. His cornerstone proposal was the creation of a Synthetic Fuels Corporation, a quasi-governmental entity with broad powers and an $88 billion budget. Congress eventually passed the Energy Security Act of 1980. The Act included six major sections mostly devoted to renewables, including solar. It also authorized the Synthetic Fuels Corporation with a budget of $20 billion (68 billion in 2021 dollars). The Synthetic Fuels Corporation's goal was to produce 500,000 barrels per day of oil-equivalent fuel from domestic sources. The "domestic sources" were primarily coal gasification, liquefaction, and oil produced by "cooking" oil-bearing shale rock.

Oil and gas production was encouraged, but the decline in conventional production since 1970 was interpreted as limiting the ability to rely solely on increased production in this sector. This limitation was exacerbated by the price control mechanisms imposed on the oil and gas sector. The relative decline of oil and gas would not be reversed until price controls were removed and, more importantly, hydraulic fracking became widespread in the industry.

Mineral production was not new to Wyoming. Coal production was a significant economic factor from early Statehood until shortly after WWII, when railroads began to shift from coal to diesel to fuel their locomotive fleets. Oil and gas production, particularly around Casper, had contributed much to the Wyoming economy starting in the early 1900s. During WWII and beyond, oil and gas generally prospered. Uranium production, supported by the Cold War subsidies, was well positioned to expand into private-sector power generation. This expansion would be defeated by a series of accidents at nuclear power stations, regulatory delays from the Nuclear Regulatory Commission, and substantial cost overruns during the construction of nuclear power plants.

But it was the force of international events and the call for domestic "energy independence" that would transform Wyoming into the "Energy State," as described by T.A. Larson in his American Bicentennial update to his *History of Wyoming*.[12]

The following section focuses on the remarkable changes compelled by the environmental/conservation movement.

FEDERAL ENVIRONMENTAL POLICY AND REGULATION

A second source of significant change during this period was the emergence of the conservation/environmental movement nationally and in Wyoming.

During the 1960s, the federal government began actively funding studies and setting standards for air and water pollution. Most of the work was related to public health threats from specific pollutants, primarily non-regulatory efforts at the federal level. Enforcement, if any, was left mainly to the states. But federal actions reflected the American public's increasing concern about human impact on the physical environment. Potential human health effects of defined pollutants and chemicals were initial areas of attention. Federal efforts also focused on land use planning, zoning, etc., as a means of managing growth. Again, the efforts were more of a carrot than a stick. Planning was encouraged through federal funding of studies and local planning efforts. Wyoming availed itself of the various federal programs and funding streams, including federal planning grants made available through the Department of Housing and Urban Development.

In the late 60s and early 70s, Congress moved towards increased regulation and greater review of environmental impacts. The significant legislation that most related to development in Wyoming were the National Environmental Policy Act of 1969, the Clean Air Act of 1970, the creation of the Environmental Protection Agency (December 1970), the Clean Water Act of 1972, the Endangered Species Act (December 1973), the Safe Drinking Water Act of 1974, the Federal Coal Leasing Act Amendments of 1975, the Federal Land Policy and Management Act of 1976, and the Surface Mining Control and Reclamation Act of 1977. These acts built upon or amended prior acts of Congress, which were less regulatory. The Clean Air Act was particularly important to coal development in Wyoming. Project Independence brought American coal to the forefront. Restrictions on sulfur emissions from coal-fired electric generation plants focused market attention on Wyoming's massive deposits of low-sulfur coal.

Most of these statutes embodied an evolving pattern of "federalism." Namely, the federal government would yield implementation of the program to the individual states if, and only if, the state developed a state-wide plan and program to achieve the same environmental and regulatory objectives. The individual states had to submit a program plan and adopt state laws sufficient to create permitting, monitoring, and enforcement provisions to achieve the national objectives. The federal government retained oversight authority, sometimes including direct enforcement if a state failed to act. This was euphemistically referred to as "state primacy." The federal government promised flexibility to allow each state to mold the program to respond to local circumstances and concerns. The federal promise would ultimately prove to be a Mary Poppins "pie crust promise, easily made, easily broken." Even with these limitations, Wyoming quickly recognized that state-run programs were the best defense against federal programs administered in Denver or Washington, D.C.

Wyoming, encouraged by Governors Hathaway and Herschler in the late 1960s and through the 1970s, developed air quality programs, water quality programs, and a mine land reclamation program. Most of these were consolidated into the Wyoming Department of Environmental Quality in 1973. The combination of Wyoming citizens demanding action and a desire to have state rather than federal regulation drove the evolution and timing of environmental protection in Wyoming.

America's environmental movement became a potent social and political force in the late 1960s and 70s. National environmental groups launched public education campaigns against the massive energy development planned in the Rocky Mountain West. They also initiated serious litigation to challenge federal agency permitting actions related to mineral leasing, energy facility siting, and grants of right of way on federal lands. Much of the litigation relied upon claims that the agencies failed to comply with the National Environment Protection Act (NEPA) requirements, signed by President Nixon in 1970.

Powerplant development in Rock Springs triggered *Sierra Club and Wyoming Outdoor Coordinating Council v. Morton* filed in Colorado Federal District Court[13] seeking to prevent the construction of the

Jim Bridger Power Plant. Plaintiffs attacked the NEPA adequacy of the Environmental Impact Statement (EIS) and EPA's treatment of air quality issues. The Court rejected the Sierra Club and Wyoming Outdoor Coordinating Council's claims and did not prevent the plant's construction. The body of case law and agency-specific NEPA regulations we know today simply did not exist when the contested EIS was prepared. The Court's Opinion reflects the fact that the EIS was started less than a year after NEPA was passed. Judicial expectations regarding proper NEPA compliance were much different in the early 1970s than today.

Of greater consequence was *Sierra Club v. Morton,* filed in the D.C. Federal District Court in 1973. The Sierra Club sought to enjoin any actions by the federal government affecting coal development in the Northern Great Plains Region—defined as northeastern Wyoming, eastern Montana, western North Dakota, and western South Dakota. The essence of the complaint was a failure to prepare a region-wide Environmental Impact Statement and other violations of NEPA. The case turned on whether a "major federal action" existed for which an EIS would be required. Plaintiffs relied on the existence of a federal coal leasing moratorium (February 1973) and the various studies underway at the national level, particularly the Northern Great Plains Resource Program (NGPRP). NGPRP was initiated in June of 1972 by Secretary of Interior Rogers Morton after the North Central Power Study was abandoned. It was a joint federal/state effort to gather and analyze data on potential development in the region. The D.C. District Court determined that the ongoing efforts were in the vein of studies and policy development. In ruling against the Sierra Club, the Court stated:

> Since there is no existing or proposed regional program or project
> or other regional "federal action" within the meaning of NEPA
> 102(2) for the development of coal or other resources in the
> "Northern Great Plains region," the complaint does not set forth
> a claim upon which relief can be granted.[14]

Plaintiff/Appellants on March 19, 1974, appealed to the D.C. Circuit and on April 12, 1974, a motion for temporary injunctive relief and expedited hearing were filed. After oral arguments on December 17, 1974, a temporary injunction was issued pending a decision by the Court. The Court ordered,

> ...the Secretary of Interior, pending further order, to take no action concerning the mining plans and railroad rights-of-way for approval in the Eastern Powder River Basin coal basin as discussed in the Eastern Powder River EIS.[15]

The Appellate Court concluded that a "major federal action" was contemplated but was not prepared to conclude that a regionwide EIS was required. The court wrote that the question of a regionwide EIS should first be left to the federal agency after the completion of several studies, most notably the Northern Great Plains Resource Program. The case was remanded to the District Court with instructions to the Government to decide as to whether a regional EIS was required within 30 days of receiving the NGPRP Interim Report. The Government was to report its decision and its rationale to the District Court and describe the role they would play in the development. An appeal was made to the U.S. Supreme Court, which reversed the decision in June of 1976.[16]

The environmental groups were not ultimately successful. The controversy surrounding the litigation and the delay in development clarified the pending development and provided Wyoming additional time to prepare for the boom years. This added time and information was particularly important to Gillette's efforts to avoid becoming "another Rock Springs."

Wyoming-based environmental/conservation groups began to emerge in 1967 with the formation of the Wyoming Outdoor Council in Lander by Tom Bell. Bell, a Wyoming native, WWII veteran, and graduate of the University of Wyoming, is credited with inspiring the active environmental movement in Wyoming. Among his contributions was the creation of *High Country News*. Starting with a small list of subscribers and nearly going bankrupt in 1973, *High Country News* became the environmental and conservation Paul Revere of its time. Bell and Governor Hathaway's relationship was almost toxic as both men had embedded convictions and held very different visions for Wyoming. Bell and *High Country News* were relentless critics of Hathaway and anyone else who did not share their vision. Wyoming Chapters of the Sierra Club and the National Audubon Society became active. Additional Wyoming-specific groups such as the Powder River Basin Resource Council, the Wyoming Wildlife Federation, and the Laramie River Conservation Council came into being. A cadre of dedicated volunteers and underpaid staff within these groups and others came to have a significant impact on Wyoming during the energy boom. As early as the 1973 Legislative Session, Wyoming legislators were held to account for their votes on various legislative matters these groups deemed important.

Conservation groups were remarkably successful in articulating the perceived threat to Wyoming's way of life posed by the massive scale of proposed energy development. Their arguments were aided by the American Presidents who pushed for energy independence based on the massive development of coal reserves in rural areas. Part of the counter-narrative nationally was to refer to those rural areas as "Energy Sacrifice Areas."

Wyoming groups did not simply mimic the larger national environmental groups. The messaging was not to "stop all growth" but to manage, control, and regulate growth. Interesting coalitions of landowners, sportsmen, community leaders, and citizens rallied around core messages of protecting air and water quality, preserving water for agriculture, building and preserving Wyoming communities, protecting hunting and fishing opportunities, and reclaiming disturbed land. In addition, those concerned about the future of the agricultural and tourism economies participated from time to time.

These coalitions enjoyed success by eschewing the national environmental rhetoric and focusing on the important issue of "preserving the Wyoming way of life." Understanding Wyoming citizens' unease with rapid change and capitalizing on the less than appealing "boom town" nature of the unexpectedly rapid population growth in Sweetwater County seemed intuitive to these coalitions. Some of the conservation groups accepted coal mining but argued for a policy of exporting coal by rail and building industrial facilities elsewhere. While Wyoming never adopted such a policy, the practical economics of electric power generation, powerline distribution systems, and a shortage of available water essentially produced the same result.

This writing focuses on the public wealth consequences of Wyoming's decision to hitch a ride on the mineral commodity train. Thus, the role of various groups, including the conservation community, need not be fully explored or documented. Hopefully, someday, someone will undertake such a task. However, their impact should not be underestimated particularly since many of these groups and coalitions were important players in supporting increases in the severance tax rates applicable to minerals.

GOVERNOR STANLEY K. HATHAWAY 1967–1975

HATHAWAY was born July 19, 1924 in Nebraska, the son of Robert and Lilly Knapp. When his mother died two years later he was adopted by Franklin E. and Velma Hathaway. He grew up on a farm near Huntley and graduated from Huntley High School in 1941. Hathaway attended the University of Wyoming before joining the Army Air Force in 1943. Hathaway served in Europe during World War II. After the war Hathaway completed bachelor of arts (1948) and law degrees (1950) at the University of Nebraska and then returned to Torrington to begin the practice of law.

Hathaway was elected governor in 1966 and 1970. He chose not to run for a third term. Shortly after leaving office he was named by President Gerald Ford to head the Interior Department. He was sworn in on June 13, 1975 but resigned on July 25 due to ill health. Since then Hathaway practiced law in Cheyenne. Hathaway died in 2005.

Source: Wyoming Blue Book. Photo: courtesy of Wyoming State Archives

ERNEST WILKERSON

Democrat WILKERSON reintroduced mineral severance taxes to Wyoming politics when he ran for governor in 1966. Republican Stan Hathaway defeated Wilkerson, but eventually presided over enactment of a severance tax and a permanent minerals fund, vastly stabilizing Wyoming's financial future.

JOHN ROONEY

ROONEY ran for governor in 1970, receiving the nomination of the Democratic party but losing to the incumbent Republican governor Stanley K. Hathaway by a 62.79% to 37.21% margin

He was appointed as Wyoming Attorney General in 1978 and served in that capacity until he was named to the Wyoming Supreme Court in 1979.

Photos: courtesy of Wyoming State Archives

GOVERNOR EDWARD HERSCHLER 1975–1987

HERSCHLER was born in Lincoln County, Wyoming, in 1918. He served in World War II with the U.S. Marine Corps. In 1949, he received a law degree from the University of Wyoming Law School. Prior to serving in the Wyoming State House of Representatives from 1959-69, he became the Kemmerer Town attorney and Lincoln County prosecutor. He served as president of the Wyoming Bar Association and as executive secretary of the State Democratic Central Committee.

Ed Herschler was first inaugurated as governor in 1975. He was reelected in 1978, and reelected a third time in 1982. He is the only Wyoming governor to serve three full terms. After leaving public office, he continued to practice private law in Cheyenne. Herschler died in 1990.

Source: Wyoming Blue Book. Photo: courtesy of Wyoming State Archives

RICHARD R. JONES

JONES served as a Republican member of the Wyoming House of Representatives and the Wyoming Senate. In 1973, Jones resigned from the Senate and ran as a candidate for the Governor of Wyoming, losing to Edgar Herschler.

JOHN C. OSTLUND

OSTLUND, from Gillette and Cheyenne, served in the Wyoming Senate from 1973 to 1978, when he resigned to seek the Republican gubernatorial nomination. He came within 1 percentage point of unseating Democratic Governor Herschler.

WARREN A. MORTON

MORTON, Speaker of the Wyoming House, representing Natrona County, resigned his seat to challenge Hershler in his re-election for a third term in 1982. However Herschler remained popular and had llittle difficulty defeating Morton.

Photos: courtesy of Wyoming State Archives

GOVERNOR MICHAEL J. SULLIVAN 1987–1995

SULLIVAN was born in Omaha, Nebraska, and grew up in Douglas, Wyoming. He received a bachelor of science degree in petroleum engineering in 1961 and a law degree from the University of Wyoming in 1964. He practiced law in Casper, Wyoming, with primary emphasis on trial practice associated with the defense of personal injury and medical malpractice litigation. Elected Governor of Wyoming in 1986, he was reelected in 1990. During his tenure, he chaired the Western Governors' Association, the Interstate Oil & Gas Compact Commission, and the Alliance for Acid Rain Control; he also was a member of the National Governors' Association Executive Committee. In 1995, after completing his second term as governor, he held a Fellowship at the Institute of Politics, the Kennedy School of Government, Harvard University. Sullivan served as Ambassador to Ireland under President Bill Clinton.

Source: National Governor's Association. Photo of Gov. Sullivan and Mrs. Jane Sullivan courtesy of Wyoming State Archives.

PETER SIMPSON
Announces candidacy

Pete Simpson announces candidacy for governor

By JOAN BARRON
Star-Tribune staff writer

CHEYENNE — Peter K. Simpson announced Thursday he will seek the Republican nomination for governor and resign as vice president for development at the University of Wyoming effective Feb. 15.

Simpson, 55, joined the university more than 18 months ago as director of the UW foundation, the private fund-raising arm of the university.

He said Thursday he will continue to give full commitment to the university job until Feb. 15 to insure a smooth transition.

"I intentionally have not con-
tacted supporters or organized any volunteer help in Wyoming's counties," Simpson said. "I trust that friends and potential supporters will understand. I simply could not walk away until the university's development effort was established and the Centennial Campaign organized."

The Centennial Campaign, he said, will be the largest capital drive in UW history.

After he leaves the UW payroll, Simpson said he will turn full attention to preparing for his candidacy. He said he and his wife, Lynne, "will be covering the state like sunshine."

Simpson said he will be making
Please see SIMPSON, A12

PETER K. SIMPSON

SIMPSON is an American historian and politician. He is a member of the Simpson political family of Wyoming. From 1981 to 1984, he was a member of the Wyoming House of Representatives from Sheridan. In 1986, Simpson was the Wyoming Republican gubernatorial nominee running against the Democrat Michael J. Sullivan.

Photos: *Casper Star Tribune* Archives

Simpson

Continued from A1

a more formal announcement in various cities in Wyoming probably in late March.

He is the son of former Gov. and U.S. Sen. Milward Simpson and older brother of U.S. Sen. Alan Simpson.

Simpson is the fourth announced candidate in the Republican gubernatorial race.

He joins state Treasurer Stan Smith, former GOP state Chairman Fred Schroeder, former Wyoming Mining Association Executive Vice President Bill Budd and Saratoga dentist John Johnson.

State Sen. David Nicholas of Laramie said he will wait until after the 1986 budget session to announce his candidacy.

Simpson predicted the variety of candidates will produce the most spirited Republican primary race in years.

He pledged to run a "clean and vigorous campaign debating the issues with a fine slate of candidates of which Wyoming citizens can be justly proud."

The overriding issue, he said, will be the state of the economy.

"All of us are going to have to address that," Simpson said in an interview. "The question of how we unify and work together to bring us out of this down time."

Simpson was educated in Cody public schools and received bachelor's and master's degrees in history from the University of Wyoming and a doctorate in history from the University of Oregon.

He taught at Eastern Oregon College, Lane Community College and the University of Oregon.

Simpson served as assistant to the president of Casper College and coordinated the initial University of Wyoming-Casper College four-year degree program at Casper.

He served as dean of instruction and assistant to the president for development at Sheridan College.

He represented Sheridan County in the Wyoming House of Representatives for two terms, from 1981 to 1985.

CHAPTER 5
MANAGING AN ENERGY BOOM:

Herschler' first 8 years

On balance, the 1974 Legislative Session was moderately successful. Governor Hathaway ably served through the remainder of his term. His announcement in December of 1973 to not seek re-election commenced the 1974 election cycle. Most observers understood this would be an exceedingly important election in setting the course for Wyoming's future.

By the end of the 1974 Legislative Session, Wyoming had fully embraced the essential elements of *the Paradox of Plenty*.

The session's singular focus was on mineral development and the capital invested in Wyoming. References to agriculture, tourism, or other sectors of the economy were protective of the status quo—not promotional. The idea of investing funds or effort to create an alternative economy was a non-starter. To some degree, this was not a conscious decision; the public, and therefore the politicians, focused on the opportunities and challenges presented by exploding growth.

Even before the severance tax, Wyoming had begun capturing wealth from the mineral industry and providing tax relief for its citizens. Starting around 1900, Wyoming created tax breaks for non-mineral taxpayers by administrative fiat. Without the benefit of constitutional or statutory authority, Wyoming simply reduced the valuation of non-mineral property for tax purposes. Such illegal but politically popular latitude was sustainable because mineral production, which remained valued at 100% of fair value, had increased exponentially. Severance taxes were used to fund state government operating costs starting in 1969. Severance revenues exceeding operating costs enabled legislative authorization of additional tax relief for citizens, agriculture, and businesses. Legislatively endorsed incremental tax relief for the incumbent population began in 1969 but received a full-throated endorsement from Governor Hathaway in his final Legislative Message in 1974. Maybe, history does rhyme. Recall Representative Brown's 1889 Constitutional Convention comment during debate on a coal tax:

> I tell you gentlemen, this tax will be the lifeblood of the state,
> will keep it up and help support it and save the people of the state
> from burdensome taxation.

Wisely, some severance tax dollars were placed in a permanent fund to partially offset future costs. One downside to creating the permanent fund was the implication that the investment income could eventually substitute for citizen support of services through taxes and fees. Wyoming largely refused to increase fuel, alcohol, and similar taxes even as surrounding states tapped these sources of revenue.

Wyoming's severance tax rates were generally thoughtful and correct. Wyoming resisted the urge felt by some neighboring states to impose extraordinarily high severance taxes—essentially a penalty tax. Wyoming remained pro-growth.

THE ELECTION OF 1974

Two elements shaped the governor's race in 1974. Foremost was how to control or manage growth in Wyoming. Voters understood that the energy boom was driven by national and international events beyond Wyoming's borders. Their confidence in Wyoming's response to the boom was less than overwhelming. Second, it appeared to be shaping up as a good year for Democrats, given the events of Watergate and political corruption in

Washington, D.C.

The months following Hathaway's announcement not to seek a third term quickly turned into a beauty pageant for prospective candidates. Republican Senators Stroock and Wallop and Democrat State Senator Harry Leimback understood the legislative limelight. Attorney General Bud Brimmer was no shrinking violet when it came to getting noticed by the public and the media. Senator Dick Jones (R-Park County) and Roy Peck (R-Fremont County) joined the pageant in less obtrusive ways.

State Senator Leimback remained committed to the Democrat primary race for governor. John Rooney, former Laramie County state representative and 1970 Democratic nominee for governor, and Edgar Herschler, a former Democratic state legislator from Lincoln County in Southwest Wyoming, would eventually join in.

During the Legislative Session, the sitting legislators enjoyed ready access to the media and exploited it with vigor. Typical was a February 3 *Casper Star Tribune* story in which Peck, Wallop, and Leimback offered positive views of pending severance tax legislation. The only non-candidate quoted was Representative Warren Morton, whose comments were more analytical than political.

The political equivalent of an "I told you so" to Governor Hathaway was offered by Ernest Wilkerson, the Democratic candidate for governor defeated by Hathaway in 1966. Wilkerson had campaigned on a 3% severance tax evenly divided between a permanent wealth fund and operating funds. Hathaway had vigorously opposed all severance taxes. Wilkerson, dubbed as the "father" of the severance tax, had returned to Casper from his New York home to visit his family. While alleging Wyoming lost $70 million by not enacting the tax in 1966, he welcomed Hathaway's support:

> I welcome Stan [Hathaway] to what was once a rather small club, or as someone, perhaps Paul [Apostle] is said to have mentioned, 'Better late to grace than not to grace at all.' [1]

The 1974 severance tax proposal was not without controversy as it moved through the legislative process. Responding to pleas from industry, attempts were made to reduce the tax. Most notably, Senator Dick Jones, who would be a late entrant to the governor's race, attempted to reduce the proposed tax by 50%. The attempt failed.

Equally controversial was Hathaway's proposal to authorize the ETSI coal slurry pipeline. Even the State Water Engineer, Floyd Bishop, told the Legislature it was "...premature in approving that specific project."[2] The legislation passed anyway, mainly on the representation that the water to be used was "salty and briny."

Legislation creating a state industrial siting process to force advance notice and evaluation of major industrial facilities passed the House with bipartisan support, garnering more than 50 votes. Legislative sponsor Rex Arney represented Sheridan County, located within the Powder River Basin coal impact area, but the bill died in the Senate due to industry opposition. The *Casper Star Tribune*'s February 10 editorial summarizing the session lauded the bill's failure, parroting industry's arguments:

> It would have required these firms to post two years notice of intentions to locate a coal gasification or some other plant. Had the measure passed, it would have compelled a year longer waiting period for some plants, in the opinion of industry observers. But it was duplicating procedures.

Wyoming's environmental groups had a markedly different view. Bart Koehler with the Wyoming Outdoor Council was disgusted with the Senate's failure even to consider the siting bill.

"The bill didn't die of its own merits," he said. "It was the victim of the Senate's desire to close down this session early and obvious political maneuvering over many issues."[3]

The death of the Industrial Siting legislation would be a pivotal issue in the coming election. Less than a week later, the Powder River Basin Resource Council joined the effort to resurrect the siting bill for the 1975 Legislative Session.

While some action had been taken in the 1974 Legislative Session, the public unease about the energy boom remained unabated, and the slurry pipeline debate had re-kindled the fear of losing Wyoming's water.

Each of the candidates approached the electorate with their own strategic plan. All strategies played against a steady drumbeat of news reports of the pending boom and problems arising in small communities already confronting unexpected levels of growth. Phil McAuley was managing editor of the *Casper Star Tribune*, Wyoming's only statewide newspaper. Under his by-line, the *Tribune* opened a series of articles on the growth projections being developed by the Wyoming Department of Economic Planning and Development (DEPAD) with an Editor's Note:

> It hasn't been released yet, but when it does, it is certain to create a furor. There are those who will be frightened and those who will bless and welcome it. It is the DEPAD 'Summary Report of Projected Population and Economic Development in the Powder River Basin'. And it affects not only the four counties in the Basin but the economies, society, politics, the very lifestyle of all Wyoming and the land. Very shortly, a series on this important study and what is conceivably in store starts today.[4]

The introductory paragraph continues the theme. "Like it or not, Wyoming appears destined quickly to shed its image of low multitudes living at high altitudes. And there is no stopping it." Working from a preliminary draft report, the story contains characterizations such as "drastic increases" and "fundamental change and rapid growth." Similar stories followed over the next few days detailing the phenomenal growth projected for Campbell and Converse Counties, driven by America's thirst for domestic energy. Not only was the region's coal an excellent energy resource, but its low sulfur content aided Federal Clean Air Act compliance.

In the early seventies, DEPAD had shifted from seeking out-of-state businesses to locate in Wyoming to helping in-state businesses and communities prepare for growth. DEPAD released *Coal and Uranium Development of the Powder River Basin—An Impact Analysis* in June 1974.[5] The response was as editor McCauley predicted—love, hate, fear, and indifference. The DEPAD report drew on existing studies, publicly announced plans, and industry surveys in creating high, medium, and low growth development alternatives (economists and planners cover their bases with varied scenarios and assumptions). The expected increase in population would not attract particular attention in most urban areas, but the Powder River Basin was not an urban area by any stretch of the imagination. DEPAD characterized the 8-county study area as having "... historically been essentially rural, sparsely populated region with a relatively static, and in some cases, declining population and economic base." Population in five of the eight counties had declined between 1960 and 1970. Two of the counties had grown by less than 4% in the same period.

Campbell County grew by 121% due to a local oil boom in the mid-to-late sixties: oil activity more than doubled Campbell County's population from 5,861 in 1960 to 12,957 in 1970. Neither Gillette nor Campbell County possessed the capacity necessary to accommodate a significant population influx. DEPAD's projected population figures confirmed Campbell County and Gillette as the center of the coal boom.

Northeast and northcentral Wyoming were not the only areas impacted by growth. In fact, part of the impetus for the DEPAD report was the difficult growth-related issues in southwest Wyoming brought on by expansions in the trona industry around Green River, construction of a massive power plant in Rock Springs, and increased oil and uranium development. Hard data for the report was virtually non-existent as many companies were not forthcoming with information about their activities. In Sweetwater County, workers were living in makeshift trailer courts, tents, and allegedly in caves. As an illustrative point, the DEPAD report noted that vehicle registrations in Sweetwater County had increased 65% between 1970 and 1973. DEPAD emphasized the need for information and planning:

> Among the problems encountered because of such growth have
> been inadequate housing and overburdened transportation, public
> utility, and service facilities. Many of these difficulties might
> have been avoided or ameliorated had local decision-makers
> been aware of company plans and the resulting economic and
> population changes. The benefits of planning for such an area
> thus become apparent, for proper planning could have helped
> guide development along lines which would assure quality growth
> in the impacted area.[6]

Community need for advance warning of population influx was part of the reason Governor Hathaway created the Powder River Basin Task Force. It was a partially effective forum for sharing information and insights. Valid criticism from environmentalists and conservationists asserted that the Task Force was stacked with industrial interests. An industrial subcommittee of the Task Force developed a study of the projected population boom to help the City of Gillette plan for the future. Brooke Beaird, the subcommittee chair, offered comments while releasing the report:

> It is a rare opportunity for industry to be the good guys for a change. If you wait until after the people are here, you will end up with a situation similar to Rock Springs.[7]

Timely, accurate information and adequate resources were recognized as essential to accommodating the energy boom and avoiding the unease and fear the lack of information creates. As Representative Warren Morton, chair of the legislative committee evaluating industrial siting legislation, observed, "I think the people of this state are frightened."[8] During public hearings before Morton's legislative committee, a representative of the company building the massive power plant in Rock Springs emphasized the lack of early information from the company.

> Pacific Power and Light representative Gary Reed said that only a year before the utility began construction on the Jim Bridger plant in Rock Springs did impact planning begin. Until that time, the City of Rock Springs did not know exactly what the company had planned to construct, Reed told lawmakers.[9]

In a sense, Rock Springs was ambushed by industrial development. But Gillette and Campbell County would be an entirely different story thanks to advance information provided in detailed federal Environmental Impact Statements, the passage of the state industrial facility siting act, and direct financial aid from the state.

Wyoming welcomed growth but had become keenly aware that rapid development without advance information and resources was not the growth it wanted. References to the difficulties encountered by Rock

Springs and Sweetwater County due to lack of any warning were simplified to "We don't want another Rock Springs."

Southeast Wyoming, which had not seen significant industrial development, became part of the energy boom when Basin Electric moved to site a new coal-fired electric power station in Platte County. Meanwhile, growth in Southwest Wyoming accelerated with oil exploration. Adding to growth worries, Pacific Power and Light announced plans to build a fourth generating unit at the Bridger Power Plant in Rock Springs.

To varying degrees, media reports in the months following the Legislative Session focused on newly announced industrial plants, water demands and disputes, the need for land use planning, the possibility of a new town in the Powder River Basin to house employees, and growth-related problems in Southwest Wyoming. Economic and social change was coming to Wyoming. Everyone knew it. Some people liked the prospect, some feared it, and some seemed oblivious. Add to the mix a pending change in state government leadership. The race was on.

THE 1974 PRIMARIES

REPUBLICAN PRIMARY CANDIDATES

On the Republican side, the early favorites were State Senator Roy Peck (R-Fremont County) and Attorney General Bud Brimmer. State Senator Tom Stroock (R-Natrona) briefly flirted with running for governor but opted instead to run for Wyoming's Congressional seat. Before deciding to run for Congress, Stroock captured a major subtext of the 1974 Wyoming election season in an appearance before the Casper Kiwanis Club. According to the *Casper Star Tribune* coverage of his talk, Stroock crystalized the available choices:

> "Do we want to become an industrial base for the rest of the
> country?" he asked, "or do we want to protect what we have...
> our open, western style of living." But new money and new
> people will threaten "our carefree, howdy neighbor lifestyle," he
> went on. "The influx of people will clog our recreation areas and
> bring problems. If we stood shoulder to shoulder with shotguns

at the state borders," he said, "we couldn't keep more people from coming to develop energy resources needed by the rest of the country. Nor should we."

Stroock emphasized that the state could control development through legislation, control of water, and taxing power. He further advocated shipping the raw materials to where the people were, by whatever means—railroads, slurry pipelines, or trucks. Stroock closed his talk by quoting a slogan he had seen, "Why make Wyoming like every place else—when everyone else wants to be like Wyoming."[10]

Senator Wallop (R-Sheridan County) echoed this nativist sentiment in a speech to the Buffalo Chamber of Commerce:

> He warned of the danger of native people finding themselves
> in the political minority as population comes with industrial
> development.[11]

Senator Dick Jones (Park County) was being discussed as a candidate but had not demonstrated the overt ambition of his fellow politicos. Roy Peck, a two-term state legislator from Fremont County, would be the first Republican to formally announce for governor in mid-April 1974. Peck asserted "quality of life" to be the central issue of the pending campaign.[12]

Malcolm Wallop, a relative newcomer to Republican politics, had worked hard in the state Senate to be the Wyoming "quality of life" guy. Of course, Wallop disclaimed any ambition for the governor's chair, but he admitted he might have to seriously consider running if the issue of industrial development and quality of life remained unaddressed. The *Casper Star Tribune* account of a late February interview with Wallop captured his effort to test the waters.

> "There is a new philosophy to run on that is not being expressed
> by either party," said Wallop, rancher-businessman, who will be
> 41 years old today. "The tone of the next four years—how we
> approach development—whether we let it happen to us or we
> take charge of it and control it," he said, is the philosophy Wallop
> claims is being ignored by rumored candidates of both parties...

"If I can hear anybody else responsibly talking these issues, I'd be the happiest guy alive and never be heard of again as a candidate for Governor," Wallop said.

Five days later, Wallop made the news with comments at a Farmer's Union Conference in Gillette. After recognizing the national need for Wyoming's coal, he said Wyoming does not owe it to the nation to become "49 stars and a smudge."[13]

Disrupted ambition visited sitting Senators Jones, Peck, Wallop, and Leimback when a Wyoming Assistant Attorney General issued a confusing opinion suggesting sitting senators could not run for governor. Wallop and Leimback were particularly incensed by the opinion. Attorney General Brimmer, perhaps the leading unannounced candidate, was no less uncomfortable than the senators as his assistant's opinion could be construed as aiding his boss's political ambitions. This inference was not justified as Brimmer had not been involved in formulating the Opinion. In fact, Brimmer quickly confirmed his view that senators *could* run for governor. On March 19, Brimmer announced he was filing a court action to gain judicial confirmation of his view.[14] The rumored candidacy of Senator Dick Jones gained new life with a news story suggesting an announcement would be forthcoming if the Supreme Court ruled in favor of the sitting senators.

A flap over who can run for governor took none of the wind from the sails of potential candidate Wallop. Speaking to the Casper Rotary Club in March, he described Wyoming's future as "…runaway industrialization leaving in its wake torn land and uprooted, alienated people." Wyoming's economy will rapidly change "…from a fairly balanced agrarian, recreational, manufacturing, and minerals to a decidedly unbalanced, hard mineral industrial society.…"

Wyoming Attorney General Clarence (Bud) Brimmer resigned as Attorney General and became the second announced candidate. According to the *Casper Star Tribune* on April 24, 1974, "He singled out forthcoming growth in the state as one of the most discussed problems and called for a balance between environmental quality and development."

As expected, the Wyoming Supreme Court ruled that the Constitutional provision cited by the Assistant Wyoming Attorney General was being misconstrued. The Court ruled that a prohibition against sitting legislators being appointed to an office was to be narrowly construed to mean what it said: legislators could not be *appointed* to office but were free to run for any elected office.

Senators Wallop and Jones immediately joined the race for governor. Jones' first comments as a candidate cited law and order as his first issue. His second and third concerns were the shortage of doctors and encouraging energy production while protecting the environment. Wallop's outline of his candidacy followed his now familiar pattern: "Wyoming is entering the most critical decade of its history; none of the other candidates have addressed the issues facing the state; if the State of Wyoming—its life and times is a one-issue campaign, then that's me."

Wallop specifically called for an industrial facility siting law and better planning. Capturing a bit of Wallop's flamboyant color commentary, the *Casper Star Tribune* article continued, "We must avoid another Rock Springs, ... A financial commitment should be gotten from industry to help offset the environmental impact ... But dollars alone will be nothing more than actions after the fact." Wallop said he wanted to prevent Wyoming from "becoming a watering hole for some people on the way to retirement somewhere else." [15]

The Republican governor's primary campaign eventually settled into a four-man race—Peck, Brimmer, Jones, and Wallop. A fifth candidate, Dr. Frank Barrett, would enter the race but withdraw before the primary vote.

Republicans convened for their convention in mid-May. By then, all five candidates had joined Wallop in pounding the drum of growth challenges and quality of life. Wallop garnered the lead paragraphs in the *Star Tribune* coverage:

> Everyone is now on the bandwagon.
>
> Early in the gubernatorial campaign, Senator Malcolm, R-Sheridan, was labeled a one-issue candidate, promoting the quality of life.
>
> "I am talking about good education, where no child should have

to go to class in a basement, a balanced economy, safe streets, sound, viable local government, and making Wyoming a place to retire and survive," Wallop said at the State GOP convention.[16]

In their fashion, each of the other candidates followed suit, speaking with vigor about the challenges ahead and the importance of maintaining Wyoming's unique lifestyle and environment. The most colorful quote award goes to Doctor Barrett: "we can have blue skies or black, rolling prairies or bomb craters, clear water or mud."[17]

Throughout the primary, the Republican candidates referred to preserving Wyoming's environment and quality of life with varying degrees of passion. Wallop was the most vocal, while Jones was most restrained. Jones often focused on inflation and other issues as important in Wyoming. Jones and Wallop had a public disagreement over zoning to control development. Jones opposed; Wallop favored. Generally, the candidates supported additional resources for growth-impacted areas. Jones, in the closing days of the campaign, criticized the idea of "grants to impacted areas," saying, "if you want to see a state go broke, just turn a bunch of legislators loose with grants."[18]

Protecting and utilizing Wyoming water was a staple of campaign appearances. The coal slurry pipeline issue forced candidates to explain their prior votes and positions. While nuanced, most of the candidates saw value in the proposal. Jones was most supportive of the legislation saying it was one of the best actions ever taken by the Wyoming Legislature.[19]

An issue only tangentially related to the energy boom was whether a new four-year college or university should be created in Casper. Albany County, the home to Wyoming's only university, was adamantly opposed to another four-year institution. Natrona County, home to Casper College, was equally committed to expanding the college into a four-year institution. Campaigning in Casper, Brimmer not only went after his primary opponents, Wallop and Jones, for apparent opposition to another four-year institution but roped in Rooney and Herschler for being less than 100% supportive. Both had essentially said the need for the institution had not been demonstrated. Leimback, (D-Natrona County) was spared as a vocal and early supporter of the Casper plan.

REPUBLICAN PRIMARY RESULTS

While Brimmer had been designated a slight favorite with Peck nipping at his heals by prognosticators and several unscientific polls, the results were markedly different. A semi-political flap in vote tallies immediately after the election would complicate the personal dynamics of the subsequent General Election.

Final tabulation of the 1974 election votes took several days. Initial news coverage Thursday after the election showed Dick Jones with a narrow 288 vote victory over surprise second-place candidate Malcolm Wallop. Representative Roy Peck was in third place, followed by former Attorney General Brimmer. Post-election, Brimmer offered the most sanguine assessment of his race, "I think we just won the polls and lost the election." Asked to assess Wallop's strong showing, Brimmer said he felt it indicated a deep concern for the environment by the Wyoming electorate. Wallop, meanwhile, called for a recount.

In seeking a recount, Wallop emphasized he was not attempting to discredit Dick Jones but expressed frustration with the other candidates' understanding of his campaign message:

> "Those guys are talking about the environment as though it was scenery," Wallop said. "I did not have one press release from my office that mentioned environment. We never did. It was they that talked about it. We talked about human issues of how you're going to live and work and play." Wallop said.[20]

When the recount results were announced on September 6, Jones' lead had gone from 288 to 814. Wallop did not win a seat on the Republican General Election train.

> The businessman-rancher said he won't urge his supporters to back either of the General Election candidates but will "let them use their own judgment. As for myself, I'll support Dick Jones," he said.[21]

Wallop held to his word and never endorsed Jones.

An important result of the primary was the emergence of a young Mike Enzi as mayor of Gillette. In his first foray into politics, Enzi captured 75% of the vote against two other candidates, defeating long time Gillette Mayor Cliff Davis. Enzi would eventually serve with distinction in the Wyoming Legislature and the United States Senate. Davis was also Speaker of the Wyoming House of Representatives having served in the body for 16 years and lost this seat in the primary election. Davis, a well-known figure in Campbell County had developed a reputation for being difficult and was viewed as the 'old guard' in a changing community. An energetic and thoughtful Mayor Enzi would take full advantage of the newly required industrial planning information and environmental laws passed in subsequent years to guide the creation of a wonderful community in Gillette.

Wallop's emergence would not have been a surprise to anyone reading the newspapers during the primary. While the candidates received some media coverage, the dominating issue was pending rapid growth and the already problematic issues in southwest Wyoming. Reports on the periodic meetings of Governor Hathaway's Powder River Basin Task Force usually involved announcements of new projects or population projections showing rapid growth. There was good reason for the candidates to opine "we don't want another Rock Springs."

Editorializing on April 11, 1974, the *Casper Star Tribune* referred to Wyoming as "...rapidly changing from an agrarian to an industrial economy...." Wyoming legislative committees attracted headlines as they formulated proposals for an industrial siting act and aid for impacted areas. For every story about politics, there were 4-5 stories about growth, water, and related problems. A sample of typical headlines in the *Star Tribune* between April and August of 1974 read:

> "Hanna seeks land to handle growth"
> "Carter oil dam proposal remains as only a plan"
> "Siting comments expected"
> "Nuclear fuel is top energy offer"
> "Impact Tour Scheduled"

"Growth spiral is biggest problem to policy makers"

"Sweetwater County works to combat doctor deficit"

"Impact Hearings to begin"

"City cites needs to handle growth"

"Panhandle plant plans may have to alter site"

"Rawlins size will double"

"Task Force to discuss development of water"

"Power plant site considered"

"Mobile home owners react at public meeting"

"Impact growth heads meet on Wyoming Municipalities"

"Impact and costs fret Kemmerer councilmen"

"Texaco gets okay for water plans"

"Gillette problems prompt discussion in hall meet"

"Bentonite activity grows on world's best deposit"

"Coal Plant predicted"

"Legislative committee okays draft for impact aid"

THE DEMOCRATIC PRIMARY

The most vocal and visible potential Democratic candidate was State Senator Harry Leimback (Natrona County). Even before he announced his candidacy, Leimback's Casper supporters were sporting bumper stickers proclaiming "Give 'em hell, Harry—Leimback for Governor" (borrowing President Truman's slogan). Democrat Ed Herschler, a former legislator from Lincoln had run unsuccessfully against Teno Roncalio in 1970 in the Democratic congressional primary. This time around he was quietly evaluating a run for governor. Herschler played coy with the press about his intentions and timing of any announcement. The *Casper Star Tribune* in its regular column entitled "Wyoming Intelligencer" reflected on another unsuccessful effort to get an answer from Herschler:

> Democrats are not the only ones interested in Herschler's
> intentions. Some Republicans are downright worried the
> respected former legislator will enter the race this year and

consider him the most formidable candidate the minority party
can offer.[22]

John Rooney, who ran unsuccessfully against Hathaway in the 1970
General Election was the first Democrat to formally announce for governor. In his announcement, Rooney made clear his expectation the
Republican candidate in 1974 would be a much easier target than unseating the formidable, popular incumbent Governor Hathaway. Rooney was
an attorney, former legislator, former FBI agent, and well-known among
Democratic voters. He listed three campaign issues—economics, water
controls and use, and transportation.

Coverage of the Democrat State Convention the weekend of May 11,
1974, found Leimback acknowledging his candidacy which he would formally announce the next week. Herschler was "keeping his intentions to
himself." Herschler made news at the convention demanding "let Arkansas
furnish the water" while amending a resolution calling for the repeal of
the ETSI coal slurry pipeline authorization. The coal slurry pipeline issue
had become increasingly heated with the revelation the first underground
water tests performed on the proposed water supply showed the water
to be potable and "...better than Gillette's water supply."[23] The slurry
advocates had promoted the pipeline with assertions the underground
water from the Madison Formation was "salty, briny" and not drinkable
or suitable for crop irrigation. The promoters had passed around vials of
saline water mixed with pulverized coal to "prove" the generally useless
nature of water from the Madison Formation.

Leimback formally announced his candidacy on May 20, 1974. In a
not-so-subtle shot at Wallop, Leimback said,

> This will not be a 'one issue' quality of life campaign. There has
> been a tendency so far in the campaign to ignore Wyoming's most
> valuable resource: its people. [24]

Leimback called for a repeal of the slurry line authorization, greater control and regulation of industrial growth, protection of Wyoming water,
preservation of agriculture lands, a four-year college in Casper, increased
pay for state employees, and tax relief.

Herschler finally announced in late May. Herschler, a Kemmerer native, lawyer, and decorated WWII Marine veteran had represented Lincoln County in the Wyoming House of Representatives for 10 years. His announcement included a reference to his sponsorship of Wyoming's first mined-land reclamation law and sponsorship of HB 208 which greatly facilitated the development of the trona industry in Sweetwater County. HB 208 is shorthand for a bitter legislative battle between the trona industry and the railroads. Prior to the passage of HB 208, the trona industry could not mine all its federal mineral leases because the "checkerboard" ownership pattern allowed the railroad to prevent mining to move from a federal mineral lease in one section to the next without agreeing to the railroads' terms. HB 208 freed the trona interests from the railroad's demands. Herschler's role in the battle gave his candidacy credibility in southwest Wyoming's "trona country." Herschler, who was well known for representing a wide variety of clients including industrial interests, was pressed on the issue:

> Questioned about an apparently open attitude towards
> development, Herschler said, "I think development is inevitable.
> It's a matter of controlling it during the time it's progressing.
> With the energy shortage, there's bound to be development.
> There's no way we can afford not to do it. The problem is to
> control it and control a way of life in Wyoming that's going to be
> beneficial to the citizens."[25]

Candidates in the Democratic primary tended to run less media-oriented campaigns. Other than a few minor skirmishes, the candidates were not particularly critical of each other apart from the Casper College issue. There may have been local issue disputes among the candidates when campaigning in the southern tier counties, but they did not garner statewide attention. In 1974, most Democratic voters resided along the southern Union Pacific route. Democratic candidates went hunting ducks where the ducks were. On the growth issue, the candidates were aggressive about state control, local assistance, protection of agriculture and Wyoming water. Herschler and Leimback vocally supported increased salaries and better treatment of public employees.

Herschler handily won the primary, sweeping the southern tier democratic counties but suffering a serious defeat to Senator Leimback in Natrona County. Both Leimback and Rooney were gracious in defeat and pledged support for the Democratic ticket.

THE 1974 GENERAL ELECTION

Herschler bypassed the victory lap and focused on the General Election. With gracious compliments for his General Election opponent and those he defeated in the primary, Herschler insisted he would be running "scared." He was not afraid to immediately reach out to the Wallop voters:

> "Malcolm made us all aware that there are a lot of people who are deeply concerned about the protection of the environment," Herschler said. "He has expressed his views on the issues. He is better known statewide, of course. There might be a lot of people who will listen to him. He's a good legislator," Herschler said.[26]

Herschler "read the tea leaves" and understood the public mood. Interest in prospective coal development had focused on the Powder River Basin with the release of a Draft Environmental Impact Statement for the Development of Coal Resources in the Eastern Powder River Basin during the summer of 1974.[27]

The analysis showed that the proposed intensive development would bring a major shift away from the agrarian economy in the Basin and would bring significant, irreversible environmental impacts. The Hathaway Administration attacked the federal analysis of future coal development. Wyoming's Department of Agriculture opined that "Narrow, one-sided, tunnel-vision people have no place in this study." Wyoming's Department of Economic Planning and Development (DEPAD) joined in by criticizing the EIS for not emphasizing jobs and a better tax base. According to DEPAD, "The environmental impact statement appears to have been prepared on the theory that when in doubt assume the worst possible result will occur."[28]

Lynn Dickey, an effective and well-liked staffer for the Powder River

Basin Resource Council, defended the EIS analysis:

> DEPAD feels the statement emphasized the undesirable aspects of
> the proposed development and ignored such positive aspects as
> more jobs and a better tax base. In the first place, the statement
> did discuss these 'positive' aspects in Volume II under socio-
> economic conditions. In the second place, the primary purpose
> of an environmental impact statement is to assess impact on
> environment, not economy. If DEPAD is willing to sacrifice clean
> environment for a flusher economy, it should say so, not decry an
> environmental document for not discussing enough economics.[29]

The Final Environmental Impact Analysis (FEIS) was released in October
1974. Primarily focused on Campbell and Converse County, it included
an evaluation of impacts in an eight-county region. *Volume II*, referenced
by Lynn Dickey, summarized the expected regional development:

> Projected development to the year 1990 within the study area
> will consist of: ten mines with plans to produce 296 million tons
> of coal by 1980, increasing to 12 mines, 858 million tons by
> 1985 and 14 mines and 1,543 million tons by 1990; construction
> and operation of a 330-megawatt air-cooled power plant, and
> a 250-million cubic feet per day gasification plant by 1980, a
> 450-megawatt air-cooled and a 500-megawatt water-cooled
> power plant as well as a second 250 cubic feet per day gasification
> plant by 1985 and another 500-megawatt water-cooled power
> plant by 1990; construction of 16 miles of road, 44 miles of
> powerline, 30 miles of coal slurry pipeline, 140 miles of rail line
> by 1980, 20 miles of road, 164 miles of powerline, 145 miles of
> rail line by 1985, and 24 miles of road, 225 miles of powerline
> and 150 miles of rail line by 1990, all of which will cause various
> impacts on the environment and its individual components.[30]

All this signaled great change for Wyoming. Total coal production for all
of Wyoming was slightly less than 15 million tons in 1973 would increase
20-fold in less than 7 years under the BLM projections. With his campaign
promise to control growth and the Wyoming way of life, Herschler would

ultimately either win or significantly reduce traditional Republican margins in the eight-county study area.

With the Wallop recount still underway, Candidate Jones and Republican Party State Chairman Jack Speight outlined the GOP campaign strategy, saying Jones approach to the General Election would be the same as the primary:

> He described the basic issues as inflation, the foremost one, and energy production, water, reclamation of our land, and the lifestyle of Wyoming. As to the mineral severance tax issue, which blossomed again as a primary focal point, Jones said he "is satisfied with the three percent severance tax. I certainly wouldn't recommend any change in the tax to the 1975 session."[31]

Drawing the contrast between the candidates was left to Chairman Speight. Speight pointed to alleged ambiguities in Herschler's positions on Casper College and the severance tax. Meanwhile, Jones spoke favorably about development and his conservative record. Suggesting added revenue from development as a means to lower taxes in Wyoming, Jones is quoted in the *Casper Star Tribune,* "...the biggest thing that can be done for workers in the low-income bracket and senior citizens is to take the sales tax off food and medicine."[32]

Herschler continued his direct appeal to Wallop voters, calling for strict environmental laws. He carefully aligned himself with the Democratic primary winner in Natrona County—Harry Leimback. He reiterated his Casper four-year college position as being based on the absence of a demonstrated need and the state's ability to support a second four-year institution.

Jones and Herschler sparred over the slurry pipeline issue as the State Engineer approved the final permits for the proposal. The Herschler campaign was active throughout September, persistently calling for stricter environmental laws and an industrial siting act in his public appearances. In Albany County, which was a Wallop county, he called for better retirement programs for University of Wyoming employees. Better pay and benefits for public employees and changes in workers' compensation laws to improve the treatment of workers was a consistent theme for Herschler.

Chairman Speight filled the traditional role of party chairman, taking shots at Herschler over alleged conflict of interest on the slurry issue because his clients included Kemmerer Coal and the Union Pacific Railroad. Candidate Jones remained quiet, prompting the *Casper Star Tribune* to pose a question through its "Wyoming Intelligencer" column:

> WHERE IS DICK JONES? — 'The number you have reached is not in service at this time' is the recording heard over the telephone at the Casper office of Dick Jones, Republican candidate for Governor?
>
> The candidate has been strangely elusive with nothing for weeks appearing in the media. Even staunch Republican supporters of Jones are inquiring of the reticence of the candidate.[33]

Jones explained in an October interview with the *Casper Star Tribune*, "he had planned his campaign to peak in the last four weeks of the campaign, the same strategy he used in the primary election."

Chairman Speight dutifully filled the void by attacking Herschler's claim of being both a lawyer and a rancher. Speight described the Herschler ranch as a "hobby" and asserted Herschler's son attended an "Eastern school." This prompted various letters to the editor, including one from the Mayor of Kemmerer, defending Herschler:

> Perhaps the running of an 800-head cow ranch is considered a hobby by Mr. Speight, but in our area it's a hell of a job.
>
> Mr. Speight says that Herschler's son, Jim, graduated from an eastern college. Jim Herschler did graduate from an eastern Wyoming college, the University of Wyoming at Laramie.[34]

A unique source of campaign funding for Republican statewide candidates was known as the "Good Government Fund" chaired by Governor Hathaway's State Planning Coordinator, Vince Horn. State Planning Coordinator is a statutory position within the Governor's Office. The funds constituted "voluntary" contributions by state employees gathered from 1971 through December 1973.[35]

The Jones campaign became more active in mid-October, pledging to create a community development corporation to give long-term, low-interest loans to industry to help offset their cost of impacts. He also called for Yellowstone National Park to be open year around.

A joint appearance by Jones and Herschler before the Wyoming Petroleum Association in Casper spoke volumes about where the oil and gas community stood. The response to Herschler was muted, but when Jones arose to speak "...the oilmen rattled cutlery with their applause...." The only new area of disagreement related to changes in agency heads after the election. Jones endorsed the Hathaway team "as one of the finest administrations I've ever seen." Herschler indicated there would be changes in agency heads but did not anticipate a "general house cleaning."[36] A more interesting story on the same day covered a two-hour meeting between Herschler and a number of environmental group leaders. Herschler revealed the results of a private poll:

> The overwhelming majority of people in Wyoming favor industry
> in the state. But a companion question revealed most people also
> thought the current administration was not controlling industry
> adequately. He added that a majority of people would favor
> stronger controls over industries in the state.[37]

Three days later, again hammering the theme of state control, Herschler told the Rock Springs Rotary, "If companies do not want to operate in Wyoming 'on our terms' they can go elsewhere."[38] *Growth on our terms* would become a defining theme for Herschler during his time as governor.

The rhetoric of the campaign would heat up, but the basic dynamic remained the same: Jones and Speight aggressively attacked Herschler's legislative record and persona, while Herschler aggressively pursued control of development in Wyoming. Polling showed Herschler winning the race.

As expected, the *Casper Star Tribune* endorsed Dick Jones for governor in the Sunday edition preceding the election. "We feel, if elected, he will ensure the continuation of good government in Wyoming. Dick

Jones, a legislator for 20 years and chairman of the Senate Appropriations Committee, has played a big part in this record of sound fiscal policies in state government. He has earned the opportunity to serve as governor in these trying times."

A sort of backhanded compliment was given to Jones as the paper weighed in on the issue of which candidate was more charismatic, an apparent topic of discussion during the campaign.

> Mr. Jones may not be a 'charismatic' candidate, but he has demonstrated thorough knowledge of all the issues raised by his opponent and has refused to engage in 'double talk' or switch positions for votes.[39]

Criticizing Herschler consumed nearly as many lines of print as the endorsement of Jones. Most of the criticism related to his character, style, and dislike for his finance chairman. Substantively, the editorial properly pointed out policy differences and Herschler's rather miserable legislative record: Herschler missed 290 votes during his 10 years in the Legislature. Jones, in 20 years, missed fewer than 10 votes.

In the same issue, the *Tribune's* "Wyoming Intelligencer" column offered an assessment of the race from the *Congressional Quarterly Weekly Report* dated October 12, 1974.[40]

> This may be Wyoming's closest gubernatorial election in nearly two decades.... In the Republican primary, four candidates each drew almost exactly a quarter of the vote.... Meanwhile, Herschler was winning the Democratic primary with surprising ease, drawing well from diverse segments of the party.

Noting Hathaway's decision not to run brought to the forefront simmering dissent within the party ranks, the *Intelligencer* article continues:

> The second-place Republican finisher, State Senator Malcolm Wallop ran an environmentalist campaign that played up his differences with the party faction that places a high priority on industrial development. Jones is generally seen as pro-development.

The portions of the *Congressional Quarterly Report* cited in the *Intelligencer* article succinctly summarized the race in mid-October and on the eve of voting.

> Jones has the advantage of Hathaway's popularity, united support from the business community and a good organization in Natrona County.... But, while Jones is respected by nearly every politician in Wyoming, he is not universally liked. Sources say he was a tough, stubborn legislator who ran his committee with an iron hand and frequently ignored the advice of his colleagues. Some Republicans fear he would not be a responsive governor.
>
> This problem is what has convinced some Democrats Herschler can win on the strength of votes from Jones' Republican enemies. A handsome, personable man, Herschler calls for orderly industrial development with an eye on environmental impact. His strategists hope this stance will attract a good share of Wallop's Republican vote.
>
> Democrats worry, however, the easy-going Herschler will let up on his campaign in the final stages. He is said to have little zest for political infighting and his reluctance to hit hard was a factor in his poor showing in a 1970 primary for the U.S. House. No clear favorite.

The voters did have a clear favorite—Ed Herschler. Governor-elect Herschler captured an unexpectedly large margin of the vote (55.9%) given the electorate was roughly 46% Republican, 38% Democrat, and 16% Independent. Herschler's margin was enhanced by his strong show-ing in predominately Republican counties. Early coverage of Herschler's victory characterized his main issues as water, environment, and impact aid to cities and towns. Editors of the *Casper Star Tribune* referred to the election as "Historic." Herschler's victory ended 12 years of Republican dominance of the Governor's Mansion. Equally historic was the shift in the Legislature to a "balance of power." Republican dominance in the House of Representatives had been reduced to a margin of 3 votes. In the

Senate, it was a tie—15 Democrats and 15 Republicans.

Like the primary, the General Election played out against the backdrop of news stories highlighting expanded energy development plans and the difficulties besetting communities and citizens impacted by rapid growth.

Oil, which had been generally stagnant or declining in Wyoming, began to increase production in 1974. New federal price controls allowed a more market-like price for newly discovered oil. Oil from older wells had generally been priced at $3.73 a barrel in 1973. New oil was quoted at $10 a barrel in 1974, resulting in a record number of oil rigs drilling in Wyoming. The new oil/old oil distinction became an administrative and regulatory nightmare. Enforcement became litigious. Hathaway celebrated the revival of the Wyoming oil industry declaring "Wyoming will have its first billion-dollar income industry in 1974." This oil boom overlapped with the coal and trona areas but also reached parts of the state which had not been previously sharing in the energy boom. Drumbeats of industrial development would continue through the 1975 Legislative Session and the four years of Herschler's first term as governor.

Two reports issued after the election reflect the momentum behind the Wallop vote in the Republican primary and Herschler's victory in the General Election. The two documents, released in December 1974, were the *Interim Report and Recommendations,* by the Legislative Select Committee on Industrial Development Impact and *Coal Development Alternatives: An Assessment of Water Use and Economic Implications,* prepared by the Department of Economic Planning and Development at the direction of the Legislative Special Subcommittee on Consumptive use of Water. The two studies and the outcome of the elections proved to be the backdrop for the 1975 Legislative Session.

COAL DEVELOPMENT ALTERNATIVES

Coal Alternatives focused on the water, population, and tax base implications of coal utilization options such as shipment out of state by railroad, slurry pipelines, in-state conversion of coal through gasification, liquefaction, or electric power generation. Representative Warren Morton (R-Casper) requested the study in his capacity as Chair of the Mines,

Minerals, and Industrial Development Committee. Morton was a force in the Legislature. An oilman and entrepreneur, Morton had been instrumental in the passage of the original severance tax. He was a pro-business engineer and "numbers guy." On its face, his study request appeared to be based on determining the consequences of committing precious water to different coal development alternatives. Presumably, the results of the study would lead to rational allocation of the scarce water resource within Wyoming. Morton articulated a concern felt by many in Wyoming—there simply was not enough easily available water to support the level of coal gasification, coal liquefaction and coal-fired power plants envisioned in the ambitious projections for in-state coal development.

The *Coal Alternatives* study avoided drawing conclusions or offering policy recommendations. Various charts and graphs within the study demonstrated the obvious: shipping coal out of state for conversion to usable energy requires less Wyoming water and creates less disruption to the local population, culture, and economy. On the other hand, in-state conversion to usable energy produces greater job opportunities, increased population, expanded tax base, and economic growth. The data would be used by those both arguing for and against growth in Wyoming. [41]

SELECT IMPACT COMMITTEE REPORT

State Senator John Ostlund (R-Johnson/Campbell County) ultimately chaired the select committee responsible for creating the thoughtful and succinct Industrial Development Impact *Interim Report*. Senator Ostlund was a successful businessman, a community leader in Gillette, and very familiar with the coal industry. Five public hearings were held by the committee focusing on the most affected areas. Early on, the Committee focused on the lack of local financial resources to build facilities needed to handle exploding populations and the absence of housing in impacted areas. Three of the report's summary conclusions served as the intellectual context for the policy discussions:

> The effects of industrial impact are and will be felt throughout
> the state. Virtually no Wyoming community will be immune to

impact problems, whether they are brought about directly or indirectly.

Coal and coal related developments are now, and for the immediate future, will continue to be the major contributors to Wyoming impact.

Though the timing of many industrial projects is uncertain, industrial impact is a present problem and is growing at an alarming rate. Because of the lead time requirements in planning and financing of public facilities, it is urgent that legislative responsibility be exercised as soon as possible in establishing statutory mechanisms whereby local governments can effectively respond to impact needs. [42]

Contrary to Wyoming's often articulated belief in controlling its own destiny, the *Interim Report* pointedly highlighted the role of markets and policies over which Wyoming exercised zero control:

There exists a severe problem in long-range planning for impact needs because the timing and character of the industrial developments depend on a large number of variables beyond our control, such as:
– Environmental constraints.
– National Energy Policy.
– Inflation, interest rates, availability of capital.
– Uncertainty regarding restrictions on federal coal leasing.
– Lack of advance notice, in many cases, of industry plans.
– Pending industry decisions on 'new towns.'[43]

The Select Committee recommendations for local government financing included a greater share of sales tax revenues, increased borrowing capability, amending legislation to allow greater sharing of the tax base for the provision of joint services among local jurisdictions, and creation of a new borrowing and bonding authority referred to as the Wyoming Community Development Authority.

Schools overwhelmed by exploding student enrollment would be given assistance through the Emergency School Loan Fund. Added revenue for impacted areas would derive from expanded sales and use tax collections and an additional severance tax to be imposed on coal. The so-called "coal impact tax" was not fully delineated. In principle, the tax would be temporary lasting only until a fixed amount of funds would be raised. 60% of the proceeds would be dedicated to highways and roads, and 40% would be for municipal water and sewer financing.

Articulated in the *Report* was a principle firmly established by the outcome of the 1974 elections:

> It was decided that every effort would be made to avoid imposing
> new taxes on Wyoming people. Where a new tax is recommended,
> it is to be imposed on coal production, which is now, and for
> some time in future will continue to be, the major source of
> socio-economic impact.[44]

This "no tax on citizens" position was not an *aha* moment. It developed gradually through 1974 as public opinion and election results became known. Confident predictions of inevitable development encouraged a far less solicitous attitude towards industry. In a discussion related to the removal of a sales tax exemption favoring industry, committee member Dick Sedar, (D-Natrona) stated in the *Casper Star Tribune*, "We don't have to kiss the feet of industry to come here anymore."[45]

The evolution of the Select Committee's work on the Industrial Impact's *Interim Report and Recommendations* demonstrates the evolution of Wyoming's attitude towards "industrialization" and who pays. Originally Senator L.V. Stafford (R-Johnson/Campbell) was chairman of the committee. Early press coverage reflects Stafford's opinion that the committee cannot solve everyone's problems. A member of the committee from Rocks Springs vocalized the dominant view that all of Wyoming was being impacted: "I don't believe there's going to be a single area of the State of Wyoming that isn't going to experience terrific impact, regardless of the presence of resources." Early committee discussions were devoid of references to increased taxes or added grant funding for local government.[46]

On June 12, 1974, the Committee met with representatives of the Wyoming Homebuilders Association. Committee member John Ostlund suggested that the state pursue ways to help individuals obtain mortgage financing for housing. A private industry panel spoke against creating a new "company town." Instead, the expected employees associated with coal activities undertaken by Atlantic Richfield Company, Carter Coal Company (Exxon), Sun Oil Company, and Amax would live in new housing developments around Gillette.

In July, Senator Stafford resigned the chairmanship to work with the Jones for Governor Committee. He was succeeded by Senator John Ostlund from the same Senate district. During meetings in August and September, the committee supported the creation of a Wyoming Community Development Authority (WCDA) to issue tax-free bonds to aid community financing of infrastructure and support individual home mortgages. Communities and individuals would remain responsible for repayment of the bonds. As support for the bonds, the Legislature would pledge one-half of one percent of the existing 3% severance tax to support a reserve for the WCDA's bond issues. Legal counsel for the committee noted potential constitutional issues for such an approach. New severance taxes were not recommended.[47]

Meanwhile, Governor Hathaway was advising a conference in Seattle that lack of water would limit large-scale development of coal gasification plants and coal-burning power plants in Wyoming, therefore, minimizing environmental problems. According to a September 21, 1973 *Casper Star Tribune* article:

> He said strip mining will actually enhance Wyoming and make
> little used lands productive. Unlike other Western areas, Wyoming
> has nothing to fear from exploitation of its rich resources,
> Hathaway said, according to news accounts.

Ostlund's committee continued to look for ways to leverage dollars and generate timely cash infusions for impacted areas. The concept of "impacted areas" remained statewide with Ostlund distinguishing between primary and secondary impacts. But again, as the *Tribune* headline proclaimed the

"Impact plan will use current taxes."[48]

On Friday, three days before election day the Select Committee began to discuss a special tax on coal to meet the revenue needs of impacted communities. Meeting again in mid-November (post-election), the Select Committee endorsed an additional severance tax on coal to raise $65 million for highways, roads, sewer, and water in impacted areas. The tax dollars would be used by local government, along with local revenues, to repay bonds issued by the Wyoming Community Development Authority. As expected, the coal industry objected. The most cogent objection was raised by Bill Budd, Executive Secretary of the Wyoming Mining Association. Budd pointed to impacts resulting from trona development and the oil and gas boom while arguing it is not fair to place the entire burden on coal. Echoes of the "no special tax on coal" from Wyoming's Constitutional Convention. Recommended impact assistance actions were finalized on December 18, 1974, including a 2% severance tax increase on coal, earmarked for a special impact assistance fund for bond repayment. Industry representatives asked the Committee to limit use of the funds to directly impacted communities. The suggestion was rejected. Coal impact taxes became, essentially, the "special tax on coal" so vigorously debated in the 1889 Constitutional Convention.[49]

1975: NEW GOVERNOR, MORE BALANCED LEGISLATURE

Statewide and legislative elections of 1974 captured a shift in Wyoming's attitude toward encouraging growth of any type, under any conditions. A shift driven by the idea that industrialization was inevitable and desirable at some level. The only question was who would manage and pay for the consequences. Six factors loomed over the 1975 Session of the Wyoming Legislature. These factors largely shaped public expectations and state actions for many years as Wyoming wrestled with market forces and federal actions largely beyond its control:

1. In the Republican primary, Wallop articulated a skeptical and sometimes critical view of growth and industrialization. Peck and Brimmer were more positive about the opportunities presented by growth but

emphasized a dedication to Wyoming's lifestyle and values. Jones tied himself most directly to Governor Hathaway in a more pro-growth style. The candidates essentially split the vote 4 ways with Jones winning by a narrow margin. Democrat Herschler handily won the General Election arguing development was inevitable but needed to be controlled. Developers were expected to offset impact costs of development on a statewide basis.

2. Impact from potential industrialization was defined as statewide. Clearly, the electorate did not support the narrow definition of impacted community offered by Morton and Hellbaum during the 1974 Legislative Session which limited potential aid to political sub-divisions experiencing "...a sudden or prolonged growth has caused both social and economic stress..." beyond the reach of local resources. All communities were impacted. Financial assistance should be statewide. Assistance would more likely be in the form of cash and not loans.

3. Protection of Wyoming's environment and quality of life were important legislative and executive branch action items. Two considerations drove this position: genuine concern about the future of Wyoming's "unique" lifestyle and fear of federal regulation from Denver or D.C. Attitudes varied widely on how to achieve these objectives.

4. Water development and utilization issues re-ignited by the slurry pipeline and trans-basin diversion discussions would remain a persistent part of Wyoming's agenda.

5. The costs of responding to development would not be borne by increased taxes on Wyoming citizens.

6. Further tax relief and expanded services for Wyoming citizens were expected.

It would be nearly two decades before Wyoming reluctantly chose a tax increase on its citizens to support existing services.

Herschler's 1975 Inaugural Address was an abbreviated event due to a terrible winter storm. His first Message to the Legislature was a more substantive reflection of his successful campaign. Titled *The Next Four Years—Growth on Our Terms*, Herschler called for industrial siting act legislation to allow communities to better understand and control growth. He encouraged support for a locally controlled land use planning program as outlined by Conservation and Land Use Study Commission created by the Legislature in 1973. Additional resources for the Department of Environmental Quality were included in this Message and the Budget Request. And he noted that amendments to the Wyoming Environmental Quality Act were required to further protect Wyoming's environment and to comply with federal mandates.

The need for water development was discussed along with the financial plight of agriculture. Greater funding for K-12 education was requested. Citizen tax relief and a severance tax increase were requested. Citing inflationary pressures, Herschler called for removal of the sales tax on food and prescription drugs. Pointing out his proposed budget was within current revenues, Herschler offered a short discussion of future revenue requirements and asked to double the current severance tax rates:

> After long and careful study, I am convinced that those requirements can best be met by an increase of the severance tax on trona, coal, oil and natural gas from the present 3 percent to 6 percent.
>
> Some may argue that this is a discriminatory tax. But is it not fair to ask those who wish to profit by the depletion of our natural resources to share the burden their activities will place on us?[50]

Themes of managed growth were not limited to statewide elected officials. The city of Gillette, in the heart of the developing coal country, had chosen Mike Enzi as its new mayor. Having watched Rock Springs and Sweetwater County's efforts to catch up with unexpected massive growth, Enzi was determined to focus on the practical problems of accommodating a possible four-fold increase in population. He expressed a desire to see Gillette not just survive the boom but become "an All-American City" with permanent housing and beautification. First on his agenda was assuring adequate sewer, water, and natural gas infrastructure. Monetary help from the state and industry was requested and expected, but he resolved to direct and control growth locally.[51]

In mid-January President Ford issued his ambitious federal energy plan focused on domestic energy production—particularly an exponential increase in coal mines and conversion facilities. (*See additional discussion in Chapter 4*) Ford's plan reminded Wyoming of the impact of events beyond our control and sharpened legislators' interest in proposals to manage impending growth.

Industrial siting legislation which died in the 1974 session, was adopted in 1975 (Wyoming House Bill 125A). The 1974 version was significantly modified during deliberations of the Mines, Minerals, and Industrial Development Standing Committee in response to industry comments. According to a memorandum prepared by the Wyoming Legislative Service Office in 2004:

> HB 125A also established new criteria for waivers of permits, exemptions, and information required by the Council. In accordance with this new criteria, facilities under construction, in operation, or as defined by W.S. 35-503.76 as of March 1, 1975, were not required to apply for a permit from the Council.
>
> This criteria declared state facilities, local government units/ agencies. Construction of railroads, electric transmission lines (not exceeding 115,000 volts), oil and gas pipelines, natural gas pipelines, coal slurry pipelines, construction and operation of oil and gas production and drilling and field processing facilities exempt from the require application and permit procedures of the Industrial Siting Council.[52]

These changes, some logical and some special interest, reflect the energy industries' ability to gain legislative recognition of their concerns. The only non-incumbent industry to secure an exemption was coal slurry pipelines. This action pleased a combination of the legislators having previously voted for the ETSI coal slurry pipeline and those supporting a "coal export" policy. The Wyoming Outdoor Council and the Powder

River Basin Resource Council had endorsed a bipartisan coal export policy resolution introduced by 16 members of the House. In supporting the resolution, Lynn Dickey the PRBRC coordinator said:

> We shouldn't be expected to pay a greater price than the stripping of our land for alleviation of the nation's fuel shortage. Large power plants in this state would irreparably damage our clean air, wide open spaces and uncrowded way of life that make Wyoming unique.[53]

Governor Herschler did not support an "export only" policy:

> On the state's energy policy Herschler said he hopes some of the state's coal and energy resources can be shipped out of state, but not all, since power plants mean jobs and a higher tax base.[54]

House Joint Resolution 22 called for the establishment of a state policy "...that favors the export of Wyoming coal for conversion to electricity or synthetic fuels closer to the centers where the energy is demanded." The House Mines, Minerals and Industrial Development summarily rendered a "Do Not Pass" recommendation.[55]

Clean air became a flash point during the Legislative Session as a battle emerged between PacifiCorp and the Wyoming Department of Environmental Quality over a proposed SO2 emissions standard proposed by the Department. SO2 standards were largely driven by federal implementation of the Clean Air Act of 1970. Herschler supported the Department's action. PacifiCorp argued the standard was too strict and sought legislative relief from a sympathetic audience in the Senate Mines and Minerals Committee. Acting quickly, under the guidance of Chairman John Ostlund (R-Johnson/Campbell County), the Committee added a moratorium on enforcement of any SO2 standard until 1977 to an otherwise non-controversial bill amending the Environmental Quality Act. Senate leadership set the bill for immediate debate. During floor debate, Senator Ostlund cited confusion in the underlying data, costs to Wyoming consumers, and potentially cost-reducing technological developments during the moratorium. Opponents of the moratorium referenced the protection of Wyoming's airsheds, potential federal takeover of air quality regulation in Wyoming, and the setting of a bad precedent by allowing one industry to seek direct relief from the State Senate. Senators Turner (R-Teton) and Wallop (R-Sheridan) and Democrats Leimbeck (D-Natrona) and Hitchcock (D-Albany) aggressively opposed the moratorium. Wallop demonstrated his taste for political theater by threatening to open a glass jar filled with SO2. Such action he said would "probably empty the chamber in three minutes."[56] The moratorium amendment narrowly passed the Senate. The contentious nature of the Senate debate engaged the public and environmental groups. The result in the House of Representatives would be very different. Members of the House committee considering the legislation unanimously rejected the moratorium. However, the House committee did add one more tax exemption removing pollution control equipment from property taxation.

State Land Use Planning legislation was enacted as Chapter 131 of the 1975 Session Laws. The Act required the individual counties and the state to develop land use goals and plans and appropriated funds to support the state and county efforts. Key to the passage of the legislation was the inclusion of language reflecting Wyoming's general affection for individual property rights. The definition of "local land use plan" specifically states "...these plans shall not require any provisions for zoning." Wyoming's general fear of the federal government found expression in the list of powers and duties of the State Land Use Commission:

> (xii) To cooperate with federal agencies and with other states, provided that such cooperation is performed in such a manner as to assure no federal intervention or control shall take place in the initial or continuing state or local land use planning process[57]

Herschler's request to double the severance tax did not materialize, however, severance taxes on trona, coal, oil, natural gas, and oil shale were raised from 3% to 4%. Coal was subject to an additional "Impact Tax" as recommended by Ostlund's Select Committee on Industrial Development Impact. It took the form of an additional severance tax gradually escalating from .4% to 2% until $120 million in total collections. Pursuant to the

Select Committee's recommendations, the sales and use tax statutes were amended to eliminate exemptions for materials stored for use in operating and maintaining interstate carriers. The percentage of state sales tax revenues going to local governments was increased.[58]

Tax relief for Wyoming citizens was very much a part of the legislative agenda of 1975. Personal property taxation was an original mainstay of Wyoming's tax structure. Post the initial severance tax, Governor Hathaway began the process of eliminating part of the personal property tax. Total exemption of personal property held for family or personal use was accomplished by House Bill No. 10. Exemptions from inheritance taxes were increased, senior citizen centers were exempted from taxation, prescription drugs were exempted from sales tax, and income limits were increased to allow more people to qualify for the homestead property tax exemption, and refunds of sales tax payments to certain income-eligible elderly citizens passed. Attempts to raise the fuel and alcohol taxes to levels commensurate with surrounding states were defeated.

Funding for K-12 education was increased by the 1975 Legislative Session but the underlying issue of equalizing funding among school districts remained unaddressed. Barely below the surface bubbled the continuing K-12 funding disparity between those school districts with significant mineral production and those without. At its core, the funding question was tied directly to the interpretation of the ambitious Wyoming constitutional provisions related to education. Development of Wyoming's water, a perennial issue, was further supported with additional funding and modest restructuring of water development programs.

Wyoming's 1975 Legislative Session ended with much congratulatory rhetoric and a sigh of relief by all involved. Dollars supporting governmental services had been expanded while providing tax relief to Wyoming citizens. Inherent tensions surrounding the correct balance between protecting Wyoming's environment and lifestyle and the need for economic development were successfully navigated. Albeit, not to the satisfaction of everyone involved. This pattern would continue for the next Legislative Sessions.

1976 BUDGET SESSION:
STATUS QUO IS GOOD ENOUGH

Discussions throughout 1975 were driven by announcements of new coal plants, coal mines, and possible renewed leasing of federal coal. Numerous studies of potential growth scenarios emphasized the magnitude of expected growth and the need for planning. Construction of capital facilities for all levels of government gathered the most traction with citizens. Local governments and education (including the university and community colleges) pushed for greater funding through increased severance taxes. But increased lobbying by the petroleum industry and effective advocacy by the executive director of the Wyoming Mining Association, Bill Budd, defeated severance tax increases and tax relief for the public.

Herschler's 1976 Message to the Legislature was short and focused almost exclusively on the budget. At the time, the expectation was for the Budget Session to deal with state spending. Herschler's Message referenced only four non-budget matters, all related to the mechanics of governing. No recommendations were offered as to the severance tax or added revenues. Nonetheless, these issues would be a significant part of the legislative debate.

From the outset, disagreement between the House Republican Caucus and the Senate Republican Caucus was apparent. House Speaker Hellbaum publicly referenced a lack of Republican unanimity on higher severance taxes. Meanwhile, Senate President L.V. Stafford announced a Republican platform including no new or increased taxes. House members advanced various severance tax proposals, none of which lived to reach the governor's desk. An attempt to add 2 cents to the gas tax to support highways was quickly dispatched. Another "coal export policy" was offered and soundly rejected. Despite individual legislators' views, the collective message of the 1976 Session was "the status quo is good enough." A view not shared by Governor Herschler.

Traditionally, the sitting governor offers closing remarks as the Wyoming Legislative Session adjourns, usually expressing thanks for the legislators' diligent efforts. Herschler took a different approach. "Governor lashes lawmakers" headlined the March 3 *Casper Star Tribune* coverage of Herschler's remarks. Offering a litany of legislative missteps, Herschler took great exception to the influence of industry lobbyists:

> He called for working through an equitable tax setup so the state could have some influence over the changes development would bring, rather than listening to the voices of company lobbyists threatening to leave the state high and dry if they are taxed or promising the state it doesn't have anything to worry about from them.
>
> "Some of these companies which are claiming to be hurt the most by our severance taxes could buy and sell Wyoming, were it available," Herschler said.

Herschler highlighted one aspect of *the Paradox of Plenty*—the increasing influence of outside interests investing their money in Wyoming.

Throughout the remainder of 1976, the pace of development continued to accelerate. Additional studies projected orders of magnitude increases in population in some Wyoming communities. K-12 education struggled to keep up with the growth in the student population. And yes, the need for added funding was a persistent talking point. Interest in oil and gas reserves in southwest Wyoming increased significantly due to successful wildcat drilling by Amoco Production in an area of Wyoming known as the Overthrust Belt.[59] The drilling would prove to be an early harbinger of significant oil and gas exploration and development.

While the Wyoming Legislature was largely inactive on the revenue front, two federal legislative actions in late 1976 would directly impact Wyoming's revenue and tax structure. Passage of the federal Payments in Lieu of Taxes program and an increase in the states' share of federal mineral royalties would put dollars into Wyoming's coffers.

PAYMENTS IN LIEU OF TAXES

In the fall of 1976, Congress passed Payments in Lieu of Taxes (PILT) legislation designed to help local governments offset losses in property taxes due to the existence of nontaxable federal lands within their boundaries.[60] Increased utilization of federal lands for development and recreation meant more people required services from local governments without property tax support from federal lands. The formula used to compute the payments is based on the number of federal acres, population, and amount of money appropriated by Congress, with funds distributed annually to local governments.

PILT funding is a perennial issue in Congress. Actual payments to local government vary over time depending entirely on the amount of funding Congress provides. Neither the original legislation nor subsequent Congressional action is intended to produce full tax equivalency. Simply stated, federal lands' full market/taxable value does not determine the payments made to local government units. However WyoFile reporting on a controversial private land purchase by the Bureau of Land Management suggested Natrona County received approximately 31 cents in taxes on the private grazing ground while securing an average of $2.67 per acre of federal ground within Natrona County.[61]

INCREASED SHARE OF FEDERAL MINERAL ROYALTIES

Congress passed the Mineral Leasing Act of 1920[62] in response to scandals, litigation, and fear of an oil shortage. The Act established a leasing program for certain federally owned mineral lands, including oil, natural gas, and coal. In deference to areas affected by federal mineral development, the Act originally allocated 37½% of the revenues back to the state of origin. This 37½% was a veritable lifeline for the Wyoming state government during the Depression and remained an essential source of funds thereafter.

From the mid-1960s through the early 70s, land use planning was a significant topic in the United States. Since the federal government controlled nearly ⅓ of the lands in the United States, focus turned to the management of those lands. Congress passed the Federal Lands Policy Management Act of 1976 as a major overhaul of policy, planning, and utilization of federal lands.[63] Wyoming's Congressional delegation had seen the early drafts of the legislation as an opportunity to increase the proportion of federal mineral royalties returned to the states. The politics of the era worked to Wyoming's advantage. The potential social, economic, and environmental impacts of developing mineral resources on federal lands, particularly coal in Wyoming, were increasingly part of the conversation surrounding the Nixon and Ford drive for energy independence. Sparked by Wyoming Congressman Teno Roncalio, and promoted in the Senate by Wyoming Senator McGee, and most aggressively by Senator Hansen, language was inserted into the bill to increase the share of federal mineral royalties, fees, and bonuses allocated to the states from 37½% to 50%. This seemingly innocuous amendment, consisting of 15 operative words tucked away in Title III, Section 317, would prove immeasurably beneficial to Wyoming for decades to come. A 50% split combined with soaring energy prices would ultimately bring Wyoming billions of additional dollars.

1977 LEGISLATIVE SESSION: BATTLES RENEWED

Herschler's 1977 Legislative Message again offered a caustic assessment of legislative inaction in 1976:

> No doubt many of the same individuals who persuaded the
> second session of the 43rd Legislature that increasing the
> severance tax was punitive will be here again this year. I am not
> suggesting that you avoid talking to them—quite the contrary—
> I would only ask that after every conversation with one of these
> individuals that you will call one of more of your constituents
> back home and ask if he or she would be damaged by an increase
> in the severance tax. [64]

Herschler's report on the state's economy and future was legitimately optimistic. Included was an observation very few Wyoming governors would ever offer "...our young people have an excellent opportunity to remain in their state and live comfortably...." Such rhetoric was music to the ears of Wyoming as a persistent political issue was, and is, the out-migration of Wyoming's youth.

Herschler's Message and subsequent legislative actions followed the pattern established in 1969—tax relief for Wyoming and increased severance taxes.

Herschler called for the removal of the inventory tax on livestock.* Agricultural interests had sought the exemption of livestock from property tax rolls from the beginning of Wyoming's taxation history. Herschler argued that the new federal Payment In Lieu of Taxes (PILT) would offset any revenue losses to the counties. While popular, the argument could not withstand mathematical scrutiny, particularly when analyzed on an individual county basis—a point highlighted in legislative debates. Counties without sizeable federal land holdings, particularly in southeast Wyoming, would lose revenue, while counties with large federal landholdings would fare quite well. Lost revenue to other taxing districts and the state was never considered. Given PILT's reliance on annual Congressional appropriation, future PILT revenues were not assured.

Driven by Wyoming's legitimate historical attachment to agriculture, the strength of agricultural representation in the Legislature, and the fact that other industries had obtained relief from the inventory tax—the legislation passed handily. The removal of livestock from the tax rolls combined with taxing agricultural lands based on productivity rather than fair market value cemented agriculture as the tax-preferred sector in Wyoming. While there were some substantive objections, it was also noted that the prime sponsor of the legislation was the Executive Director of the Wyoming Stockgrowers Association. Removal of the inventory tax on livestock was among the first actions of the Legislative Session.

Herschler requested added tax relief for Senior Citizens through expanded property tax exemptions and increased sales tax refunds.

Herschler weighed in on the allocation of the added 12½% federal mineral royalty distribution. The distribution of the existing 37½% would remain undisturbed. As to the additional distribution, Herschler recommended 60% go to cities and towns based on population, 20% be divided among the state's seven community colleges, and 20% be allocated to the

---

* While referred to as the inventory tax on livestock, it is more appropriately described as a tax on personal property held for commercial use.

State Farm Loan Board to address special impact problems. His recommendation reflected the sense that all of Wyoming was being impacted by federal resource development and conformed with the federal intent to address impact issues through the added share of federal mineral royalties. Allocation of these monies would prove controversial until the final hour of the session. Ultimately the added revenues were divided between highway construction, cities and towns, discretionary impact grants for cities and counties, and a nascent public school construction program.

Central to Herschler's Message was a request for a 1½% added severance tax on coal, trona, and uranium to support a $250 million fund for capital construction. The tax would expire when collections reached $250 million (1.22 billion in 2022 dollars). A recently completed study had estimated $280 million in capital construction needs for state institutions, the University of Wyoming, the state government, and the community college system. Herschler argued the fund would build the "permanent physical wealth of the state...." Herschler also argued that failure to act now with the severance tax option would mean future Wyoming taxpayers would be forced to bear the financial burden of capital construction. With minor modifications, this proposal was enacted as Chapter 155 of the 1977 Session Laws.

Legislators had their own plans for severance tax increases, proposing various tax rates targeting different minerals, with the aim of meeting perceived near-term needs or adding to the permanent savings. None of the proposals reached the rate of Montana's coal tax. Conventional wisdom was Montana's rate would prohibit development—a result deemed undesirable by most Wyoming legislators and citizens.

Extensive, and sometimes angry, severance tax debate produced the passage of a second severance tax measure. Chapter 189, Session Laws of 1977 was summarized by the Wyoming Legislative Service Office as:

> Increased severance tax on coal by 1.6% for CY 77 & 2% for CY
> 78 until $160 million collected; increased severance tax on coal
> by 1.5% for water development account; increased severance tax
> on coal by 1% for highway fund; increased severance tax on coal
> by .5% to PWMTF (total 10.1%); increased severance tax on trona

THE PARADOX OF PLENTY

by 1.5% (total 5.5%); increased severance tax on uranium by 3.5% (total 5.5%).[65]

As for tax relief for senior citizens, the requested increase in the elderly sales tax refund passed, but the expanded Homestead property tax exemption was rejected.

Legislatures tend to act in the context of the times. The context in 1977 was primarily the drumbeat of ongoing and expected energy resource development. Impact problems were real and increasingly reported by news organizations. The Census Bureau estimated Wyoming's population growth since 1970 was 17.4%. Coal and uranium were the primary focus but hopes for federal deregulation of oil and gas pricing encouraged development. In early 1977, data showed the United States was again 50% reliant on imported oil. Natural gas shortages were problematic nationwide, and Wyoming's oil community was not sympathetic. Under the February 2 *Casper Star Tribune* headline "Oilman: easterner's ordeal is good news for Wyoming," several Casper oilmen cheered federal action increasing the regulated price of natural gas and held out hope for ultimate de-regulation:

> Although industry spokesmen remain pessimistic that the
> nation will see total deregulation of natural gas supplies by the
> federal government, all agree, that if it comes, exploration and
> development in Wyoming will only be limited by the supply of
> rigs and drilling equipment.

Just as with coal and uranium, federal policies and markets controlled the prospects for oil and gas resource development in Wyoming.

Southwest Wyoming, particularly around the community of Evanston, became a focal point for the future development of massive oil and natural gas reserves in a geologic formation referred to as the Overthrust Belt. Media outlets had begun to provide statewide coverage of growth issues in Evanston and the surrounding area. A February 13 editorial in the *Casper Star Tribune* announced—"Boom towns have become a way of life in Wyoming."

Environmental concerns remained evident as legislation was

introduced to deny permits for energy generating or conversion plants if more than 50% of the output was to be exported beyond Wyoming's borders. (Senate File No. 194, Died in Committee) Staff positions were added to the Wyoming Department of Environmental Quality, and various amendments were proposed to the Act. Some of the amendments passed. Unsuccessful efforts were undertaken to repeal the state land use planning program adopted in 1975. Education funding in terms of absolute dollar amount and equalization of funding between rich and poor school districts were hot topics. Little was done on equalization. Of course, K-12 education funding was increased.

While several decades pre-mature, federal agencies and others began discussing Wyoming's potential to host wind and solar energy facilities.

1978 LEGISLATIVE BUDGET SESSION

1977 saw continued emphasis on developing Wyoming's energy resources. Wyoming ranked fifth among America's fastest-growing states with a 22% population gain between 1970 and 1977, according to a glowing editorial in the *Casper Star Tribune*.[66]

Coal development moved towards more mines with reduced expectations of multiple coal liquification and gasification facilities. While several companies continued to work towards developing such facilities, financing and technical/environmental issues posed significant hurdles. Water availability and public opposition to transferring agricultural water to industrial use created their own problems for conversion plants. Major mining complexes with rail transport beyond Wyoming's borders appeared to be the course of future coal development. Heightened interest in uranium, oil, and gas was evident in the news stories and public discussions.

Allegations of corruption in Wyoming, particularly in the boomtown of Rock Springs and within the Herschler administration in Cheyenne, garnered national attention in mid-1977 when CBS *60 Minutes* hosted by Dan Rather dedicated two weekly segments to alleged corruption in the booming energy state. A bit of dramatic license was exercised when CBS titled one of the segments "High Noon in Cheyenne."[67] By early summer of 1977, Herschler felt compelled to ask the State District Court in Cheyenne to convene a statewide Grand Jury to investigate the wide-ranging allegations. In November of 1977, the Grand Jury began its work.

The coal and uranium industry had become an increasingly important part of the Wyoming economy. The role of company lobbyists and the Wyoming Mining Association impacting public policy was now equivalent to that of the Petroleum Association of Wyoming and oil company lobby-ists. Similarly, Wyoming environmental/conservation groups (along with their national counterparts) were devoting added resources to lobbying state policies and perspectives.

Governor Herschler's 1978 Message to the Legislature emphasized Wyoming's economic and public revenue health. He conceded that his recommended budget was another in a series of expanded state budgets reaching back to 1969. Herschler requested additional state funding to offset the gradual termination of social service and public welfare county mill levies started under Governor Hathaway in 1971. Termination of mill levies was a tax reduction for Wyoming property owners. Additional tax relief was proposed for the elderly and disabled through sales tax refunds. Herschler did not ask for an increase in severance taxes this time. A 1% increase in the severance tax on oil was pre-filed by Representative Larsen (D-Albany County), excluding natural gas, as a nod to public anger over the increasing utility bills. The legislation failed to be introduced.

Unanticipated events forced Herschler to quickly address the failure of a key legislative effort to address growth impact issues. Days before the Legislature convened, the Wyoming Supreme Court struck down a key provision of the Wyoming Community Development Authority Act (WCDA) passed in 1975. WCDA created capacity for the state to issue long-term bonds for upfront funding of infrastructure projects needed to handle population growth. Population growth usually occurs before a tax base is developed to fund new infrastructure. The WCDA provision had allowed bonds to be paid off over time— after the plant or mine was built and subject to taxation. Relying on Constitutional requirements limiting the state's ability to incur debt beyond current revenues with-out a vote of the citizens, a divided Court found the WCDA structure unconstitutional. Contentious and confusing debates ensued as solutions were offered and rejected. Long-term bonding authorized only by the Legislature proved unworkable. Unless the Constitution was changed by a majority vote of the citizens, the only option available for direct, upfront impact aid was limited to grant funding or direct dollar distributions to local governments.

Herschler had harsh language for the legislative effort to preclude mines from the jurisdiction of the Wyoming Industrial Siting Council. As passed in 1975, the Industrial Siting Act applied to certain facilities whose "construction costs" exceeded a specified dollar threshold. Defining "construction costs" was left to the administrative discretion of the Wyoming Industrial Siting Council (ISC). Initially, the definition of construction costs was relatively narrow, which meant mining complexes may or may not have been included. As the energy boom evolved, it became clear that mining complexes would be a significant source of impact. Through rulemaking, the ISC revised the administrative definition of construction costs to capture the cost of creating a mining complex more realistically. Reflecting the increased power of the mining industry, some legislators objected to the rule change. In the prior Session, legislation was passed to allow legislative review of administrative rules. Based on this review, the Legislature could pass an Order negating the offending rule. The other option would be to amend the Industrial Siting Act outright to exclude mines from the Council's jurisdiction. A bipartisan group of legislators chose the seemingly less controversial route of an Order striking down the rule.

Less controversy would not be the outcome. Environmental/conservation groups and community leaders from impacted areas immediately opposed the legislation. Herschler's Message to the legislators reflected his original objections to the administrative rule legislation and his background as a lawyer:

> My objections, then as now, are based on constitutional
> concerns. I will refer only to the revision of the Industrial Siting
> Act rules. Rather than facing the issue and your constituents
> squarely and passing legislation which specifically says major
> mines are covered or not, this body will consider an order to

disapprove the administrative rule. The Legislature cannot have it both ways. It can either write complete, precise legislation and eliminate the authority to promulgate rules and regulations by the executive agencies, or it can write general legislation coupled with administrative rulemaking. Under the latter, it cannot then attempt to write the administrative rules. As Governor and as a lawyer, I am not sure what the passage of such an order would mean other than that the Legislature has failed to meet its responsibilities. In any event, this Legislature should carry through on the commitment of the 1975 Legislature to protect the people of this state by requiring major developments, including mining, to be reviewed under Wyoming's siting laws.[68]

The Legislative Order passed the Senate 20 to 10. The strongest proponents were two senators, Robert Johnson (D-Sweetwater County) and L.V. Stafford (R-Johnson/Campbell County), from legislative districts with significant mining interests. Warren Morton (R-Natrona County) was the chief proponent in the House. House passage was secured by a vote of 40 to 21. The legislative debate focused on high-minded constitutional issues and tension between the executive and legislative branches, but everyone understood the real issue was whether major mines would be subject to review. Herschler vetoed the Order. The veto was narrowly sustained with the aid of a few brave-hearted Republicans who resisted significant pressure from their peers.

Attempts were made to resurrect restrictions on siting council jurisdiction through amendments to other legislation and a specific bill in the Senate. Senate debate on the mine exclusion legislation tended to focus on constitutional issues and legislative intent. The House debate on the Senate bill focused directly on the issue of mines and related human impact. Nonetheless, the House narrowly passed the new legislation and sent it to the governor. Governor Herschler again vetoed the measure.

Fault lines were accelerating as coal and uranium mining interests gradually moved from outsider to significant in-state industries. Siting council jurisdiction battles further defined the fault lines within Wyoming politics.

The 1978 Budget Session passed limited tax relief and no tax increases. Action was taken to secure state enforcement through the Wyoming Department of Environmental Quality of the federal Surface Mining Control and Reclamation Act. Thus, continuing the Wyoming pattern of preferring state over federal enforcement of Congressionally approved environmental laws. Water development programs were re-configured to facilitate more timely and logical development of the state's water resources.

A fact not lost on any of the players, in or out of the Legislature, was the pending election of 1978. Numerous Republicans were contemplating a contest with Governor Herschler, whose public standing was significantly damaged by the allegations of corruption and the convening of a statewide Grand Jury.

THE ELECTION OF 1978

Governor Herschler was an extremely vulnerable incumbent. Extensive coverage of the alleged corruption in Rock Springs and Grand Jury indictments against some members of his administration bumped the stories of boomtown growth off the front page. Herschler's ties to southwest Wyoming were used against him to feed public suspicions that he was somehow involved and possibly linked to mob activity in Las Vegas. Given the advantage of Republican voter registration and Herschler's tarnished reputation, the knives were out.

The public press covered announcements of industrial development throughout the state, including coverage of mounting problems faced by impacted communities and school districts. But the scent of scandal, Grand Jury indictments, and subsequent convictions garnered most of the public's attention. Dramatic events over the summer would add fuel to the corruption fire. In July, a Rock Springs city drug investigator was shot and killed by the Rock Springs Public Safety Director. The investigator, who was scheduled to testify before the Grand Jury two days later, was shot sitting in the back of an unmarked police vehicle.

Two strong, well-qualified, and well-funded Republicans entered the Republican primary—John Ostlund (state Senator) from Gillette and

Gus Fleischli (former state representative) from Cheyenne. Early indications were that either Republican candidate would emerge victorious in November. Ostlund and Fleischli engaged in a spirited and sometimes acrimonious primary contest. Ostlund secured a substantial victory on primary day.

Herschler was challenged in the primary by Margaret McKinstry, a 63-year-old former university extension agent.

McKinstry was largely unknown and unfunded. Nonetheless, slightly over one-third of the Democratic primary voters rejected Herschler's candidacy. Herschler barely carried Sweetwater County, home to the city of Rock Springs and a key Democratic stronghold. McKinstry endorsed Ostlund in the General Election. Adding to the Democrat's problems, President Jimmy Carter was deeply unpopular as his policies included scuttling construction plans for numerous Western water development projects, including some in Wyoming. Suffice it to say, Herschler was more than 25 points behind his Republican General Election opponent. In the greatest understatement of the campaign, Herschler admitted to being a "slight underdog."

Herschler's primary campaign had been low-key and lackluster. To the extent it was active, it carried a calculated message aimed at the General Election. He confronted the corruption issue directly and emphasized his role in calling for the Grand Jury, funding it, and supporting its independence. Mindful of the continuing impact issues throughout the state, he emphasized the "growth on our terms" theme. Shortly before primary election day, Herschler proposed a ⅓ reduction in property taxes for businesses, industry, and homeowners to be funded by a 5% increase in the severance tax on all minerals. For good measure, Herschler proposed removing the sales tax on the value of vehicles traded in when purchasing a new one. Wyoming citizens generally objected to taxes, and the idea of paying sales tax on the value of a vehicle traded in to buy a new one felt like double taxation. It was a persistent and personal irritant every time taxes were paid on a new vehicle. Fleischli and Ostlund immediately panned the proposal. Herschler responded with harsh criticism for Ostlund before a single primary ballot had been cast:

"I am disgusted that the Republican Party's leading candidate can't act like anything other than a mouthpiece for the Wyoming mining industry and its narrow special interests," Herschler said.

"A clearcut choice is emerging in this election between my point of view, one that says the companies that mine in Wyoming must meet their social responsibilities to Wyoming, and the point of view—that of John Ostlund—that says Wyoming owes these companies a free lunch," said Herschler. [69]

Most observers (and candidate Herschler) understood that if the campaign's dynamic remained unchanged, John Ostlund would likely be the next governor. Herschler, the admitted underdog, set about redefining the election as a referendum on the theme of "growth on our terms." Immediately on the attack, Herschler's campaign went after Ostlund's opposition to the property tax relief proposal, his opposition to severance taxes, his support of a moratorium on air quality standards and the coal slurry pipeline, and the pro-growth positions he had taken over the years. Herschler painted with a broad brush, disregarding Ostlund's support for the original coal impact tax and other measures to resolve population impact funding.

For unknown reasons, the Ostlund campaign was relatively absent from the battlefield for nearly six weeks. Perhaps, they were confident the corruption issue would carry them through the General Election. As often as not, Ostlund's campaign staff or the State Republican Party Chairman responded to Herschler's attacks with attempts to keep the campaign focused on corruption. Meanwhile, Herschler sought to explain and defend his record, manage current issues, and offer proposals for the future. His efforts were coupled with a not-so-subtle design to paint Ostlund as working for himself and industry interests. Grand jury and corruption issues continued to dog Herschler, but he, or his campaign, confronted them directly each time, returning the message to "growth on our terms."

In late October, the Herschler campaign launched its own character attack. Alleging Ostlund was a "captive of the mineral industry" based on documents demonstrating Ostlund's ownership of certain coal land interests, which entitled him to a 1 cent per ton payment for each ton of coal mined. Based on the potential coal tonnage to be mined, Herschler's campaign estimated Ostlund would receive payments totaling $2.4 million.

Ostlund's campaign response was to accelerate efforts to focus on Herschler's corrupt character and his failure to develop water.

A *Washington Post* article in late October had an entirely different take on the Wyoming governor's race than a previous article in August.[70] The article recounted State Republican Party Chairman Castberg's earlier victory prediction:

> We're going to win this election on the crime and corruption
> issue. Ed Herschler is carrying a big load of garbage around, and
> we're going to poke it.[71]

Noting that "...Ostlund inexplicably pull [sic] back his television advertising at the same time Herschler started campaigning," the article states, "...Ostlund is carrying some heavy burdens of his own...." The *Post* summarized the race in rather harsh terms. "If the rival candidates for governor can be believed, Wyoming voters this year face a choice between an incumbent tainted by scandal and corruption and a challenger who is in the hip pocket of the big energy companies." Ultimately the *Post* deemed the race too close to call.

Herschler won the General Election by the narrowest of margins with 50.9% of the vote. Neither candidate's reputation was enhanced by the election of 1978. Other than the hard-core partisans, no one was terribly enthused about the choice presented.

Both candidates were better men than the electioneering would suggest. If the *Post's* characterization of the election choice was correct, growth on Wyoming's terms and tax relief were the choice of the electorate by the narrowest of margins.

Herschler was eventually cleared by the Grand Jury in a report filed after the General Election.

1979 LEGISLATIVE SESSION

In January 1979, the Legislature convened against the backdrop of an ugly campaign season. Press coverage in 1978 was split between the Grand Jury, the killing of Detective Michael Rosa, and the booming growth throughout Wyoming. National press coverage of growth issues presented a desolate and uncomplimentary image of Wyoming. Positive stories about development stood out due to their rarity.

Gaining press coverage was the oil and gas development emerging in the Overthrust Belt in southwestern Wyoming. Billion-dollar investments were underway. Incentivized by OPEC's decision to raise oil prices in 1979 by 14.5% and the increasing likelihood of dissolution of federal price controls—oil and gas development was set to explode in southwest Wyoming. OPEC price increases and national emphasis on coal usage fueled optimism for increased coal production in 1979 and beyond.

Governor Herschler's Message to the Legislature contained a brief reference to the 78 elections and his interpretation of the results:

> The 1978 election was as difficult and painful as any in recent memory.... The single most important message I received on the campaign trail is that it is time to devote increasing energy to making Wyoming the kind of state we want to live in.[72]

After a glowing report on Wyoming's economy and the larger-than-projected state revenues, Herschler immediately opened an argument in favor of a permanent property tax reduction/severance tax increase. He defended his campaign theme by clarifying his proposal, explaining that the effective tax increase for industry was 3%, not 5%. Industry could offset the increased severance tax with a ⅓ reduction in their property taxes. Given the makeup of the Legislature and its leadership, the proposal was doomed to fail. But Herschler devoted three pages of a nine-page speech to the topic. Three paragraphs stand out in his rhetoric:

> I served in this Legislature not too many years ago. The Wyoming Legislature used to be criticized because all we worried about was branding, dehorning, irrigating, and railroads. All we worried

about were Wyoming problems; we were too provincial.

From what I read in the papers it appears that we now have a number of cosmopolitan legislators. We now worry about the profit and loss statements for Kerr-McGee, Carter Oil Company, Atlantic Richfield, Amax, Sun Oil, Stauffer Chemical, and the rest of the energy industry. I am amazed at the concern we show for those companies who find ways to make money from our resources, have their headquarters outside of Wyoming, and deposit their profits in such small financial institutions as the Chase Manhattan Bank.

I welcome these companies to Wyoming, but I am not persuaded that occasional trips to their western properties by corporate directors and the annual invasion of company lobbyists at the Hitching Post* give them the right to dictate Wyoming tax policy.[73]

Note the specific reference to oil and gas companies' expansion into the mining business. Driven by the national push for coal and uranium and the absence of the controls hobbling oil and gas production, Kerr-McGee, Exxon (Carter Oil), ARCO, and Sun Oil, among others, entered the mining business in the 1970s. Most of them exited the mining business within a decade. Coal mining was never their core business, and they were happy to leave it behind.

The property tax relief/severance tax bill was introduced in the House of Representatives and referred to the Revenue Committee. It was returned to the House with a "Do Not Pass" recommendation adopted by the Republican majority on a party-line vote. The proposal died without any floor debate. No surprise there.

Republican Speaker of the House Warren Morton (Natrona County) had dismissed Herschler's speech as a "rehash" of the campaign pitch for property tax relief/severance tax increase. One day later, the *Casper Star Tribune's* Editorial Board took Morton to task for ignoring the tax relief

---

* The Hitching Post Inn was once a major Cheyenne landmark. It was sometimes known as "The Second Capitol" because so many state legislators stayed there when the legislature was in session. It was destroyed by a fire in 2021.

issue. Included in the editorial were verbatim quotes from the sitting State Republican Party Chairman:

> Whether or not you accept the governor's proposal for tax relief, you must acknowledge the citizens of Wyoming are asking for revisions of our tax structure in some manner. If you fail to acknowledge their needs, you may well jeopardize our majority position and your future as well.[74]

The expected public uproar over the failure of property tax relief was fanned by Governor Herschler's persistent references to legislators catering to "special interests" while ignoring the needs of the average citizen. In response, the House Republican leadership devised a proposal that reconciled their objections to severance tax increases with the need to deliver some form of property tax relief. As introduced, the proposal limited property tax relief to dwelling owners and was funded for one year with a $10 million general fund appropriation. For many occupied dwelling owners, it did roughly produce a ⅓ property tax reduction. The 10 million dollars could offset the cost of a ⅓ property tax reduction for selected homeowners because residences were no longer taxed on fair market value as envisioned by Wyoming's Founding Fathers. Through illegal administrative actions over many years, residences were only taxed at 10% of fair market value. Businesses were not given property tax relief. Republican leaders were happy. Tax relief was temporary, and no severance tax increase was required. Of course, the sales tax refund program for the elderly and disabled was extended.

With the Legislature solidly controlled by the Republicans, the legislative issue was settled. The political problem was a different question. Various attempts to resurrect the Herschler proposal and separate severance tax proposals were offered and debated. None were successful.

The slurry pipeline debate was resuscitated by legislation to authorize Texas Eastern Transmission Company to use 20,000 acre-feet of surface water to move Wyoming and Montana coal to the Gulf Coast. Under this proposal, water would be impounded in new reservoirs along the Little Big Horn River in Sheridan County, Wyoming, just south of the Montana border. Appealing aspects of the proposal included: actual development of Wyoming's unused water resources; the reservoirs could store more water than the 20,000 acre-feet required by the project, the excess water would be made available to the State of Wyoming; and it appealed to those who wanted Wyoming coal shipped out of state rather than converted to electric power in Wyoming. The initial response to the proposal was curious to positive. Environmental/conservation groups offered conditional support pending further information and resolution of outstanding issues. The only outward opposition came from the railroads and traditional opponents of exporting water.

Discussions over the ensuing weeks raised more questions than answers. Environmental groups withdrew their conditional support and serious local opposition emerged. In addition, the State of Montana threatened litigation since the reservoir construction would affect flows of the Little Big Horn River into Montana. Project sponsors simply could not resolve the issues within the legislative schedule. Compromise legislation was adopted, outlining three project options to be considered and negotiated by the governor and project sponsors within 90 days. If contract negotiations were successful, the governor would sign the contract. One interesting provision of the legislation removed slurry pipelines from the list of projects excluded from consideration by the Wyoming Industrial Siting Council (ISC). ETSI's slurry pipeline remained outside ISC jurisdiction as their authorization pre-dated the siting council act. Herschler allowed the legislation to become law without his signature.

In his letter to the Legislature explaining his action, Herschler noted the proposal had arrived at the Legislature without sufficient advance notice. With the significant number of unanswered questions, it was appropriate to spend additional time evaluating the proposal to determine whether to move forward.[75] Ninety days of negotiations did not resolve the issues, and Montana continued to threaten legal action. Herschler ultimately rejected the slurry contract arguing there were simply too many unanswered questions.

Legislative attempts were again made to weaken and modify the Industrial Siting Act based on continuing industry objections to the time and effort involved in meeting the Act's requirements. While the efforts gained some traction, they were ultimately unsuccessful.

Other issues addressed in 1979 included additional ways to assist impacted areas, increased education funding, new facility construction, and modest supplemental budgets for selected agencies. Wyoming's water development efforts were again revamped with the creation of the Wyoming Water Development Commission.

Every Legislative Session vents its anger at the federal government, usually taking the form of some joint resolution calling on Congress or the President for action on a particularly irritating issue. In 1979, the confrontation was more direct. As part of the national effort to respond to the energy crisis, the Federal Highway Administration had lowered speed limits to 55 mph on all interstate highways.[76] From the beginning, this angered motorists, particularly in Western states. In 1979 Wyoming joined an effort to increase all state speed limits to 65 mph. The response from the Administration was to simply say, "no more federal highway money if you raise the speed limit." After much wringing of hands and gnashing of teeth, the Legislature abandoned the speed limit increase.

1980 LEGISLATIVE BUDGET SESSION

Growth and population impact continued to be news in Wyoming. The coal and uranium impacts attracted less attention simply because they had become "old news." Coal production in 1980 would reach 95 million tons compared to 7 million in 1970. Oil and gas development was the "new news," particularly in southwest Wyoming around Evanston. Unrest in Iran and OPEC led to supply questions, and the limited oil production in the United States gave rise to price spikes in the oil field and at the pump. Federal price controls were relaxed, creating positive market signals and encouraging greater oil and gas development. However, positive signs were muted by discussion of a windfall profits tax designed to capture what some believed to be exorbitant profits by major oil and gas companies.

In March of 1979, the Three Mile Island Nuclear Power Generating Facility Unit 2 Reactor suffered a partial meltdown. While there were relatively small releases of radioactive material, the public reaction spelled immense trouble for the nuclear power industry. Wyoming's uranium industry also suffered a meltdown. The cancellation of proposed nuclear plants destroyed the demand for uranium.

In April of 1979, the Iranian Revolution replaced the Shah of Iran with religious leadership hostile to the United States. In November of 1979, the American Embassy was overrun, and employees were taken hostage. International oil markets were in turmoil.

A 1975 well in Utah rekindled expanded development in the Overthrust Belt that included parts of Wyoming. Limited development of the area had occurred for decades. By 1979, numerous promising new fields had been discovered in Utah and southwest Wyoming. The boom was on. Oil production in the Wyoming portion of the Overthrust Belt was slightly over 2.5 million barrels in 1978 and grew to more than 7.5 million in 1980. In 1979, area companies conceived the Overthrust Industrial Association. It would be formalized in 1980 with 36 participating oil and gas companies and related service/supply firms.

Cities, towns, and counties throughout Wyoming exerted pressure for added funding for basic infrastructure—streets, roads, sewer, water, etc.—citing a need for personnel and programs in order to respond to growth and development.

Thirty days before the Legislature convened, the Wyoming Supreme Court, referencing prior Opinions dating back to 1971, issued its decision in *Washakie County School District No. 1 v. Herschler*. The original Court decision issued on January 13 relied on hard numbers to show the financial disparity between rich and poor school districts. In an Order Denying Rehearing and Responding to Requests for Clarification, the Court removed any ambiguities about its initial decision:

> The court's decision herein again finds unconstitutional the state's
> system of school financing in failing to provide equal protection
> in violation Section 34, Article 1, Wyoming Constitution,
> compatible with Section 1, Article VII, Wyoming Constitution,
> requiring a 'uniform system of public instruction.' Undue delay
> in implementing the court's decision would only be doing a

disservice to the educational needs of the state with respect to financing. However, upon reconsideration, it appears advisable that the time for compliance with the court's direction be extended for a further brief period. [77]

The Washakie Court allowed the state until July 1, 1983, to bring educational financing into constitutional compliance. The Court's patience had been tried by the failure to heed its earlier opinions. This would not be the last word from the Wyoming Supreme Court on educational finance. Litigation would continue for decades to come.

Funding inequities had been papered over by successive governors and legislatures for years. An uneasy peace between rich and poor districts was purchased by increased spending based on a classroom unit. Total dollars spent increased, but the disparities remained largely unaddressed. In response to the Supreme Court decision, the Legislature chartered a committee responsible for crafting a solution for implementation by 1983.

Republicans dominated the Legislature. Even before the Session convened on February 12, 1980, the Republican leadership stated their opposition to any severance tax increase. However, they did offer extended residential tax relief subject to available appropriation and limited additional funding for local governments. Neither proposal was to be funded by new severance taxes.

Governor Herschler's 1980 Legislative Message began by extolling the wonders of the Wyoming economy. The unemployment rate was the lowest in the nation. More people had jobs in Wyoming than ever before. Personal income had risen 18% over the last three years. State government finances were equally rosy, although inflation drove costs well beyond expectations.

Under the rules governing Budget Sessions of the Wyoming Legislature, no bill (except the appropriations bill) could be introduced without ⅔ of the House (42 members) or ⅔ of the senators (20 members) voting in favor of introduction. In those days, the rule was generally followed in good faith. Non-budget proposals were thereby limited. Herschler's request for only eight non-budget items reflected the discipline of the body. Two of the governor's requests are relevant to this discussion.

Extensive amendments to the Wyoming Environmental Quality Act were needed for Wyoming to comply with the federal Surface Mining Control and Reclamation Act requirements. While controversial in some respects, passage was assured as Wyoming legislators preferred regulation from Cheyenne rather than control from the nation's Capital.

Renewing his quest for increased severance taxes, Herschler asked for an added 4% excise tax on coal, uranium, and oil and gas. 1½% would be distributed to local governments, ½ percent to the General fund, and 2% to the Permanent Mineral Trust Fund. The allocation to the Permanent Mineral Trust would more than double the 1½% placed in the PMTF by Constitution. While lobbying for the PMTF portion, advocates attempted calculations of the fund's growth over the coming decades. Impressive numbers were produced but were ultimately unpersuasive. In retrospect, the PMTF would likely be double today's fund balance had the proposal been adopted. Since the annual income from the fund is used to underwrite current government expenditures, doubling the corpus seems like an attractive idea in hindsight.

While the tone of Hersherler's Message was moderate, his language was direct:

> Finally, we should be building our permanent fund to meet
> the crisis that inevitably will occur when our non-renewable
> resources and those who have been extracting them will be gone.
> It is difficult for me to comprehend some of the rhetoric that is
> being extolled by those who believe the mineral giants are now
> overtaxed and will leave if we require them to pay their fair share
> of the taxes.
>
> I would remind you that a corporation makes the same sound
> as a street, or a school building or a road, or a sewage lagoon,
> or a water pipe, but unfortunately only the corporations have
> spokesmen with vested interests, who are more concerned and
> motivated by a profit and loss statement than they are for the
> welfare of their fellow citizens. I urge you to reconsider your
> past commitments relative to severance tax and give favorable
> consideration to this Bill. [78]

Nine attempts were made in the House to introduce severance tax increases, but none of the proposals were ever debated on the floor of the House since 42 votes were necessary for introduction. An analysis of the nine proposals shows that 18 (all Republicans) of 62 members voted against every severance tax proposal. Forty-four of the members voted for one or more of the severance tax proposals. If all 44 had voted "Aye" on the same proposal, the severance tax debate would have reached the floor of the House. Several of the proposals garnered more than the 32 votes necessary for passage. Before the Legislature adjourned, Herschler accused the House Republicans of engineering the voting patterns to allow individual legislators to say they voted for a severance tax, meanwhile assuring none of the measures received the requisite ⅔ vote for introduction. Herschler's assessment of the voting pattern was mathematically demonstrable. Motivation remains a matter of opinion.

Following the rejection of the last House severance tax proposal, Speaker of the House Warren Morton (R-Natrona), House Majority Leader Russ Donley (R-Natrona), and Senate President L.V. Stafford (R-Johnson/Campbell) attacked the newspapers and television media for unfair coverage of the severance tax issue, claiming the media was pro-severance tax and failed to cover the anti-severance tax story. Notably, House Speaker Pro Tem Bob Burnett (R-Albany), a severance tax supporter, did not criticize the media coverage.[79]

On the same day, the head of the Wyoming Petroleum Association (WPA) testified to the Senate Committee, considering a constitutional amendment to allow the voters to decide whether to add another 1.5% severance tax on oil and gas. The proposed constitutional amendment would have divided the proceeds 50% to the Permanent Mineral Trust Fund and 50% for permanent capital improvements. None of the money would support general government. WPA called the proposal "greed, not need." Referencing current revenue flows and an anticipated revenue boom based on oil and gas development in the Overthrust Belt, WPA argued the state had funds to finance the next two years "...making any additional tax on oil and gas punitive and unnecessary."[80] WPA's argument ignored the fact that none of the proposed revenues were to be used to finance the general government in the next two years—or ever. The proposed constitutional amendment would not survive.

Herschler, legislative leadership, and the mineral industry supported changing severance taxes from annual payments to quarterly payments. Not required as a matter of law, but perhaps by the politics of the moment, the legislation gave mineral companies a one-year holiday from severance tax payments. Severance taxes would simply not be paid on 1980 mineral production. A fact footnoted on page 8 of a 2010 report entitled *Wyoming Severance Taxes and Federal Mineral Royalties* prepared by the Wyoming Legislative Service Office.[81] The language reads, "no severance tax assessed on 1980 production, because assessment changed from being based on prior year production to being based on current year production in 1981." This tax holiday was understood by the sponsors but not widely discussed within the Legislature or the press. The total 1980 assessed value of minerals for taxation purposes was $4,026,165,628. The severance tax holiday for mineral companies meant approximately $270 million would not be collected (969 in 2022 dollars).

Two bills affecting the jurisdiction of the Industrial Siting Administration gained introduction in the House. House Bill 110 would have limited the purview of the industrial siting council to social and economic considerations. It was never debated and died on General File. House Bill 127 and Senate File 74 were counterpart bills designed to bring major gas processing facilities proposed by Amoco and Chevron in southwest Wyoming under the Siting Council jurisdiction. Senate consideration was indefinitely postponed, essentially to allow the House bill to proceed. Speaker Morton (R-Natrona) was successful in amending the House bill in a manner which may have precluded jurisdiction of the currently proposed facilities. As amended, the bill passed the House and was forwarded to the Senate. Senate action by Committee Chair True (R-Natrona) further watered down the bill, and it was ultimately listed as "indefinitely postponed."[82]

Resurrection of the Little Big Horn River coal slurry pipeline authorization to export 20,000 acre-feet of Wyoming water was sought through legislation sponsored by two Sheridan County legislators, but it failed to gain the necessary ⅔ vote for introduction in the House of Representatives. The same fate awaited the bill when introduction was sought in the Senate. Heated exchanges occurred post-failure between Herschler and supporters of the proposal.

Talk of other coal slurry pipeline proposals came and went. The ETSI pipeline was a serious endeavor that encountered stiff opposition from the railroads, railroad unions, some landowners, and states along its 1800-mile route. Federal eminent domain legislation that would have solved many of the pipeline problems died quietly in the summer of 1978. Eventually, practical obstacles and declining energy prices were the death knell for slurry pipeline discussions in Wyoming.

Homestead exemptions for property taxes were converted to an increased Homestead Tax Credit, increasing property tax relief for residences. Sales tax refunds to the elderly and disabled were continued. A proposed three-cent per gallon fuel tax for highway construction failed on introduction.

Republican leadership was sensitive to the revenue needs of cities, towns, and counties and supported various proposals, so long as they did not include an increase in severance taxes.

A fiscally responsible attempt by Speaker Morton (R-Natrona) to require local governments to utilize their existing taxing authority before seeking state assistance was soundly rejected.

1980 POST LEGISLATIVE SESSION

1980 was a tough year in America. The Iraqi invasion of Iran exacerbated the oil supply disruptions of the 1979 Iranian Revolution in September of 1980. Oil prices peaked in 1980 at $35 per barrel (126 in 2022 dollarsh). Rapid interest rate increases triggered by the Federal Reserve's efforts to clamp down on inflation contributed to a growing recession in the American economy. In April, the prime rate for bank lending reached 20%. Second-quarter mortgage interest rates in Wyoming ranged between 14–17%. Local government and school district construction bonds were difficult and sometimes impossible to sell. Iran still held 50 American hostages while release negotiations showed little progress.

However, Wyoming's economy continued to prosper. In April 1980, Wyoming's unemployment rate continued to decline with an expectation of further declines as the summer construction season opened. President Carter, though not a fan of oil import fees, imposed an oil import fee of nearly $5 a barrel. Petroleum prices accelerated oil and gas exploration and production in the Overthrust Belt. Kemmerer in Lincoln County and Evanston in Unita County were feeling the brunt of development impacts, with projections of future growth being 20–30% in the next few years. The Overthrust Industrial Association, led by Chevron, Amoco, and Champlin Petroleum, was already donating funds and undertaking studies of projected growth.

Coal production increased, and prices were favorable. Increased energy costs damaged the national economy and pinched family budgets throughout America. Congressional Representatives from non-energy-producing states began to push for limitations on severance and other taxes imposed by producing states. Two clouds in Wyoming's economic sky were reduced farm income and depressed uranium prices. Reduced uranium demand would lead to layoffs in the industry. At the same time, Exxon announced it was moving up its drilling schedule for the development of uranium resources in the Sunlight Basin.

Industrial expansion continued to add population. Wyoming believed the U.S. Census Bureau had undercounted our total population. Personal income in Wyoming was up. The National Director of the Bureau of Land Management, in a ceremony in Cheyenne, offered the observation, "More than any other Western state, Wyoming will bear the brunt of the national program to accelerate the development of energy resources...."[83]

Coal gasification plants, additional power plants, and new mines were very much under discussion in the state. President Carter's version of energy independence included significant subsidies to advance coal conversion and oil shale development. The passage of the federal Energy Security Act of 1980 created the Synthetic Fuels Corporation, intended to supercharge efforts to convert coal to synthetic fuels. The legislation authorized $88 billion for loans, loan guarantees, and subsidies for coal conversion facilities and oil shale development. The Energy Mobilization

Board Act of 1979 was introduced in the U.S. Senate in the fall of 1979. The Energy Mobilization Board (EMB) was intended as a companion piece to the creation of the Synthetic Fuels Corporation. EMB powers included the ability to override state and federal environmental and siting laws to develop domestic energy resources. Projects selected by the EMB as priority projects could avoid compliance with federal, state, and local development restrictions. Suffice it to say, the EMB was attractive to some in industry and adamantly opposed by citizen groups, conservationists, and most states, not the least of which was Wyoming. Suddenly the notion of public land states becoming "energy sacrifice areas" moved from theatrical rhetoric to a potential reality. Congressman Dick Cheney saw Wyoming coal as a likely target for the federal Synthetic Fuels Corporation.[84]

Cities, towns, and counties continued the search for more financial assistance from the state to respond to growth. Fights over water quantity and quality continued with varying levels of intensity. Looming barely in the background was the struggle for school funding equalization. A battle royal between rich and poor school districts was inevitable—rich districts did not want their funding diminished, and poor districts, with the backing of the Supreme Court, were demanding a bigger slice of the pie.

Former governor and Secretary of Interior Stan Hathaway noted the counter-cyclical nature of Wyoming's economy, pointing out that times were bad in Wyoming and good nationally when he took office in the mid-1960s. In 1980, times were bad nationally and great in Wyoming. Nonetheless, Wyoming should not consider itself a separate nation. Mindful of the ongoing severance tax discussions, Hathaway expressed a view held by many Republican leaders. An excerpt from the April 4 *Casper Star Tribune* captures the moment:

> The former Governor and Interior Secretary, now a Cheyenne attorney whose clients number large energy companies, also criticized those who would increase taxes on energy development in Wyoming.

> "That has to be self-defeating when we consider ourselves part

of the nation," he said, adding, "Wyoming can't think of itself as another Saudi Arabia."

On August 20, 1980, a Casper Republican candidate for the Wyoming House of Representatives released a poll showing "nearly half" of Natrona County Republican voters favored an increase in the severance tax even though the Republican legislative leadership from Casper had fought Herschler's severance tax proposals.[85] 1980 was an election year, and severance taxes would be an election issue.

A catalyzing event was an announcement by Governor Herschler that he would ask the legislators to approve a 3% increase in the severance tax on oil and gas. Herschler deferred the question of added-on coal tax while protecting uranium and the trona industry. The 3% would be divided between cities and towns (1.25%), highway construction and maintenance (1.25%), and counties (0.5%). Herschler cited the considerable impact oil and gas production was creating in Wyoming. He also noted that the oil and gas companies were allowed to deduct local taxes from their obligations under the federal windfall profits tax. The battle lines were clearly drawn when Herschler referred to the "overblown rhetoric of the oil and gas industry, the Republican leadership and the Wyoming Heritage Society..." as "flim-flam."[86]

Two controversial water issues confronted the pending Legislative Session. First, the Sheridan-Little Horn Water Group again proposed a coal slurry pipeline using water from the Little Big Horn River. The second was a growing movement to recognize in-stream flow as a beneficial water use. Proponents of legal protection for in-stream flows argued that allowing water to remain in a stream or river channel would preserve Wyoming's heritage of wildlife, fishing, and recreation. Proponents also highlighted the increasing economic value of travel and tourism to Wyoming's economy.

In the 1980 presidential election, Ronald Reagan swept Wyoming. His coat tails, political action committee money, and petroleum industry money again assured GOP control of the Legislature—made easier by the national Democratic Party's movement away from issues of importance to rural America.

Before the end of the year, a proposed $2 billion coal gasification plant planned in Wyoming would seek federal assistance. Tri-State Generation and Transmission continued its evaluation of potential sites for a power plant and pledged to help communities deal with the impact.

1981 LEGISLATIVE SESSION

Herschler's 1981 Message to the Legislature reflected the generally upbeat attitude of citizens and legislators alike. Wyoming was prospering as the national recession took hold. A series of comments in the opening paragraphs seem to capture the hopes and fears of Wyoming:

> It is true that development was very great during the 70s, but it is now my conviction that the next 15 years will see unparalleled development in Wyoming. The combination of the pressure for development of the overthrust belt and synthetic fuels program will dwarf the development pressure of the last 10 years. We must continue to keep strong those environmental programs which have made Wyoming a leader among the Western states.
>
> There is one other point which I would like to make in regard to the protection of Wyoming's lifestyle. [references federal push to develop domestic energy resources] I expect that federal policies will... push the states to develop energy resources in a manner which better suits Chicago and San Francisco or even Washington. The pressure, in and of itself, will not account for the particular needs of Wyoming's people.... I have, in previous years, fought hard against attempts to dictate Wyoming development policy by slowing the process through unnecessary and useless federal regulations and policies. I would like to serve notice that I will be equally inclined to resist any federal efforts to compromise Wyoming's future through policies designed to make the state an energy sacrifice area.[87]

Governor Herschler proposed an aggressive agenda for a Legislative Session already confronting a record number of proposals offered by individual members. In keeping with Wyoming's pattern of encouraging state primacy in enforcing the federal regulatory scheme, Herschler requested amendments to the Environmental Quality Act enabling Hazardous Waste and 404 Permitting programs.

On the state level, requests included:

1. Amending the Industrial Siting Council jurisdiction to include the gas processing facilities planned for the Overthrust Belt and the Synthetic Fuels industry in coal country. Industrial siting had evolved into a forum for communities and project sponsors to negotiate company-sponsored impact assistance prior to obtaining a permit.

2. Added funding for the water development account, authorization for Game and Fish to appropriate unappropriated water to sustain instream flows, a substantial tax on the export of water, and renewed opposition to coal slurry lines.

3. A severance tax increase of 3% on oil and gas to be distributed to cities, towns, counties, and the highway fund. Emphasis was given to the needs of local governments and the wealth extracted from Wyoming by the extractive industry relative to their tax burden. It was noted that 90% of all extracted minerals are exported from Wyoming.[88]

From the outset, it was clear that this General Session would be very different from the 1980 Budget Session. The prior Speaker of the House and the Republican majority had successfully defeated severance tax proposals. Under Wyoming's Constitution, tax increases must originate in the House of Representatives. The new House Speaker Bob Burnett (R-Albany County) was a supporter of a severance increase and would allow the drumbeat to be heard. Speaker Burnett adopted this position, even though the Republican Party hierarchy reiterated their coded anti-severance tax message. According to the State Party Chairman,

> "We've taken the position we've always taken on the severance tax...that is, we'll identify the valid needs and apply our sources of income against them," he said. "If the income is inadequate, then an increase will be considered," he added.[89]

It was a colorful session with significant antagonism between the House and Senate as they managed an overly aggressive agenda. Mechanically the General Session was a failure as many agreed-upon measures simply died as the clock ran out. With agreement from the legislative leadership, Governor Herschler immediately called a Special Session, and normal rules were suspended. In two days, 26 legislative measures were passed and forwarded to the governor. In total, two hundred and two measures covering a broad range of issues became the law of Wyoming.

Prior to the legislative debate on the oil and gas severance tax increases, President Reagan had accelerated the schedule for decontrol of the price of oil, allowing it to become effective in January rather than in September 1981. Among the reasons for immediate decontrol was the desire to encourage domestic oil exploration. Wyoming's State Geologist described the Overthrust Belt as the most significant Wyoming oil discovery in fifty years. The estimated minimum reserves were 2 billion barrels of recoverable oil. While price controls on natural gas remained in effect, President Carter had previously doubled the allowable price for new gas produced from "tight sand" formations such as those found in southwest Wyoming. Industry representatives encouraged the belief that the added price incentive would increase Wyoming production.[90]

Increased taxes seemed a safe bet with greater oil and gas production on the horizon. Ultimately, House and Senate votes reflected the existing fault lines within the Republican majority. Democrats were solidly in favor of the increase, and more than enough Republicans voted "aye" to easily pass the measure.

Oil and gas severance taxes were increased by 2% rather than three, the lion's share of the new revenue earmarked for cities, towns, and counties. The remainder was divided between the Permanent Mineral Trust Fund, the Highway Fund, and a new subaccount within Water Development. The added money for water development was "…for the improvement of water projects in use and completed prior to 1970."[91] Agricultural interests who relied on outdated irrigation projects built by the federal government many decades ago established this account to gain public funding for rehabilitation and improvements of their decaying infrastructure.

1981 would be the last time a severance tax increase would pass.

Within a few short years, Wyoming's energy economy would be challenged. Rather than look to build an alternative economy, the state's response was usually to authorize various tax breaks requested by industry. A Legislative Service Office report documents more than 40 different "Mineral Tax Incentives" between 1983 and 2020.[92] This response was driven by industry pressure and the mistaken belief that changes in state tax policy could somehow overwhelm national and international events and market forces. It is difficult to discern any measurable effect on mineral production over the 37 years.

Legislation brought by Senator Stroock (R-Natrona County) added staff in the State Auditor Jim Griffith's office to audit the records of producers of valuable mineral deposits in Wyoming on both federal and state lands. Senator Stroock, a Casper oilman, was a smart, strategic leader on various issues related to health care, conservation, minerals, and economic development. According to the legislative enactment: "The purpose of the audits is to ensure that the state is receiving all of the state and federal mineral royalties to which it is lawfully entitled."[93] Near unanimous passage was assured since the audits would benefit not only the state but also landmen, citizens, and agricultural landowners owning a royalty, overriding royalty, or other interest attached to mineral estate.

Jurisdiction of the Industrial Siting Council was expanded to include gas processing facilities, synfuel facilities, and railroads.[94]

Chapter 145 of the 1981 Session Laws provided additional sales and use tax distributions to impacted areas. Sales and use tax payments would spike during the project construction period, and local governments were granted an increased share of sales tax distributions during the construction. In effect, some funds destined for state coffers were redirected to local governments impacted by facilities subject to the Industrial Siting jurisdiction. This legislation enjoyed broad support as it provided impact areas a reliable funding source and reduced the project sponsors direct obligation to fund impact assistance.

Instream flow issues were generally unaddressed. Legislation was introduced to allocate a portion of the income from the Permanent Mineral Trust Fund to support wildlife conservation and recreation. The proposal engendered considerable debate but was eventually defeated after the agricultural community mounted forceful opposition.

Legislation for state regulation of hazardous waste passed the House, despite opposition from the oil and gas industry. Ultimately it died in a Senate committee.[95]

A package of educational bills intended to satisfy the requirements of the 1980 school funding equalization decision passed, along with a significant increase in Classroom Unit funding. Eventually, this plan would also be ruled unconstitutional by the Court.

Coal slurry legislation was rejected, as was an attempt to remove sales tax from the purchase of food. Other items were exempted from sales tax, and public schools were exempted from the gas tax. Moving in an entirely different direction, House Bill 439 would have done away with more than 100 existing sales tax exemptions and reduced the statewide rate from three percent to two percent. This would have significantly expanded the state's tax base. Nearly all sales, including professional services, would bear the tax under HB 439. The bill's net effect was revenue neutral—the tax base would be diversified, but the rate of taxation was reduced. While the proposal was essentially fair, those interests which would suddenly become subject to sales tax were incensed. Having passed the House after contentious debate, the proposal died unceremoniously in a Senate committee. Representative Pete Simpson (R-Sheridan County) was a co-sponsor of the legislation, which would haunt his 1986 bid for governor.

The elderly and disabled sales tax refund was continued, as was the property tax exemption. Proposals to increase cigarette and liquor taxes to levels commensurate with surrounding states failed to leave the starting blocks. The House Transportation Committee proposed a fuel tax in response to a request from Highway Department officials, but the increase was rejected. Wyoming citizens saw no need to increase sales taxes, fuel taxes, or any other fee or tax, even though surrounding states had done so. Why add taxes to locals when we can rely on mineral taxes?

THE REMAINDER OF 1981

1981 would be a year of recession for the United States. Wyoming was not entirely immune, but the overall impact was muted. High interest rates drove up the cost of living. As Wyoming participated in the savings and loan/banking crisis, available credit was diminished. Numerous Wyoming banks would be permanently closed or closed and reorganized. Uranium was challenged by a lack of demand and alternative sources of supply. Some uranium facilities laid off workers. Texaco's refinery in Casper was set for closure. Powder River Basin coal markets remained solid, but uncertainty surrounded pending actions related to the federal Clean Air Act. If requirements of the Clean Air Act were reduced, the attractiveness of Wyoming's low-sulfur coal would decline. Energy Development Corporation laid off workers at its underground bituminous coal mine in southwest Wyoming, pending better market conditions. Agriculture was hard hit by interest rates and low prices. Coal leasing had been revived over the objections of the environmental community. The coal industry viewed the revived process as complicated and cumbersome but continued to pursue leasing. Construction jobs declined slightly. However, the oil and gas industry, buoyed by better prices and Reagan's support for natural gas deregulation, continued to build facilities and employ Wyoming citizens. Oil prices peaked in 1980. A modest decline came in 1981, but no one predicted a steep drop in prices. Wyoming's unemployment rate reached 5.2%, the highest rate since 1975.[96] Still much lower than the national unemployment rate, which hovered in the 8–9% range for most of 1981. Wyoming's federal bankruptcy court records showed a significant increase in bankruptcy filings.

Media stories focused on growth and impact problems associated with oil and gas development in southwest Wyoming. Overthrust development was expected to bring in 4,000 new bodies in the summer of 1981. Records of the Wyoming Oil and Gas Conservation Commission demonstrated that oil and gas companies planned to drill a record number of wells in 1981.

While northeastern Wyoming was learning to cope with the impact of mining expansion, the prospect of two or more major coal conversion facilities in the next 5–7 years created considerable concern. These coal conversion facilities were dependent on funding from President Carter's

Synthetic Fuel Corporation. Prospects for funding seemed positive. Newly elected President Reagan had yet to show his distaste for the market interference inherent in the Synthetic Fuels program.

The State Board of Equalization (the state taxing authority) had proposed updating and equalizing property tax assessments throughout the state. Such updates and equalization were required by the State Constitution, which mandated "equal and uniform" taxation throughout the state. A relatively recent "fair market value" determination was essential for applying the Constitutional provisions. Most property appraisals had not been updated since 1967. Updated appraisals would mean increased taxable value. Such proposals were met with solid citizen objections. At a hearing in Rock Springs, 500 angry citizens shouted, "let industry pay."[97]

Citizen groups marshaled forces around a petition to force the Legislature to act on the instream flow issue. The effort had considerable momentum but engendered significant legislative opposition.

Results from the royalty audit program created by Senator Stroock and Auditor Griffith were impressive. Within the first month, $7.8 million (24.2 million in 2021 dollars) in delinquent royalties were identified.

1982 would be an election year for Wyoming's governor. Herschler had been elected to two four-year terms. No governor in Wyoming history had been elected three times. Herschler remained coy in November of 81, suggesting he was deciding between running for senator, governor, or just withdrawing from politics.[98] Former Republican Speaker of the House Nels Smith had already made his interest in running for governor abundantly clear. Republicans decided Herschler was vulnerable on the water development issue, but before they could fully develop the point, Herschler announced he would ask the 1982 Legislature to support an ambitious $600 million water development program. Republican leaders, including the State Party Chairman and the Senate President, lambasted Herschler as suddenly supporting major water development only because he was planning to run for a third term.

Warren Air Force Base in southeastern Wyoming was consistently seen as a likely location for the new MX missiles which President Reagan planned to deploy as part of America's updated nuclear deterrent.

The population boomed 41.3% between 1970 and 1980, according to the Census Bureau. The increase in population was nearly equivalent to the entire population of Wyoming in 1910.[99]

Wyoming's legislators were set to convene in Cheyenne for a short Budget Session. Republicans remained firmly in control.

Herschler's water plan enjoyed broad bi-partisan support even before the session began. His proposed budget, the largest in state history, drew some critique. But most legislators understood they would ultimately spend as much or more than Herschler recommended.

A tale of two industries appeared in the *Casper Star Tribune* on February 8, 1982, one day before the Legislature was set to convene. Prospects for the uranium industry remained gloomy. Demand for yellowcake had plummeted due to the Three Mile Island nuclear accident (1979), licensing delays at the Nuclear Regulatory Commission, and inflation-based construction cost overruns. Employment in the industry had dropped from 5,000 to around 2,000 workers. On the same page was a story predicting "major growth" in Campbell County driven by mining, slurry pipelines, and synthetic fuel plants. A study projected as many as 7,000 new employees by 1986.

On day one of the Legislature, even before Herschler's Message was delivered, legislation was considered to mollify the public's fear of property tax increases. Wyoming's system was allegedly based on a determination of the current fair market value of the property. An assessment ratio (a percentage of actual value) was applied to the fair market value to determine the assessed value of the property to which tax rates were applied. This assessment ratio was by administrative and political decree, sanctioned by neither the Constitution nor statutes. Over multiple decades it had brought tax relief to Wyoming residents and businesses. The locally elected County Assessor determined the fair market value for homes and most businesses. As elected officials, County Assessors were not exactly aggressive about keeping fair market value appraisals up to date. Further, County Assessors as independent elected officials may or may not choose to follow guidance from the State Board of Equalization. Recent litigation highlighted the practical and constitutional issues with the system's operation.

Legislators and the Board of Equalization agreed the system needed an overhaul. Most fair market value determinations pre-dated the boom and the associated increases in property values. They even agreed on the basic approach, which would ultimately increase property valuations. A scathing *Audit of the Ad Valorem Division of the State Board of Equalization* undertaken by the Legislature was released in September of 1981.[100] The Audit detailed the deterioration and mismanagement of the state's property tax system since 1900. Action had to be taken, or the Court would step in. Legislators' fear of facing an angry electorate in 1982 froze the committee into inaction.[101]

Herschler's 1982 Legislative Message to the joint session of the Legislature was optimistic about Wyoming's economy and finances. Contrary to the national recessionary trends, Wyoming's employment and personal income were higher than ever. Unemployment was 4% compared to a national number of 9%. Herschler spent little time pitching his budget proposal as the debate was already well underway.

Water development and a Budget Stabilization Account were his major proposals. Three bills would support water development. One, was to immediately appropriate $114 million (approximately 350 million in 2021 dollars) for project construction. A second bill would streamline the procedures for project approval. And finally, a list of projects to be pursued and hopefully constructed. With some legislative tinkering, the water development program would be adopted.

Herschler's proposal of the Budget Stabilization Account reflected the uncertainty of Wyoming's economic future. Under this proposal, an amount equal to 5% of the general fund expenditures would be set aside as a hedge against future revenue declines. Herschler cited four areas of fiscal uncertainty: continued cuts in federal grant programs to the states, potential legislation in Congress to limit the state's ability to impose a severance tax, the impact of the continuing national recession, and finally, the most lasting consequence was Congressional discussions suggesting a relaxation of clean air standards. According to Herschler, "This could greatly affect the demand for low-sulfur Western coal, resulting in the loss of severance tax monies and the weakening of the coal industry in our state."[102] Adoption of the Budget Stabilization Account was the first practical legislative recognition that the bloom could fade from the rose of mineral development.

Herschler supported in-stream flow legislation as "vitally needed." Vigorous debate ensued with the Senate and House creating different versions of an in-stream flow bill, but conference committees failed to reconcile the differences, and the measure failed.

Legislation was advanced to fund the construction and improvement of livestock processing facilities in Wyoming, initially focusing on a lamb processing plant. The legislation was not part of a cohesive plan to develop an economic alternative to minerals. Instead, it was a response to the lack of local facilities to process livestock into marketable products. Increasingly, meat packing was being consolidated into fewer and fewer national companies. The meat packer monopoly left Wyoming producers with few options for marketing their products. Considerable controversy arose related to ownership of the facility, including allegations of a conflict of interest with the sponsor, Senator Eddie Moore (R-Converse County). The financial viability of the entire enterprise was seriously challenged during the floor debate.[103] This measure, of dubious constitutional validity, would pass, but no facility would ever be built.

Annual renewal of the tax relief and refund measures were accomplished without substantive legislative debate. K-12 education funding was again increased.

Severance tax action took an interesting about-face. Since 1969, severance tax debates had been on whether to increase rates or leave them alone. In 1982, Representative Russ Donley (R-Natrona County) was angry when his proposal to reduce the severance tax rate on uranium failed to be introduced. According to a February article in the *Casper Star Tribune*, "The measure...by itself would not have restored the industry to health, Donley admitted, but it was one thing the state could have done to address the industry's troubles." The bill failed to gain the ⅔ vote necessary for introduction. The vote was mainly along party lines, with only two Republicans voting against introduction. The Republicans voting against the measure correctly observed that this small tax change would not solve the industry's problems. Representative Donley's position—*it won't change things, but it is something Wyoming could do*—would echo for decades. Such measures, sometimes time sincere, sometimes political and self-serving, were promoted mainly on the mistaken premise that Wyoming could single-handedly change the course of commodity markets.

During the period of tax "incentives," the Legislature funded two separate studies on the value of mineral tax incentives. During a fiscally difficult period in 1997, the Legislature created Tax Reform 2000, consisting of legislators and citizens. According to Senate Enrolled Act 56, 1997 General Session:

> The mission of the committee shall be to recommend standards
> and options for developing a fair, viable and economically
> competitive state and local tax structure capable of generating
> sufficient revenues to meet expected needs in the future.

The Tax Reform 2000 effort included an extensive study entitled *Mineral Tax Incentives, Mineral Production, and the Wyoming Economy.*[104] Simply summarized, the study concluded that mineral tax reduction incentives do not significantly increase production but may have a tangible impact on state revenues. Following the detailed analysis, the Tax Reform 2000 executive summary explicitly states: "The committee does not recommend a decrease in mineral taxes."

Tax Reform 2000 provided an equally candid assessment of Wyoming's circumstances: "Wyoming's tax structure contributes to the lack of economic growth in the state."

Tax Reform 2000s assessment of the tax structure was correct. So long as growth and new population fail to bring in a commensurate tax base to support the new public service demands, neither the industries bearing the major tax burden, nor the citizens fearing personal or business tax increases and diminution of public services, fully support economic growth.

A second study directed by the Legislature in 2018 (House Enrolled

Act No. 63) called for a study directly focused on the impact of Wyoming taxation policy on the exploration, development, and production of petroleum products. A similar conclusion was reached:

> Higher tax rates do not discourage exploration and production—it depends more on geology.[105]

Both studies concluded that development is a function of commodity price and the value of the prospective mineral resource. State leaders ignored both studies as they were contrary to the political forces at play.

THE GOVERNOR'S RACE OF 1982

1982 would be the year the national recession caught up with Wyoming. No such concern would be evident during the campaigns. Hampshire Energy was still planning a $2 billion (5.82 billion in 2021 dollars) coal conversion facility in the Powder River Basin. Even though oil prices had moderated, exploration and production activity in Southwest Wyoming continued apace. Coal production in northeast Wyoming continued to expand, and prices remained solid as much of the production was governed by multi-year contracts. Coal production in southwest Wyoming was challenged. While the coal was higher in Btu content, it was slightly higher in sulfur content, and some utilities complained of ash problems during combustion.

Former representative Nels Smith, a tall, deep-voiced rancher from Crook County, announced his candidacy for governor very early. Representative Smith enjoyed support from the party leadership and was the odds-on favorite to win the Republican nomination. Governor Herschler, as expected, announced he would seek an unprecedented third term as Wyoming's governor. Herschler may have overdone playing coy. Suggesting at one point that he remained undecided but his decision might simply be based on the "flip of a coin."

Shortly before the Republican primary, Nels Smith withdrew from the race, citing health reasons. Republican party leaders gathered at the Casper Ramada Inn to quickly select a viable candidate to run against Herschler. Former Speaker of the House Warren Morton courageously accepted the short straw. Morton and Herschler would easily win their respective primaries. General Election 1982 would prove to be a hard-fought race between two men who had clashed over severance taxes, environmental protection, and government spending. At times, the race took on the flavor of two old soldiers fighting old battles anew.

Republicans were determined to regain the governor's chair and deny Herschler an unprecedented third term. Herschler was attacked for moving too slow on water development, allowing exponential growth in government, mismanaging the ETSI coal slurry pipeline water dispute with South Dakota, and his commutation of prisoner sentences. Herschler's flippant attitude about whether to run again or not, combined with his early lackluster campaign efforts, gave credence to Morton's charge that Herschler was tired and would be ineffective in a third term. In their turn, every important Republican in the state took a swing at Herschler for a variety of perceived errors and failures.

Herschler was determined to have his eight-year record as governor vindicated. Herschler touted his accomplishments under the "growth on our terms" banner. Herschler made his case by pointing to the funds distributed to communities for infrastructure, the fiscal wealth of the state, the effectiveness of the Plant Siting legislation, balanced environmental legislation, and a general sensitivity to the protection of Wyoming's unique lifestyle. These issues carried an explicit rebuke of Morton for having voted nine times against severance tax increases, resisting funding for needed social programs, and having a less than supportive attitude towards local governments. In a sense, Herschler's strategy was a replay of 1978, with Morton cast as the special interest candidate and Herschler as a man of the people. Completely ignored by the Herschler campaign was Morton's early support for severance taxes and environmental protection.

Neither candidate focused on the economic storm clouds that were forming just over the Wyoming horizon.

Two other considerations shaped the race. Morton was easily among the most intelligent, thoughtful, and well-educated (a degree from Yale) people ever to seek the governor's office. But his personal style and rapid-fire staccato speech pattern did not sit easily with the average voter.

Herschler relied on humor and occasional jokes to maintain a rapport with voters. In an irony of political life, a near-fatal blow to Morton's candidacy came from his friends. A Denver oilman of considerable prominence sent out a fund-raising letter to the oil and gas community extolling Morton's support for the industry. Of course, the letter fell into the hands of the Herschler campaign. The oilman's full letter was published in the newspapers as "Exhibit 1," proving Herschler's opponent was a special interest candidate.

Herschler won resoundingly in November. Even he was surprised when he carried 21 of 23 counties. But the next four years would be very different from the eight years of Hathaway and the first eight years of Herschler.

CHAPTER 6

Boom Becomes Bust

By the time the 1983 Legislature convened, the reality of the national recession had reached Wyoming. The drilling rig count in July 1982 was down to 120 compared to 193 in July 1981. Oil prices declined as OPEC and other oil-producing nations engaged in public arguments about production and price goals. Coal production remained high, but the growth in coal production moderated. In August, unemployment reached its highest level since 1963. A contrary indication was the increase in total employment in Wyoming during the first three quarters of the year. This total employment trend was reversed in the fourth quarter. The railroads laid off 600 workers. A future drilling boom was projected in the Riley Ridge area in southwest Wyoming, but it had yet to materialize. WyoCoal Gas canceled their proposed coal gasification plant near Douglas. Hampshire Energy's $2 billion synthetic fuel began to falter when Standard Oil of Ohio withdrew its financial support. December would bring an announcement that the plant had been canceled. In December, the state again reached an eleven-year high in unemployment. While Congressional funding for the MX missile remained uncertain, its ultimate location in Wyoming seemed confirmed.

In September, a consensus estimate of state revenues was issued by a joint committee of the legislative and executive branch agencies. Gary Glass, State Geologist, summarized the results, saying, "most significantly, this forecast predicts that the total mineral valuation for 1982 will actually be less than that of 1981—something that hasn't happened since 1972."

Herschler's third inaugural address was markedly different from prior years. Wyoming's weakened economy made for a somber event. Having referenced the underlying themes of "growth on our terms," Herschler reframed the message for the new times:

> Herschler said the state must avoid the temptation of yielding to pressures to abandon the balance between economic development and environmental protection for the 'illusory promises of short-term economic gains.'

Herschler's Message to the Legislature began by contrasting the past eight years with future prospects. While his discussion focused on 1975 to late 1980, a more appropriate time frame would have been 1969 to 1981. After the perfunctory opening remarks, Herschler moved immediately to the altered circumstances:

> Eight years ago, Wyoming faced a future of unprecedented growth, and that growth continued until late 1980. During that period of time, there was increasing exploration, development and removal of our energy resources; the financial institutions of the state experienced growth beyond anyone's expectations; our population in the last decade increased by almost 50 percent; our unemployment rate was, at a time, less than 3.5%; tourism reached an all-time high; even agriculture seemed to be holding its own. We were seeking solutions to boomtowns, balancing our growth, maintaining our Wyoming lifestyle, continuing opportunities for quality education, and caring for human needs.
>
> We in Wyoming are now seeing a very different set of circumstances. Our position, in relation to other states, remains excellent. However, our rate of growth slowed, and the latest

unemployment rate is 6.9%—the highest it has been since 1964. Our revenue projections that were so optimistically rosy just 18 months ago are now dropping at an alarming rate. For example, it was estimated that sales and use tax revenues would grow at an approximate annual rate of 18% but have, in fact, only grown at a 3% rate in the last year.

The National economy, with seemingly chronic inflation, more than 12 million unemployed, and a projected deficit for this fiscal year of $200 billion, has caught economic pneumonia. Our vulnerability to the national economy has been clearly demonstrated the past year and a half. As a result, we have caught the proverbial economic sniffles.

In retrospect, "economic sniffles" was an optimistic diagnosis. Before moving to specific legislative proposals, Herschler offered a candid assessment of Wyoming's situation:

Wyoming's people and its economy remain dependent on agriculture, tourism, small business, and the development of our energy resources. One other fact remains the same as 1975—Wyoming remains subject to external forces beyond our control. These two facts define the range of problems and limit the opportunities for action by state government. In order to move forward, Wyoming must diversify its economic efforts and reduce our susceptibility to external forces.

The legislative resolution of the school funding equalization issue pinpointed by the Supreme Court in *Washakie v. Herschler* required significant legislation to implement the Constitutional amendments approved by the voters in the 1982 election. The legislative measures were endorsed by Herschler and adopted by the Legislature. Emphasis on the continued development of Wyoming's water resources, including rehabilitation of existing irrigation projects, was the other concern pushed by Herschler. With some tinkering, the Legislature chose to stay the course.

Herschler did not request additional taxes or added tax relief. Legislation to double the tax on liquor to support alcoholic treatment programs passed the House and died in the Senate committee. (HB 54) Representative Tom Jones (R-Park County) was not surprised by the Senate committee's action, "I knew the committee was stacked against me with three liquor dealers and one who doesn't like my bills." Meanwhile, legislation was passed to reduce the annual fee for retail liquor licenses. Expansion of tax refund for elderly and disabled died in a House committee. (HB 174) Of course, the Homeowners Tax Credit was amended and funded.

Legal authority for the State Auditor to participate in joint audits with the federal government and other states was sought. The added audit authority expanded the effort to assure Wyoming and its citizens were capturing all the mineral royalties and taxes due. Legislative endorsement was extended.

Herschler offered a modest proposal for diversification of Wyoming's economy—a program to promote the filming of motion pictures in Wyoming. Surrounding states were capturing significant economic benefits from film production. With its magnificent vistas and open spaces, Wyoming was a logical location for such activity. House Speaker Russ Donley (R-Natrona) panned the proposal before it was even formalized, saying "...it won't work." A January 11, *Casper Star Tribune* article summarized Donley's views:

> He said it is difficult to attract industries to Wyoming because of the state's elevation, location, and climate.

Senate File 39, creating the office of motion picture development easily passed the Senate. It died when the House Appropriations Committee Chair (Tom Jones-Park County) said the bill was not a high priority for the committee. Herschler offered two proposals to pressure companies and contractors to use in-state labor. Both received a warmer legislative reception.

The creation of a Wildlife and Conservation program was again on the legislative agenda. Senator Tom Stroock (R-Natrona) had advocated such a program for many years. Herschler offered his own proposal for a wildlife trust with a job component in the form of a Youth Conservation

Corps. Observers noted that Herschler did not mention the in-stream flow proposals. Herschler later explained the decision as a tactical calculation based on its prior failures when he did endorse an in-stream flow bill. "I thought maybe they would think it was their idea and might pass one." The agricultural community in the House killed in-stream flow and the wildlife fund proposals.

Much of the wrangling during the session derived from competing estimates of future revenues by the legislative and executive branches. This was not a Budget Session, so relatively modest budget recommendations were considered. Nonetheless, Speaker Donley (R-Natrona) was particularly vocal in highlighting the matter. Donley chose to make the issue personal, including charging Herschler with employing "political rhetoric."

Ultimately it was more a matter of degree than direction. All the estimates demonstrated reduced revenue expectations, but that did not equate to the state being broke. State Auditor Jim Griffith identified several liquid savings funds which remained untapped. The *Casper Star Tribune* undertook a detailed analysis of various fund stashes ("coffee cans" in legislative lingo), which could be used if necessary. With some budgetary belt-tightening, the "coffee cans" should support state government for 3½ years beyond the current biennial budget period. A National Conference of State Legislatures found Wyoming had the largest surplus of General Funds in the nation as of mid-1982.

A thoughtful and far-sighted proposal for the use of General Fund surpluses was offered by Senator Frisby (R-Park County) in Senate File 84 entitled *Cash Basis for General Fund*. Frisby's proposal would place 50% of the surplus over 113% of the prior total general fund expenditures for the prior biennial budget in a special reserve account ("budget reserve account"). Only the earned income from the Budget Reserve account would be available for appropriation. In theory, the account would grow to the point of supporting the annual General Fund expenditures. Further, the measure was intended to limit the growth in expenditures to 13% per budget cycle. Frisby's proposal narrowly passed the Senate and was killed on final reading in the House. An exact explanation for the bill's defeat is not available. One cannot but wonder what Wyoming's finances would look like today had Frisby's approach been adopted. Annual spending in excess of annual income remains a conundrum for the legislative and executive branches.

Declining revenue expectations meant early death for proposals to reduce the severance tax on iron ore and uranium, along with several new sales tax exemptions. An optional 1% sales tax on lodging, meals, and liquor by the drink ("resort tax") would be seriously considered but ultimately rejected. A severance tax reduction for underground coal to benefit a mine operated by Carbon County Coal Company near Hanna became law.

A brief dustup over economic development arose when GOP legislative leadership criticized Herschler for not offering more specific proposals in his Legislative Message. Representative Donley (R-Natrona) led the charge suggesting he was working on some ideas but was not prepared to discuss them. Senate Vice-President Turner (R-Sublette/Teton) touted potential severance tax reductions, increased loan assistance for agriculture, and a sales tax break for farm machinery.

Proposals for increased agricultural loan assistance may have been spawned by the State Farm Loan Board moving against delinquent state agricultural loans. Wyoming had not foreclosed on agricultural loans since the 1930s. Most severance tax reduction bills would be introduced by Republican legislators, arguing that reductions would equate to increased production. Industry lobbyists were quick to promote the theory while making no commitments to increase production.

Senator Roy Peck (R-Fremont County) offered a more tailored approach to severance tax revenues and growth. Peck's proposal would set aside 5% of all severance tax income in a "reinvestment tax credit account." Monies would be disbursed to mineral companies demonstrating the money would be "...used for capital that would increase the state's tax base and create new jobs." While the measure failed to gain full legislative approval, it was the only severance tax proposal reflecting a disciplined tie between tax relief and tangible benefits for the state.

Legislators pushed to reactivate the Department of Economic

Development and Planning (DEPAD). Pre-energy boom, DEPAD was expected to promote industrial and water development in Wyoming. During the boom, the expectation changed to helping communities respond to population impacts. The economic downturn restored interest in DEPAD promoting economic growth. Representative Fred Harrison (D-Carbon County) sought a substantial budget increase to support economic diversification as the "...lifeline to Wyoming's future." House Appropriation Chair Jones (R-Park County) defeated the proposed budget increase. Instead, a "strong message" was sent to the agency to reorganize, re-focus, and report back to the next Legislative Session. Strong words but no dollars and no specific direction.

Commuter airline subsidies in the form of guaranteed ticket purchases by the state were also advanced as assisting tourism and industrialization. Legislation did pass to expand the use of state aid to airports. Over the coming decades, various forms of subsidies would be employed to address air travel issues in Wyoming.

In the early to mid-80s, large banks and credit card companies were seeking to relocate to states which would allow them to charge higher interest rates on unpaid credit card balances. To encourage these companies to relocate to Wyoming, Senators Stafford (R-Campbell-Johnson) and Taggart (R-Big Horn) introduced two bills to de-regulate interest rates. Both measures died in the Senate Revenue Committee. South Dakota would ultimately be the beneficiary of the credit card company relocations.

Significant controversy erupted when Senate President Eddie Moore (R-Converse) and House Speaker Russ Donley (R-Natrona) offered legislation to authorize three slurry pipelines (eventually reduced to two pipelines). One of the pipelines known as the *Aquatrain* was being advanced by W.R. Grace and the federal Bureau of Reclamation. Together these entities were evaluating a:

> ...proposed 1,200-mile pipeline project [costing] about $2 billion
> to construct. It would run from southwestern Wyoming to
> Southern California and perhaps even to New Mexico.

The joint federal-private pipeline is designed to use salty water now spilling into the Colorado River to wash huge plastic bags filled with coal or even soda ash, clay and grain from the intermountain area to southern California markets and ports.

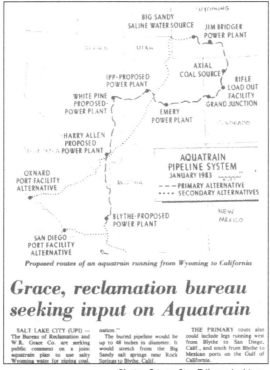

Grace, reclamation bureau seeking input on Aquatrain

SALT LAKE CITY (UPI) — The Bureau of Reclamation and W.R. Grace Co. are seeking public comment on a joint aquatrain plan to use salty Wyoming water for piping coal, nation."

The buried pipeline would be up to 48 inches in diameter. It would stretch from the Big Sandy salt springs near Rock Springs to Blythe, Calif.

THE PRIMARY route also could include legs running west from Blythe to San Diego, Calif., and south from Blythe to Mexican ports on the Gulf of California.

Photo: *Casper Star Tribune* Archives

The second slurry line would be for coal transport relying on 20,000 acre-feet of water diverted from the Little Snake River to eastern Wyoming.

Legislative proponents argued that the state could make big money selling the water. Proceeds of the sale would be devoted to other water development projects. Speaker Donley simply asserted that the projects would create thousands of jobs. Moore and Donley also contended that the projects were essential to keep Montana from stealing Wyoming coal markets. Opponents reflected on the speculative nature of both proposals and urged the completion of further studies and identification of actual market support before proceeding. The Wyoming Outdoor Council

(WOC) generally opposed the export of Wyoming water. Based on an independent consultant study, WOC contended that the projects were not rational from an economic point of view. As expected, Herschler vetoed the legislation arguing that the Legislature had put "the cart before the horse" and that the approval of water export was premature. Herschler announced his opposition to the bill in an early February appearance before the House Rules Committee. Herschler deemed the proposal premature, challenged the assertion of thousands of new jobs when the ETSI slurry pipeline only proposed to create 349 jobs, and expressed a fear Wyoming would lose control of its water once it entered interstate commerce.

1983 was a contentious session. Wyoming knew energy markets and policy had changed but struggled to formulate a strategy to adapt. Republicans ignored the realities of external energy market forces, instead believing a few percentage point changes in local severance taxes would overcome the influence of national and world markets. Admittedly, this belief was encouraged by corporate lobbyists and small in-state producers. Herschler recognized the fallacy of the Republican legislators' assumptions but offered little in the form of an alternative strategy. Proposals submitted by other legislators were given short shrift as they fell outside the walls of Wyoming's existing wheelhouse. In total, Herschler vetoed ten bills, including one which would have reduced the fine for exceeding the 55-mph speed limit to $5. This latter veto may have been the most controversial.

THE REMAINDER OF 1983

Throughout the remainder of 1983, Wyoming was the land of mixed messages. Evanston, in the heart of the Overthrust Belt, confronted increasingly overcrowded schools. Lusk, located in Wyoming's least populated county, braced for a major population impact related to the construction of a new rail line to haul coal to the Midwest. Oil rig counts statewide remained low, construction work declined, and reports of record unemployment were common. Coal production remained steady, but related construction decreased significantly. Towards the end of the year, Evanston and southwest Wyoming felt the decline in construction workers with money to spend.

Worldwide oil demand was declining, and production was increasing. Ongoing economic and political battles within OPEC and other oil-producing nations drove world oil prices ever lower. Casper's oil community drew a straight line very early in the year, between declining world prices and declining rig counts in Wyoming. Wyoming Senator Malcolm Wallop, a free trade advocate, called for a tax on imported oil to maintain a domestic price of petroleum sufficient to encourage exploration and production.

November and December saw the closing of the iron mine in Lander. Comments on BLM's draft Environmental Impact Statement for the Riley Ridge development in southwest Wyoming were mixed. The Riley Ridge proposal consisted of four large gas processing plants and associated wells. BLM was proceeding with the NEPA process even though most companies had shelved or delayed their development plans. Exxon's push to develop a massive natural gas and helium project at Shute Creek in southwestern Wyoming was the exception. Various closures and lay-offs were announced, particularly in uranium and coal.

Wyoming's Legislature would be called to a Special Session, lasting only two days, in early August of 1983. The increase in unemployment had severely drained Wyoming's unemployment trust fund. Insolvency would occur before the 1984 Session could convene. Everyone knew the issue was serious and acted accordingly. In less than two days, intra-fund and federal borrowing were authorized, various changes in the unemployment system were completed, and everyone went home. A temporary fix averted the crisis.

In early November, the consensus revenue estimates for Wyoming showed a relatively modest decline. Herschler would subsequently propose a bare bones budget, cutting spending by nearly $200 million. The legislative majority endorsed the concept of a bare-bones budget but worried the revenue estimates remained too high. As events would unfold in 1984, the legislative and executive branches had different definitions of "bare bones."

1984 LEGISLATIVE BUDGET SESSION

By 1984, a rhythm had developed for the legislative process. Budget Sessions convene in mid-February. governors provided the proposed budget the preceding December to facilitate a full legislative review of the state budget. House and Senate Joint Appropriation Committee members convene in advance of the full Legislature to consider the governor's recommendations and prepare their own budget proposal.

As was traditional, the Joint Appropriations Committee scrutinized individual agency budgets and modified Herschler's 1984 recommendations. A scattershot of agency budget reductions was standard fare. Cutting the Governor's Office budget, having state employees pay for parking, jettisoning state support for the Wyoming Beef Council and Wyoming Wheat Commission, resisting pay increases for state employees, and one-year rather than two-year funding for some programs, including the entire Department of Health and Social Services, limiting funding increases for the University of Wyoming and the community colleges—all were indicative of the Committee's attitude.[1]

Herschler's budget recommendations did not include funding for homeowner's tax exemption that year, and, of course, the Appropriations Committee seized on the absence of tax relief funding. Technically, the requested funding should have been in the State Treasurer's budget request. Treasurer Stan Smith (Republican) was drug into the fray for failing to include it. Seeing a politically opportune opening, the Appropriations Committee added $8.5 million to support the continuation of the popular tax relief program. It was one thing to discuss austere budgets and belt-tightening but quite another to suggest Wyoming citizens were not entitled to continued tax relief. Especially in an election year.

The Appropriations Committee would eventually claim to have cut the budget by $25 million in addition to the $200 million agency funding requests originally denied by Herschler, all accompanied by great legislative fanfare and equivalent grumbling by the governor and executive branch agencies. A February *Casper Star Tribune* editorial began by observing, "it is hard to imagine so many lions roaring at so few mice." The editorial pointed out that the 'real' budget cuts by the Appropriations Committee amounted to $10 million. "...the entire fight is over perhaps one-half of one percent of state spending...." Wyoming's total state budget was $2 billion.[2]

During this budget dust-up, modest declines in expected revenue and increases in 'carry-over' funds (funds not spent in the current biennium) were announced by the consensus revenue estimating group and the State Auditor's Office.

Typical of the economic news were two stories in the *Casper Star Tribune* on the 4th of January. One headline announced a "mini-boom" in Sweetwater County. Driving the potential mini boom was a power plant scrubber retrofit, work on Chevron's proposed fertilizer plant, and the anticipated construction of a gas processing plant by Exxon. A second headline noted Arch Minerals was closing its Seminoe No. 1 coal mine near Hanna. This pattern persisted as layoffs and closures often paired with expansions or modest new projects. Demand for state impact assistance loans had declined, diverting the money to other purposes was considered by the Legislature.

Hard numbers showed an increase in total employment and personal income over the last year. Coal production, if not price, was expected to increase. Wyoming could now claim to be the second-largest coal-producing state in America. In late January, the statewide drilling rig count fell for the sixth straight week. Boomtimes had moderated, but the economy remained relatively strong. A sense of unease was afoot.

An uncertain economic future continued the focus on the Department of Economic Planning and Development (DEPAD). Representative Tom Jones (R-Park County) was preparing legislation to redefine DEPAD as a vehicle to provide direct assistance to city and county economic development efforts. Referencing the prior session's directive to DEPAD to get to work on the economy, Jones observed, "...I don't think they have done a thing besides produce a brochure."[3] A Fremont County legislator (Scott Ratliff-D) announced legislation to legalize slot machines to facilitate local economic development.

Early in the fourth quarter of 1983, Herschler had appointed a ten-member "Governor's Industrial Development Task Force" chaired by Jerry Delano (R-Casper). Its report to the Legislature on January 10, 1984, was within the bounds of the status quo. Notable among the recommendations:

> The state should place the highest priority on the retention and expansion of existing industries.

> The state should work to diversify the state's economy as a means to expand the economy and diminish the effect of cyclical and long-term employment fluctuations.

> Development of water remains one of the highest priorities for strengthening the state's permanent economy.[4]

These recommendations are echoes of Wyoming's historical approach. Delano's testimony to the Joint Mines Minerals and Industrial Development Committee reinforced the message:

> Delano said the state's economy should diversify within the already-existing framework of tourism, agriculture, and energy-related industries.

> He pointed out that 'high tech' industries are not a long-range solution to economic diversification in Wyoming.[5]

The Task Force report called for the creation of an Economic Development Board, centralization of industrial revenue bond authority, use of state investment funds to augment loan dollars from the federal Small Business Administration and Farmers Home Administration, and a tiered severance tax structure for companies using minerals for manufacturing within Wyoming, and greater promotion of Wyoming as a place to do business.* Committee Chairman Senator Diemer True (R-Natrona) agreed with the recommendations and commented directly on the diversification issue. According to True:

---

* The tiered tax preference for in-state mineral processing imitates 1966 gubernatorial candidate Wilkerson's "no severance tax" on minerals processed in Wyoming.

> Recruiting high-tech types of industrial development for which
> there is no local outlet…is not practical. For example, in order
> to attract high technology, you need a significant educational
> institution. We have one in the state—that's the University of
> Wyoming. You are not going to recruit high-tech companies to
> Laramie, Wyoming.

The Task Force recommendations received a far less positive response from the Joint Appropriations Committee. After several Republicans expressed reservations, the Committee chose to punt the ball to the full Legislature.

A prescient but little-noted seminar of scientists, economists, and political leaders convened at the University of Wyoming on January 11, 1984. State representative and Casper geologist Jim Barlow succinctly defined the concern.

> Wyoming's minerals will not run out. What will run out is
> society's use for Wyoming's minerals.

Other panelists pointed to declining oil prices and increasing competition within the coal market as problems for Wyoming. Suggested solutions ranged from state-sponsored research for enhanced oil recovery, fighting freight rates imposed by the railroad monopoly, and converting coal to liquid products. A nod was given to diversification, but mainly in the context of the existing economic structure. A suggestion offered by UW economics professor Shelby Gerking to change the state tax structure in order to reduce our dependence on mineral revenues merited scant discussion or press coverage.[6]

Property tax reform remained a painful discussion. It was generally accepted that Wyoming's property tax system was broken—not all taxpayers were treated equally—thus, a court challenge to the system based on Wyoming's Constitution would likely be successful. Throughout 1983, the Joint Revenue Committee struggled to develop a legal and politically palatable solution (meaning no tax increases on Wyoming citizens). Returning to the constitutionally mandated fair market value tax assessment was *not* a politically palatable option.

Initially, the committee proposed a tiered tax system with residences taxed at the lowest tier in conjunction with a statewide reappraisal of all property. A day before the session convened, the committee backed off the proposal and simply supported a statewide property reappraisal. House Revenue Committee Chair Ron Micheli (R-Uinta) expressed his disappointment with the committee's action. While the reappraisal would proceed, the House Revenue Committee chose to exclude agricultural lands from a fair market appraisal. Testimony from Doran Lummis, a Republican member of the Wyoming Tax Commission, explained that ag lands were already exempt from fair market valuation (meaning price established between a willing buyer and willing seller):

> We already have a method of valuing agricultural land today, and
> I can't personally see what good would come of a market appraisal
> of agricultural land when we're not going to use that method to
> value that particular class of property.
>
> I would hope that we could re-value all the taxable property.
> Taxable property would include industrial, commercial,
> residential, non-agricultural lots and land.[7]

Both as a member of the Tax Commission and an agricultural landowner, Lummis understood that agricultural land had been exempt from fair market valuation since Hathaway had begun to value agricultural land based on agricultural production rather than fair market value. Production value did not even approximate fair market value.

Herschler announced he would not be running for a fourth term. Pundits debated whether it was wise to announce his intentions so early in his four-year term.

Titled *Wyoming in the 1980s: Economic Development in a Period of Limited Revenues,* Herschler's 1984 Legislative Message captured the sentiment of the times. Much of the Message was devoted to disputing the Joint Appropriations Committee's proposed budget, which had (modestly) modified Herschler's budget priorities. Herschler immediately drew battle lines:

> I will naturally contrast my philosophy with the activity of the
> Joint Appropriations Committee. I refer to 'activity' because
> I cannot discover a coherent theme in the majority members'
> conduct. To suggest that they had a theme would be like
> suggesting that my grandson's finger painting should replace the
> Mona Lisa.[8]

Considerable rancor surrounded budget discussions, yet the final result was anti-climactic. Accounting for the inevitable second-year program funding, the difference between the Herschler and legislative budgets was $1.9 million out of nearly $2 billion. Venting hot air over declining revenues and pending economic decline did not diminish the political need to fund services desired by Wyoming citizens.

Herschler called on the body to confront "the extremely complicated issue of developing Wyoming's economy." Referencing the multitude of economic studies, conferences, task forces, and reports, Herschler limited his request to three items needing legislation:

1. Authorization for the State Treasurer to buy $50 million in federally guaranteed small business loans at favorable interest rates, so long as the lower rates were passed onto the borrower. Herschler hoped this would encourage small industry expansions and creations rather than refinancing existing debt.

2. Creation of an Economic Development Board to ramrod state economic development efforts. A strong citizen board was vital in providing guidance and maintaining a connection to the private sector.

3. Legislation to designate the Wyoming Community Development Authority as the non-exclusive authority for the issuance of tax-favored industrial revenue bonds as authorized by the federal government.[9]

Aware of efforts by the House leadership to delay action, Herschler closed his economic development argument with a sense of urgency,

> I strongly disagree with those who suggest that we wait until next
> year to act on the proposed economic development program.

> I doubt that the people of Wyoming will tolerate a legislative
> decision that suggests that these economic problems are not
> important enough to be considered this session.[10]

Herschler supported the creation of an Enhanced Oil Recovery Institute at the University of Wyoming and more significant investments in airports as economic development measures.

The purchase of federally guaranteed loans and the Enhanced Oil Recovery Institute easily passed the Senate and the House. Also passed was broad legislation adding bonding authority to the Wyoming Community Development Authority (WCDA). Beyond $100 million in new bonding authority, WCDA was granted ambitious and extensive authority to develop and fund new and existing economic activity in the state. Care was taken in the drafting of the legislation to avoid implicating the "good faith and credit" of the state. Ideally, the projects would secure repayment of the bonds without direct government assistance.[11]

The Economic Development Board sailed through the Senate. Speaker Donley chose a procedural route to kill the bill in the House. The *Casper Star Tribune* described the events.

> House Speaker Russ Donley, however, stifled the bill by refusing
> to waive rules needed to expedite the bill's movement through
> committee hearings.
>
> In response to whether his action was a personal vendetta against
> the Governor or a responsible decision on behalf of the entire
> state. Donley chuckled and said he was "acting on behalf of the
> state." [12]

Donley then proceeded with a litany of Herschler's errors, including vetoing his slurry pipeline bill, increasing severance taxes, and responsibility for the recession.

Economic development and diversification were discussed, but very little new money or effort materialized. An important issue—maybe not so much.

Expanded education funding was not controversial. Nor was a move

THE PARADOX OF PLENTY

by larger, richer districts to increase their share of the pie. Representative Jack Sidi (R-Natrona), who ably handled most of the work on school finance reform, offered the opinion that the new system was working better than expected.[13]

Water and property tax reform proved contentious. Previously approved projects were attacked and modified. Water users in the affected areas realized that the construction of water projects could mean winners and losers. Nonetheless, water project funding continued. Property tax reform was a different matter. Individual legislators promoted reform measures, none of which passed. The seemingly innocuous proposal to fund the reappraisal of taxable property (excluding agricultural lands) engendered controversy during and after the session. Shortly after the Legislature adjourned, taxpayers understood property reappraisal meant increased taxes. Demands for tax increase limitations and a special Legislative Session to protect taxpayers immediately erupted. The Wyoming Tax Commission suggested deferring any taxable value increases until after the mass reappraisal was complete. A freeze did not occur. Herschler's decision to veto the homeowner tax relief program, which provided approximately $75.00 to nearly 100,000 households, added to taxpayer anger,

Akin to legislators, Wyoming citizens recognized public revenues were declining but expressed no interest in bearing a greater share of the burden.

1984 POST LEGISLATIVE SESSION

In early January 1985, Governor Herschler offered an assessment of 1984:

> Things weren't rosy, but they also weren't as bad as they could
> have been. We've been trying to recover from the recession, and
> we have had to deal with a lot of unemployment this year.

As the recession continued, ETSI announced it would not be building the coal slurry pipeline. Some retail stores closed throughout the state. Exxon and Chevron began construction on gas plants in southwest Wyoming, creating a mini boom for nearby communities. Taxpayers were again angry when property tax bills went up in June. By September, both political parties and Herschler offered proposals to re-establish the homeowners' tax exemption/credit. Massive snowstorms and subsequent flooding took a toll on the agricultural industry. The in-stream flow issue was back in the news with the certification of requisite signatures to create a ballot initiative. The November elections saw the Republicans increase their majority in the Wyoming Legislature. Thirty years of price ceilings on about half of the nation's natural gas production were set to end in January 1985. Consumers were assured their gas bills would not increase due to steadily declining oil and gas prices. An end to natural gas price controls was welcome news in Wyoming, but the low-price environment was expected to limit new drilling activity.

1985 GENERAL LEGISLATIVE SESSION

Honoring tradition, the House and Senate Republican majorities elected new leadership. Representative Jack Sidi (R-Natrona) and Senator Gerald Geis (R-Washakie) approached the session with a more constructive, less confrontational attitude. Likewise, Herschler adopted a much less antagonistic attitude. Relations between the two branches were much improved. Generally, citizens and elected leaders recognized that the energy boom was mainly in the rear-view mirror. The effects of the national recession were easing, but unease about the future inspired talk of the need for economic development. And talk they did. "Economic development" was used to support everything from a new state economic development agency to severance tax breaks, more agricultural loans, general government spending, water development, and an endless list of other items. The Joint Mines and Minerals Committee was convened to, in the words of Senate Chairman Diemer True, "explore the issue of whether environmental regulations hinder economic development."[14]

Before the session's January 8th commencement, legislative surveys found property taxes (the broken system and rising tax bills) to be the biggest issue, with economic development a distant second. Emphasis was added to anti-taxation sentiment shortly before the session convened when the State Board of Equalization signaled an increased property tax assessment ratio of 25% for non-agricultural lands, effective March

1, 1985. This action translated into higher prospective taxes. Legislative attitudes were not improved when one member of the Board, Republican Doran Lummis, sanctimoniously awarded the title "gutless wonder" to the Legislature for past inaction on property tax matters. As the session approached, everyone knew the citizens expected relief from the prospect of paying more taxes even if the state constitution mandated it.

Herschler's Legislative Message offered a long list of desired legislation and budget adjustments. His rhetorical energy focused on property taxes, economic development, and severance taxes.

PROPERTY TAX

Elected officials and citizens had disregarded Constitutional mandates for "uniform and equal" taxation since 1900. By illegal administrative fiat, several different and unequal property classifications ("tiers") of property had been developed, each assessed differently. Residents and agriculture were the prime beneficiaries of the decades-old broken system. Not a big surprise; most voters owned property within these two classes. In March, a *Casper Star Tribune* article succinctly described the system:

> The state currently uses countless methods to arrive at the assessed, or taxable, value for different types of property. Town lots are assessed at 8 percent of current market value, residences and commercial buildings at 25 percent of 1967 replacement values, and utilities are 'all over the place' according to Warren Bower, director of the state's property tax division.

Lack of coherent tax policy, sloppy administration, and unequal tax burdens were nothing new. In 1933, the same circumstance was cited by the Griffenhagen Study, which preceded the adoption of the first sales tax in Wyoming. Broad recommendations for tax reform and improved administration of the tax system were rejected in 1933 and again in the 1960s and 1981.

Herschler sidestepped the "blame game," casting a wide net of responsibility. After observing the tax discussions as generating more heat than light, Herschler continued:

We are all guilty of fueling the fire. As Governor, I have not
always been forceful enough in explaining the ad valorem tax
system. The State Board of Equalization has not delineated nor
followed a coherent plan. The County Assessors have been too
willing to stand for election on a platform that blames everyone
else for the problem. The Legislature probably doesn't deserve the
title 'gutless wonder' recently awarded it by Commissioner Doran
Lummis. However, the legislative proposals have sometimes been
parochial and political rather than substantive. Even when one of
your members offers a constructive proposal, it is usually defeated
before it reaches my desk. [15]

Mindful of the politics, Herschler announced he would not allow the
Board of Equalization's proposed tax increase to go forward. He did support a constitutional amendment to legalize the current de facto property
tax tier system along with legislation forcing disclosure of property sales
prices to keep fair market values up to date. Herschler had previously
vetoed legislation freezing changes in assessed (taxable) value. He again
spoke against the various "freeze" proposals under legislative consideration. Legislative optimism permeated early discussions attempting to
correct Wyoming's unconstitutional tax system. Optimism quickly gave
way to reality, and only the financial disclosure of sales price legislation
became law. As hope of substantive legislation faded, Herschler took the
pressure off the legislators. With the help of the two Democratic members
of the Board of Equalization, Herschler established rules to maintain the
status quo until a statewide property reappraisal was completed in 1987.
Equalization Board member Doran Lummis, who voted against maintaining the status quo, accused Herschler of being a "master manipulator." A
moniker Herschler took as a compliment.

The Chairmen of the respective Revenue Committees, Senator
Bob Frisby (R-Park County) and Representative Ron Micheli (R-Uinta
County), offered proposals and expended great effort to reach a legislative majority. They understood the problems and knew legislative inaction
would ultimately force the courts to act. Even after accommodating the
agricultural interests in formulating the tiered tax system, a legislative

majority could not be mobilized. Opponents of property tax reform even argued that reforms would hinder economic development.

Viable tax reform meant some taxpayers would pay more, and most legislators chose not to risk the ire of the voters. Wyoming was accustomed to excellent public services and low taxes. Utah's State Tax Commission had studied the ten surrounding states and found Wyoming's average household tax to be the lowest in the region.[16] A circumstance quite acceptable to Wyoming voters.

Property tax relief in the form of the Homestead (homeowners) Exemption was re-established.[17] The Senate wanted a double exemption to make up for the lack of tax relief the prior year, but the House declined the offer and stuck with one year. No veto this year. Herschler gladly signed the bill, in part to avoid the verbal bricks thrown in his direction the prior year. Tax refunds for the elderly and disabled were also renewed.[18]

ECONOMIC DEVELOPMENT

Wyoming's economy was recovering from the recession, with total employment back to 1981 levels, the unemployment rate had dropped six percentage points compared to prior years, and per capita income was up by over six percent.

Herschler encouraged the Legislature not to allow current optimism to deter efforts to build a resilient economy capable of surviving sudden shifts. Herschler chided the Legislature for its failure to act even after their own Legislative Service Office had issued a report in 1980 encouraging greater funding and effort for industrial development. Herschler contrasted legislative inaction with the 28 local governments already creating their own economic development efforts. He renewed his call for an Economic Development Board. Recounting that his original proposal had passed the Senate in 1984 and died in the House, possibly because it was an idea from a Democratic governor, he reminded them that the citizen committee recommending the proposal had a Republican majority. A second reason for the 1984 demise was that it created a new agency. Herschler offered to discuss combining the new Board with the existing

Department of Economic Planning and Development.

The Senate Minerals, Business, and Economic Development Committee considered a broad range of proposals—from an international trade office, low-interest loans, and a variation of Herschler's proposal sponsored by Senate President Gerald Geis.[19] The Senate would eventually settle on legislation to create the new board, terminate the Department of Economic Planning and Development (DEPAD), and transfer the functions to the new Board. This action reflected a general dissatisfaction with the performance of DEPAD and the current director. The House Business and Commerce Committee persuaded the House to pass legislation much more protective of DEPAD and the status quo. Serious conflict between the House and Senate ensued until the last day of the session, when a compromise created the Economic Development and Stabilization Board. DEPAD was terminated, a new leadership structure was put in place, and most of the functions were transferred to the new entity. However, significant new money to support economic development and stabilization would not be forthcoming. Legislation is one thing; substantive funding is a horse of a different color.

Language was included in the legislation requiring the new Board to cooperate with the Wyoming Community Development Authority (WCDA). Legislation in 1984 had given the WCDA broad economic development and bonding authority. Ambitions for the program faltered when viable projects simply could not be found. In addition, WCDA needed more than operating funds; it needed additional seed money to fund new businesses. WCDA proposed an ambitious economic development plan funded by a $20 million low-interest loan from the Permanent Mineral Trust Fund (PMTF). The plan ran aground when attorneys from the Legislative Service Office and the Attorney General's office concluded WCDA could not borrow from the PMTF because it was not a political subdivision of the state. WCDA changed its strategy to borrowing $5 million in federal mineral royalties. A House committee killed this proposal due to the federal restrictions on the use of federal mineral royalty dollars. With the money gone and the ambitious plan dead, the only bone supporters could throw the WCDA was a commitment to cooperate.

Session Laws for the 1985 session contain several other tentative economic development steps. Chapter 124 provided one-year funding to promote international marketing of Wyoming commodities and technical assistance to the companies involved. Chapter 188 directed the state to assist local communities with access to federal funds available under the National Trust for Historic Preservation. Chapter 171 appropriated additional state dollars to match locally funded efforts for tourism promotion.

Rejected proposals included subsidies for private air carriers, a new program for marketing and development in the Department of Agriculture, and water development funds for low-interest agricultural loans.

Reduced compliance with environmental regulations was offered in the name of economic development. Legislation was advanced to reduce and extend reclamation schedules for non-coal mines closed due to depressed commodity markets.[20] As passed by the House, the legislation included additional monitoring and extended interim stabilization periods for mines no longer in operation. Pathfinder Mines Corp., owner and operator of a uranium mine in Fremont County, pushed hard for an amendment to allow operating mines to "stretch out" their reclamation obligations while they remained in operation. Nyla Murphy (R-Natrona County), the original sponsor of the bill, passionately opposed the amendment saying, "it would lead to the 'rape' of the state with the possible indefinite postponement of reclamation on non-coal mines covering many acres."[21] In an emotional debate, the House rejected the amendment, but Senate committee led by Diemer True (R-Natrona County) inserted a variation of the proposed amendment into the bill. Eventually, the measure reached Herschler's desk and was vetoed. Herschler viewed the bill as giving preferential treatment to a particular segment of the mining industry, noting the Department of Environmental Quality could provide the relief Pathfinder sought, subject to specific factual demonstrations by the company. As expected, Pathfinder decried the veto.

SEVERANCE TAXES

Herschler supported extending the Coal Impact Tax, which was set to expire. Coal impact taxes were collected only until total collections

reached $160 million—a a threshold soon within sight. Local govern-
ments throughout Wyoming largely supported an extension of the tax
as a source for necessary infrastructure funding. Restrictions on local
taxing ability and local politics had left communities with little choice
but to ask for state funding. Extending the tax seemed unlikely since the
coal industry had emerged as a powerful force in Wyoming. Bill Budd,
the Executive Secretary of the Wyoming Mining Association, effectively
argued that the needs of communities truly impacted by coal development had been met. He warned that funds would now be extended to
local governments beyond the definition of impact.

Legislators did not extend the Coal Impact Tax, however another way
was found to extend mineral-based funding to local governments. Local
governments were given a share of "excess" federal mineral royalties.
Federal mineral royalty income had increased well beyond original expectations when the federal government raised royalty rates from 17 cents per
ton to 12½% of the adjusted market price. Local governments substantively and politically won the day. More mineral money was headed their
way. Severance tax opponents won because the Coal Impact Tax was not
extended. Coal production in 1984 was 130 million tons compared to 95
million tons in 1980.

Multiple proposals were offered to reduce the severance tax on oil and
gas as economic development measures. Herschler reminded the body
of their rejection of his prior request to fund a detailed study of whether
modifying the severance tax structure would encourage added in-state
processing or production:

> Thus, we are being asked to forego funding of needed
> government programs in exchange for hazy promises of possible
> economic growth. I am sure various lobbying groups will offer
> a great deal of information. I hope you will evaluate it carefully
> before you act. It is also necessary to evaluate the cumulative
> effect of all of the proposed changes.[22]

The Legislature would reject a "high-cost coal producers" tax break
intended to promote added production in southwest Wyoming. Herschler

vetoed a severance tax break for "wildcat oil production," arguing the definition was too broad and the oil and gas industry should bear some risk like any other business. Tax breaks for tertiary oil production escaped the veto pen.* Herschler's argument for signature was two-fold: the tax break applied only to tertiary recovery programs started after July 1, and a small tax break might encourage companies to recover oil otherwise left in the ground. Herschler also signed a severance tax break for "oil mining," a production method not yet demonstrated in Wyoming.

A severance tax bill that never reached Herschler's desk demonstrated the increased power of major oil and gas companies in the Wyoming Legislature. Senator Tom Stroock (R-Natrona) and Representative Jim Barlow (R-Natrona), both intimately involved in the oil and gas industry, proposed legislation to clarify the taxation status of CO2. Carbon Dioxide had long been considered a waste gas but now had commercial value in enhanced oil recovery efforts. The state contended that the taxable rate was 6%, while Chevron argued that the applicable rate was 2%. The other major player in the CO2 fight, Exxon was initially neutral but eventually opposed the legislation. By narrow margins, the Senate and the House passed legislation clarifying 6% as the applicable rate but deadlocked on other provisions. Lobbying by Chevron and Exxon created significant opposition to the bill. The bill died in a House/Senate conference committee. The balance of power had shifted in the Legislature since the 1970s.

Herschler expressed continued support for aggressive water development, particularly two projects which were ready to break ground. Water development, in general, had come under attack from the Wyoming Heritage Society, an industry-supported policy advocacy group. A white paper, primarily drafted by former Speaker Warren Morton, called for a re-evaluation of the water development program, recommending that current projects be delayed or shelved. The Heritage Society's paper said Wyoming already had surplus water available for industrial development. The ten water-hungry coal conversion plants originally projected would not be built.

* "Tertiary oil production" is an expensive production method used to capture oil left in the ground by traditional oil and gas wells

The Heritage paper further argued that Wyoming's financial fortunes had declined, and the state could no longer afford to fund the creation of water projects to meet speculative demand. Ironically, as a gubernatorial candidate in 1982, Morton campaigned against Herschler, charging the incumbent governor with failing to pursue water development aggressively. Legislative leaders reacted angrily to the attack on the water development program. They stayed the course and approved the advancement of the projects.

In-stream flow legislation was considered again and failed. Funding was increased for K-12 education. Of note was the decision by the Governor and the Legislature to tap the rainy-day fund to help fund the state budget. Expenditures exceed anticipated revenues.

Speaker Jack Sidi characterized a generally harmonious session:

> The Legislature, he said, wants to wait and see what happens to
> oil prices, to agriculture, and to interest rates nationally because
> all will have an effect on the future of the state.[23]

Herschler agreed the session was harmonious but characterized the outcome as akin to an ostrich, the "hiding-your-head-in-the-sand legislature." While applauding the good faith effort on economic development, Herschler described the legislative action as a "...rearrangement of the deck chairs on the Titanic:"

> Unfortunately, the Legislature failed to realize that simply
> changing personnel and renumbering statutes is not enough. If
> we are really serious about economic development, we should
> spend the necessary money to promote the state's economy as
> aggressively and effectively as possible.[24]

Wyoming leaders detected the frailty of our commodity economy but remained unsure of what to do. Representative Tom Jones emphasized the importance of development from within the state rather than looking to recruit large outside industries in a presentation to the Republican Caucus.[25] Funding for such activities was limited and largely symbolic. Legislative leaders understood commodity market forces dictated

Wyoming's future but still supported marginal severance tax breaks as though they could change fundamental economic forces.

Charting a course into the uncertain future was disconcerting. A self-evident path forward was not available and decisive action carried risk. Thus, the status quo largely prevailed.

THE REMAINDER OF 1985

Exxon and Chevron continued the construction of plants in southwest Wyoming. The actual workforce needed for those projects continued to exceed original estimates, and employment and population grew in the area. Statewide unemployment rates were tolerable, but the total number of employed people declined. Workers who had moved to Wyoming for the construction boom jobs were moving on. An *Associated Press* story, reprinted in the *Casper Star Tribune* in December, said Wyoming had the highest percentage of homes in foreclosure in the nation. Three state-chartered banks and two national banks failed in the first eleven months of 1985 (a smaller percentage than suffered by many other states during the bank/savings and loan crisis). According to the State Bank Examiner, banks in Wyoming increased assets in 1985.[26]

The *Casper Star Tribune* undertook an analysis of lending in Wyoming. An extended headline in December summarized the findings: "Wyoming banks cut total spending; worst post-war credit crunch; credit-worthy borrowers few, so money shipped out of state." Interviews with Wyoming bankers pointed to a lack of credit-worthy borrowers and increased audit and lending requirements as driving the problem. The story went on to suggest things would likely get worse.

Capital availability has been a problem in Wyoming since Territorial Days. Over the years, numerous efforts have been undertaken to address the issue. From early statehood, governors traveled to visit the national banking and investment community seeking backing for Wyoming businesses. 1985 would see an effort to develop indigenous capital. In March, the WCDA announced funding of a significant economic development study by the Fantus Company of Chicago, Illinois, to "...address how to produce venture capital in the state." James Peck, "who will work on the venture capital report, said that lack of private investment is probably Wyoming's greatest weakness at this point."[27]

Meanwhile, the state's economy chugged along. Annual coal production increased slightly. Oil, natural gas, and trona production remained steady. Uranium production declined as the national interest in nuclear power continued to wane. Agriculture, already suffering low prices and increased foreclosures, was hit by terrible winter storms in the fall.

On the political front, various Republicans were testing the waters in the race for governor. Some announced, others coyly performed as unannounced candidates. Democrats interested in running for governor were much more cautious. Pundits put forward various names. Bill Rector, a well-respected Democratic state senator and businessman from Cheyenne articulated one other factor weighing on the minds of Democrats, "I think Ed Herschler is a tough act to follow. It's like a coach going in to take over Bear Bryant's show."[28] Republicans enjoyed a considerable registration advantage, and after 12 years of a Democrat, conventional wisdom held that the next governor would be a Republican.

Economic development was the *soup de jure* at meetings and conferences, large and small, throughout the state. Proposals ran the whole gambit. Former Governor Hathaway called for cutting the severance taxes while adding, "...tourism will never be more than a fringe benefit to the economy because the state's climate is too cold and inadequate transportation [sic]."[29] State Treasurer Stan Smith, now a candidate for governor, proposed using revenue generated by the State Liquor Commission to support the issuance of economic development bonds, advancing the novel view that money received by the state for managing wholesale liquor sales was not state money. From Smith's perspective, this money was not subject to constitutional limitations related to pledging state dollars to repay bonds.

The issue of Wyoming's broken and unconstitutional property tax system was woven into the public discourse. Citizens complained about current tax payments and threatened political retribution if taxes increased in the future. Elected officials, generally sympathetic to taxpaying voters, quickly identified someone else as the responsible party. Thoughtful discussions were as rare as hen's teeth.

Oil prices in 1985 continued the decline which began after the 1980 peak. The rate of decline seemed moderate in the first half of the year. No one expected a significant uptick in prices or anticipated steep declines. As the Reagan administration struggled with growing federal deficits, potentially unfavorable federal tax policy changes were under discussion. Major oil and gas companies trimmed their exploration and production budgets. Many smaller companies were not expected to survive. Mergers and acquisitions to add reserves were not uncommon. Discussions between OPEC and non-OPEC oil-producing nations were increasingly tumultuous. Industry experts anticipated events would settle and expected oil prices to rise, possibly in 1987 or early 1988. No one, including the Wyoming Consensus Revenue Estimating Group (CREG), seriously expected the international oil price war to crash from $27 to less than $10 per barrel in 1986 (from 64 to 24 in 2020 dollars). In the fall of 1985, Herschler built the executive branch budget on CREG's seemingly conservative pre oil price-war revenue estimates. CREG estimates assumed oil prices in the mid to low 20s for the coming two years.

1986 HERSCHLER'S LAST YEAR: DECLINE TURNS TO BUST

In preparation for the Budget Session, the Joint Appropriations Committee convened on January 6th. Revised revenue projections for the next two years showed only a modest decline due to oil and gas price adjustments—not enough to worry committee members but enough to enhance arguments against executive branch spending. Herschler had submitted a flat budget with a 3% inflation factor for costs and employee wages.

World oil prices remained in turmoil. OPEC's control of oil production and price had been dramatically eroded. Oil production by non-OPEC affiliated countries had rapidly reduced OPEC's share of the world oil market. Successive failed meetings of the oil-producing countries seemed unlikely to stem oil production and related price declines. OPEC countries, determined to hold on to market share, were threatening to open the production spigot and further depress oil prices worldwide. Prospects of an oil price war were openly discussed, but most observers thought or hoped it would not happen. Wyoming's oil community was deeply concerned and oil companies were rethinking prospective drilling and production budgets. Unprecedented volatility was the name of the game. Press accounts suggest spot prices (oil sales not subject to long-term contracts) as low as 8 or 10 dollars per barrel.

Data from the U.S Energy Information Administration that tracked futures contracts for oil priced at Cushing, Oklahoma, was more reliable but equally volatile. Future delivery contracts for January 7–11, 1985, averaged above $25.50. Futures pricing reached as much as $30 per barrel in 1985 to close out December at over $26. When the legislative Appropriations Committee convened the first week of January 1986, futures were still around $26. By the time Herschler addressed the Legislature in February, futures were trading around $15. Each dollar decline in oil prices appeared to reduce state revenues by one to two percent.

Federal budget cutbacks by the Reagan Administration and the Graham-Rudman federal budget amendment threatened several significant funding sources Wyoming relied on. A *Casper Star Tribune* analysis under the headline "Reagan's budget proposal would hit Wyoming hard" detailed cuts to federal airline subsidies, agricultural programs, federal mineral royalties, education, local governments, etc.

Turmoil in the energy markets did not markedly change the Consensus Revenue Estimating Group (CREG) income projections for the next two years. In retrospect, believing oil prices would remain above $23 for the next two fiscal years was overly optimistic. Still, legislative appropriations committee members accepted the projections and adopted a proposed legislative budget essentially consistent with the executive branch budget prepared in November of 1985. Total expenditures for the next biennial budget would be 10% higher than the past budget when the Legislature adjourned on March 15, 1986.

Wyoming's economy was not improving. Unemployment rates in late 1985 were two percent higher than in 1984. Unemployment rose even though many of those who had lost their jobs left the state looking for work elsewhere. Wyoming's State Bank Examiner predicted more banks would fail in 1986.[30] According to a WCDA-funded study, Wyoming had a great business and tax climate but lacked financing from local banks, venture capital, and insufficient government-supported financing options for industrial development. An industrial development financing program created in 1984 to leverage added WCDA bonding authority was declared unworkable. Wyoming's declining economy, lack of Wyoming bank participation, and strict requirements from out-of-state banks defeated the program. Money simply was not flowing to Wyoming businesses under the program.[31] Blaming Casper's economy, poor lending practices, and insider transactions, the State Bank Examiner closed the American National Bank of Casper.

The temporary administrative property tax freeze on agriculture, commercial, and residential property was extended through 1987. Some upward assessment ratio adjustments were made to industrial property but were expected to be offset by including depreciation in the calculation of assessed value.[32] A study by the International Association of Assessing Officers identified a need for better education of county assessors, actual enforcement of state laws related to assessment, and more explicit assessment guidance. Try as they might, in this election year, legislators could not avoid the property tax "hot potato."

Bill Budd, former legislator and Director of the Wyoming Mining Association, announced for governor with a platform focused on economic development. Budd understood that while legislators may be focused on the budget, the public worried about the economy.

Herschler's Legislative Message was optimistic, referencing wise decisions made in the past. He referred to differences between his proposed budget and the appropriations committee bill, but much of his Message was devoted to the insurance availability crisis confronting Wyoming.

Noting the gubernatorial candidates' use of the buzzwords "economic development," Herschler sought to reframe the discussion:

> I would submit to you that our real objective is not development
> for the sake of development. Our real objective today should

be the same as it was ten years ago, twenty years ago, or even
one hundred years ago. That objective is economic progress.
Economic progress means the development of our state's
resources, including our people, in a manner that benefits us
today and for generations to come.[33]

Herschler pitched restoration of the appropriation committee cuts to the
Economic Development and Stabilization Board. He requested nearly
a half-million dollars to support WCDA and EDSB's efforts to create a
venture capital fund. In response to the lack of business development
loans, Herschler proposed asking the voters if they wanted to change the
Constitution to authorize loans to private businesses in an amount not
to exceed 1% of the state's assessed valuation. Each legislative chamber
would require a two-thirds vote to appropriate general fund dollars to
a revolving loan fund for economic development. Herschler requested
agricultural investment in the form of state authority to purchase individual agriculture operations and lease the land back to the operator with
an option to buy. He asked for legislation allowing the state to create
international trade zones.

Continuing financial support for the Wyoming Futures Project was
included in the proposed budget in a nod to longer-term planning. This
ongoing public/private partnership examined the state's resources and
options for economic progress. Controversy arose surrounding some
of the group's recommendations and harsh language evaluating the
University of Wyoming's contribution to the state's economic progress.
Pressure from the university forced a rewording of the evaluation.

Herschler renewed his request for a constitutional amendment to
legalize Wyoming's tiered tax system. A Revenue Committee proposal
to rely on statutory changes was explicitly rejected as raising taxes on
agriculture and small businesses. He pushed water development, including funding for ten new projects.

Legislative deliberations were relatively calm, but most of the Budget
Session was spent on non-budget items. Herschler's constitutional
amendment authorizing limited use of general fund dollars (approximately $70 million) to assist business initially died in the Senate but was

renewed in the House with easy passage (54 ayes, 9 noes) of a similar proposal sponsored by a House and Senate Joint Committee. Senators passed it (25 ayes, 5 noes).[34] An agricultural investment authority to buy distressed farm and ranch operations and lease back to the owner gained introduction in the Senate, but it died in Committee[35] due, in part, to the Wyoming Stockgrowers opposition to the idea of the state owning more land.[36] Authorization for the state and other entities to apply for foreign trade zone status passed.[37] An economic development measure promoted by the oil and gas industry was a sales tax exemption for the movement of oil rigs, including disassembly and assembly.[38]

In early statehood days, the Wyoming Legislature preempted the ability of local governments to impose sales taxes without the express authorization of the Legislature. Local jurisdictions with significant tourism economies applied pressure for the authority to charge an additional sales tax on tourism activities. The added funds would be used only to promote and expand the local tourism economy. Legislators finally consented to an additional sales tax so long as voters within the jurisdiction approved it.[39]

Americans were developing an appetite for lean grass-fed beef. Wyoming sought to enter this marketplace by creating a Wyoming Lean Beef Committee. Committee responsibilities included defining and enforcing standards, establishing, and protecting a "Wyoming lean beef" name, licensing the trademark use, and collecting royalties. The statute is detailed and thoughtfully written, but no money was appropriated to fund the task.[40] Finally, Chapter 106 of the Session Law appropriated $102,000 to the University of Wyoming College of Agriculture to "… develop a study to assist and increase value-added agribusiness opportunities in Wyoming."

Acknowledging that pipelines were needed to move Wyoming's abundant natural gas to market, a joint resolution was adopted supporting the construction of a pipeline to move natural gas from southwest Wyoming to Kern County, California.[41]

Other legislative economic development efforts that were unsuccessful included:

– Coal severance tax reduction

– Creation of a venture capital corporation,

– A state lottery

– Funding for a proposed study to build a state-owned railroad

– And various gambling proposals.

Legislation was passed authorizing the State Treasurer to "deposit and invest" $100 million of state funds in Wyoming banks at a 3% below market rate, so long as the lower rate was passed on to "...persons borrowing funds for agricultural or commercial purposes which will create or maintain jobs in Wyoming...."[42] Governor Herschler vetoed the measure.

Economic development discussions in 1986 carried the refrain that "Wyoming's low taxes will attract all kinds of industry." After all, Wyoming has consistently ranked among the most tax-friendly states in the nation. Successive politicians of all stripes have touted Wyoming's low tax environment. Experience is a tough teacher. The lesson is that low taxes alone have not and will not bring industry clamoring to cross our border. If low taxes were the magic key, Wyoming would have the most diversified and vigorous economy of the lower 48 states. Discussing low taxes as an economic development tool may simply disguise our personal preference for low taxes.

The Wyoming Heritage Society and former gubernatorial candidate Warren Morton were unsuccessful in delaying or derailing water development. The Wyoming Water Development Commission and at least ten legislative measures passed funding various projects. Faced with the prospects of a successful citizen drive for instream flow legislation, the agriculture community relented and passed a modified version of an instream flow law.

Property tax reform was again debated, and modest procedural bills were successful, but a statutory proposal to solve the issue died as it appeared to increase taxes. The proposed Constitutional amendment to sanction the existing tier system was also defeated. The proverbial "tin can" was again kicked down the road.

Legislators left town confident their decisions were wise, and the budget was austere, disregarding notes of caution offered by those concerned about declining energy prices. Everyone took heart in the money saved for future years. Senate Appropriations Chairman Tom Stroock (R-Natrona),

> ...praised Herschler's 'prudent' budgeting and his planning for
> the future in calling for the budget reserve funds...to save up
> some of the boom-time wealth for the future.[43]

Budget reserve dollars were not the only funds available to support state expenditures. Various other accounts held funds well beyond current spending.

WYOMING'S ECONOMIC DOWNTURN CONTINUES

1986 brought additional bank closures, fire sales for housing in Hanna after the coal mines closed, oil prices below $13 per barrel, and additional layoffs in the oil and mining sector. Independent oil operators were hit hardest and first. Drilling activity in March fell, year over year, by 50%, but 47 rigs continued to operate. Drilling continued to decline. Rocky Mountain operations suffered more than the rest of the United States, and Wyoming suffered the most. Complex geology and challenging drilling conditions were to blame.[44] Commercial credit continued to contract. Uncertainty in the energy market caused Exxon and others to delay major construction scheduled for Wyoming. Wyoming's economy was akin to a cork floating on the stormy seas of international markets and events. Oil-producing states called for a tax or tariff on imported oil, but President Reagan opposed an import tax. Much of the country shared his view that low energy prices helped the American economy.

Agriculture continued to be squeezed by low prices and high interest rates. The Legislature had rejected the proposal for the state to buy distressed agricultural operations and lease them back to the prior owner with an option to purchase. Wyoming's five elected officials sitting on the state Farm Loan Board decided to resurrect a similar plan for farmers and ranchers who had borrowed money from the state. Only properties subject to foreclosure by the state would qualify for this relief.

Up 37% from the prior year, Wyoming's unemployment rate was 9.3% in August (compared to the national number of 6.8%). The total number of employed people fell by 6%. These trends would continue throughout the year. Raymond Plank, head of Apache Corp. and Co-Chairman of the Wyoming Futures Project, wryly observed, "...the largest employer of geologists is now McDonald's."[45]

Adding to the economic pressure, a discouraging note for Wyoming coal producers arrived from Washington, D.C. Scientists and policymakers had long argued that sulfur dioxide (SO2) emissions from coal-fired power plants were major contributors to acid rain. President Reagan had resisted acid rain control programs. In March of 1986, Reagan reversed course and entered an agreement with Canada to reduce acid rain-causing emissions (primarily SO2) from power plants and other sources. Potential problems loomed for Wyoming's low-sulfur coal producers. Wyoming's coal was attractive to Midwest utilities because emissions from the low-sulfur coal were lower than the more sulfur-rich coals in the Midwest and Appalachia. Burning Wyoming coal met existing SO2 emission standards without added capital investment, but if new SO2 standards were adopted and utilities were forced to meet standards through the installation of smokestacks and "scrubbers," Wyoming's low-sulfur advantage would evaporate. Wyoming's leaders pushed for a policy of achieving SO2 compliance by installing scrubbers *or* burning low-sulfur coal. Expensive smokestacks and scrubbers were the solutions preferred by Eastern and Midwestern coal and economic interests.

Mineral royalty and tax income drifted significantly lower than projected when state budgets were adopted in February of 1986. Legislators would be forced to cut budgets in 1987. Beyond the state-level concerns, cities, counties, school districts, and special districts all confronted the budget-cutting dilemma.

1986 GOVERNOR'S RACE

Eight Republicans were identified as candidates for governor before the Legislature adjourned on March 15, 1986. State Treasurer Stan Smith, Senator Dave Nicholas (R-Albany County), and Representative Pete

Simpson (R-Sheridan County and brother of US Senator Al Simpson) already held elected office. Former House Speaker Russ Donley, director of the Wyoming office of the conservative Center for Constitutional Studies, had recently served in the legislature. The remaining candidates were not elected officeholders. Fred Schroeder, a Douglas businessman and former Chairman of the state Republican Party; John Johnson, a dentist from Saratoga; Bill Budd, former Director of the Wyoming Mining Association and Jim Bace, a computer programmer for the Laramie County School District, rounded out the early list. Smith would eventually withdraw from the race and run for re-election as State Treasurer.

The heart of each campaign was economic development. Jim Bace focused on the agricultural economy. Bill Budd pitched streamlining government regulation and a business-friendly attitude. During the Legislative Session, Bill Budd was the most forceful economic development advocate favoring the constitutional amendment to allow the use of state funds to help private businesses. Simpson referenced the economy as the overriding issue of the campaign. Schroeder opposed using state funds to start new businesses and called for regulatory streamlining. Donley saw the state of the economy as driving the discussion in the primary. He touted his experience, ability to make hard decisions, and knowledge of state government. Nicholas' announcement was short on details but relied on his experience in government and private business. Eventually, he came out against state loans to private businesses and would consider severance tax reductions. The closing month became a two-person race between Simpson and Budd. Simpson barely won the right to face the Democratic nominee in November. Less than ½% separated Simpson from Budd when the counting was done.

The Democratic primary was a much less dramatic affair. Initially, the odds-on favorite to be the party's nominee for governor was Ford Bussart, a well-known former state senator from Sweetwater County. Bussart was contemplating the race when political newcomer Mike Sullivan, a generally conservative attorney from Casper, announced he would seek the Democratic nomination. Sullivan's announcement was low-key and avoided taking positions on issues. Sullivan touted his experience on various community boards and as a lawyer. Bussart eventually rejected a run for governor, saying he did not want to "preside over the near-economic wasteland" he believed Wyoming would become. Sullivan cruised to an easy primary victory (70.92%) over three relatively unknown candidates. Prospects remained that the next governor would be a Republican. Twice as many votes were cast in the Republican primary compared to the Democratic primary.

Pete Simpson and Mike Sullivan squared off in the General Election. Economic development was the top-line issue. Of equal importance were stylistic and leadership qualities—unquantifiable but still consequential. Sullivan and Simpson both courted the state employee vote during the primary. Sullivan staked out a position that included a possible reduction in the state workforce and grim prospects for pay raises. Simpson's position in the primary was more favorable to state employees. However, his position changed in the General Election, as pointed out by Sullivan in their first debate, noting Simpson changed his mind after gaining the state employee endorsement.[46] Simpson's legislative record occasionally put him on the defensive. Simpson had co-sponsored a revenue-neutral sales tax proposal to reduce the effective rate but expand the type of items subject to sales tax. Sullivan lacked a legislative record to attack but fell prey to the lack of experience argument. By November, the stated policy differences between the candidates were limited but significant on a few critical issues.

Simpson adopted the no new taxes pledge on the general issue of taxes. Sullivan opposed tax increases but did not rule them out if essential services were threatened. Sullivan opposed severance tax reductions. Simpson favored limited decreases, such as for wildcat wells. Sullivan favored a constitutional amendment to address property tax reform. Simpson offered the appointment of a citizen council to study the issue. Sullivan would not take uncommitted money from the water development fund but would divert the current revenue flowing into the fund for three years. Simpson would withdraw uncommitted funds from the water development account but continue construction of authorized projects.

Public attitudes about Wyoming's changed circumstances were fluid.

How bad was it really, and how long would it last? Were circumstances transitory, lasting only as long as the OPEC struggle continued? Were the changes fundamental, and should Wyoming adapt? Responses varied from calls for fundamental re-examination to a simple prayer, "Oh Lord, grant me another boom. I promise not to mess it up."

Fears related to "how bad is it?" were stoked by former Governor Stan Hathaway. In February, Hathaway gave a speech declaring Wyoming was in the worst condition since the Great Depression. "Not a recession—a depression right now." Hathaway acknowledged the role of national and international factors beyond our control, but warming to his topic, Hathaway blamed the Wyoming mineral industries' woes on "over-regulation and over-taxation"; "we've gone too far in imposing ever-higher severance taxes"; and the "press is responsible for Wyoming's image as a bad place to do business."[47] A *Casper Star Tribune* columnist offered Hathaway a less than kind rebuke, including references to his law firm representing Exxon and Pacific Power and Light.[48] The discussion re-emerged about a week before the election when the *Casper Star Tribune* printed an *Associated Press* story under the headline "Wyoming fared better in Depression than now."[49] Much of the article highlighted the discouraging state of agriculture but also noted that Wyoming's rig count was the lowest since 1967. Economists and historians from the University of Wyoming, including historian T.A. Larson, offered an objective response. According to Larson, half of Wyoming's banks failed during the depression, 17% of the population was on relief in 1935, and unemployment reached 16%. Larsen closed with this observation:

> "Most of the people squawking now weren't even born then," he said. "They don't know what they are talking about."[50]

Sullivan won with 54% of the vote. His lack of legislative baggage and relatively measured approach to the future carried the day. Simpson was a well-qualified and strong candidate cursed with legislative baggage and nasty divisions within the Republican party exacerbated by a contentious, seven-candidate primary.

In November and early December, OPEC discussions moved towards a sustained target price of $18 per barrel. While encouraging, progress was insufficient to justify optimism. Wyoming's Consensus Revenue Estimating Group (CREG) had begun reducing the estimated state revenue for the coming years. In May 1986, Herschler issued an executive order reducing the state budget by 3.3%. Some legislators questioned the legality of the executive order. Herschler argued that the revenue estimates had crashed through the floor. The original budget was based on oil prices of $22–24. A revision of the CREG estimates issued on May 16 projected oil prices of $13 and $10.50. In addition, the predicted levels of coal and natural gas production had been reduced.[51] The dramatic effect of OPEC's turmoil could not be denied. The Governor and the Legislature had adopted a budget in mid-March based on projected oil prices in the low twenties. A few months later, projected oil prices were slightly over $10.

To quote the salesman huckster, "wait, there's even more." On December 16th, CREG provided revenue estimates dramatically lower than those provided the prior month. Soon-to-be Governor Sullivan would need to cut budgets approximately 10% more than the budget reductions imposed by Herschler in May and again in his December 1 budget. Herschler immediately imposed a hiring freeze and ordered two days of unpaid leave for state employees.[52] In early December, Herschler had asked the Wyoming Water Development program to delay the construction of an authorized dam to make funds available to support the general government.

Senate Appropriations Chairman Tom Stroock (R-Natrona), fully engaged in the oil business, offered a candid assessment of the future:

> The Legislature, he said, should move slowly and count on four
> more tough years. While it's raining out there now, I think the
> storm is liable to last four years.[53]

Stroock offered light criticism of Herschler's original budget but "... admitted that he personally never thought oil would drop below $20 per barrel."[54]

Wyoming's mineral boom had blossomed for more than ten years. The unparalleled growth and prosperity were stunning. Mineral production since 1900 supported (unconstitutional) tax relief for non-mineral taxpayers, reducing revenue from the statewide mill levy and contributing to the need to adopt a sales tax in 1935. In the 45 years preceding the sales tax adoption, the annual statewide property tax generally ranged around 4–5 mills. For 35 years after the adoption of the sales tax, the statewide mill levy hovered around 1.5. After the severance tax was adopted in 1969, the mill levy for state government support was never imposed again.

Severance taxes and federal mineral royalty payments supported expanded services at all levels of government and reduced citizen taxes. In 1986, OPEC burst the bubble of economic growth. Wyoming had inadvertently fallen into another trap of the commodity curse; it had not invested or developed an alternative economy to support jobs and governmental services.

Wyoming's new governor, Mike Sullivan, had a full buffet of challenges. It would prove to be a difficult eight years.

For better or worse, the Constitutional questions surrounding property taxation would be resolved before the end of Sullivan's first year in office. The Wyoming Supreme Court forced action on the property tax front before the end of Sullivan's first year in office. In December of 1987, the Court declared that the historical system of de-facto tiered property tax assessments violated the Wyoming Constitutional provisions related to equal and uniform taxation.[55] Rather than conform the tax system to the mandates of the original Constitution, the Constitution was amended in 1988 to delete the original language of Article I, Section 28 requiring "all taxation be equal and uniform."

Further, the 1988 Constitutional Amendment removed the original requirement in Article 15, Section 11 that "all property...shall be uniformly assessed for taxation." The new Article 15, Section 11 enshrined the multi-tiered tax structure invalidated by the Court's decision. The Constitutional Amendment abandoned the founding fathers' notion of taxing property based on fair market value as determined by a willing buyer and a willing seller. Instead, "all taxable property will be valued at it's full value as defined by the legislature except agricultural and grazing lands which shall be valued according to …" productivity. The legislature, not the marketplace, defines "full value."

Conforming to the original Constitutional language would have meant increased taxation for all property, except mineral production. That was not going to happen. Better to simply modify the Constitution to maintain some version of the status quo. Wyoming's historical reliance on mineral production taxes and federal dollars to support public services was enshrined in our Constitution.

EPILOGUE

"The future's vital, and only, constituency
is the conscience of the present."
— *George Will,* Washington Post[1]

Wyoming checked most of *the Paradox of Plenty* boxes, including a near singular focus on the extractive industry. But *the Paradox of Plenty* fails to account for regions or states capturing significant personal and public wealth from the extractive industry. A Paradox of *Prosperity* might be more descriptive of the public revenue balance sheet. This is not an argument for reducing taxes on the extractive industry. Extractive industries are and will continue to be an essential and vital part of Wyoming. And they should be supported. A useful inquiry would be whether it is time for us to share a greater proportion of the cost of public services and to diversify our economy for future generations.

Our citizens have not demonstrated a willingness to accept fewer governmental services. Everyone talks about reducing government, except for the services personally important to them or their family. The roller coaster of federal dollars, mineral taxes, and federal mineral royalties have produced temporary restrictions on services but has not altered our basic appetite.

As to diversifying our economy, public revenue has provided only a small percentage of the funding needed to address it. We have, as

Herschler described, "rearranged the deck chairs" several times. The Natural Resources Board was replaced by the Department of Economic Planning and Development in 1969. Since then, we have had the Economic Development and Stabilization Board, the Department of Commerce, and most recently the Wyoming Business Council. This latter effort was sold as a state and private funding effort, but the private funding never materialized. The basic strategy for promoting economic growth has been to rely on Wyoming's status as among the least taxed states in America. Comparative data with other states suggests the basic strategy is inadequate to the task.

The historic ledger demonstrates significant investment in public infrastructure and services. But the single largest investment of federal dollars, mineral taxes, and federal mineral royalties has been in tax relief (or tax avoidance) for our citizens, businesses, and agriculture. Multiple generations, beginning shortly after statehood, have shifted the burden of supporting public services to the minerals industry. This was possible because the utilization of Wyoming's mineral storehouse increased over time. Property tax support for state government ended with the passage of the severance tax in 1969. It is difficult to recall the last time a property tax bond issue was used to build a state, local government, or school district building. According to the Wyoming Taxpayers Association, we pay only about 20% of the actual costs of the public services we receive as citizens. The difference between the cost of the services we receive and the taxes we pay is referred to as the funding "gap." We are not exactly the rugged, carry-your-own-weight Westerners embodied in the Cowboy Ethic adopted by the Legislature and signed by me, as Governor.[2]

Our low taxes and unbalanced tax structure have both advantages and disadvantages. Wyoming is a magnificent place to live for those moving towards the end of their careers with some financial security. Wyoming is a financially attractive place for those who accumulated a nest egg or fortune elsewhere and are seeking refuge from taxation, enhanced by significant but inexpensive public services. Wyoming is simply a better place to conserve wealth than to build wealth. For a younger generation hoping to build a future and generate their own wealth, it is less attractive. A traditional commodity-driven economy may not generate enough jobs or the type of jobs sought by a new generation. Inherited wealth or land or mineral holdings will allow some young people to remain in Wyoming. Others, fully understanding the trade-off between lifetime earnings and a desired lifestyle, will opt for Wyoming's lifestyle. These hearty souls, like our pioneer ancestors, find a way to make a living and build a life in Wyoming.

The funding gap discourages serious economic development/diversification efforts. If added population is not accompanied by sufficient additive tax base, the gap grows. Major taxpayers bearing the freight to bridge the gap cannot enthusiastically support economic development that brings in more people without an accompanying increase in the tax base. Equally problematic is a calculation on the part of current inhabitants equating added population to overcrowding, a more diverse population, increased taxes, and a reduction in available services.

A perennial question in Wyoming is "how long can we rely on mineral taxes, federal mineral royalties, and federal dollars"? An answer was nearly forced in 2020/2021. The combined effects of COVID and an oil price war between Saudi Arabia and Russia crashed the Wyoming economy. Oil prices were temporarily negative, the drill rig count dropped to zero, coal demand and price plummeted. Public officials at all levels were considering Draconian budget cuts and whispering the dreaded T-word—taxes. Conveniently, the much maligned federal government rode to the rescue with a flood of federal COVID dollars for both the public and private sectors and mega-funding for infrastructure. Thanks to a massive infusion of federal dollars, a war in Eastern Europe, increased income from Permanent Funds, and a significant spike in energy prices, Wyoming likely has plenty of public funding for several years to come. There is indeed a boom—in public revenue. Hard decisions are not required nor expected.

In explaining inaction, we tell ourselves: "we have always been a boom-and-bust economy." This statement contains a grain of truth enhanced by perception and convenience. Wyoming Decennial Census data since 1910 suggests a steady but modest population growth on a statewide basis through 1970. Wyoming lost population in the decade of the 1960s despite the emergence of the uranium and trona industries. There were periodic "mini-booms" in limited geographic areas of the state. There were "price and revenue booms" when external events drove up the price of oil or other commodities. But the first and only statewide boom came in the 1970s—driven by world events that compelled national policies to focus on the development of domestic energy resources. It was further accelerated by environmental regulations, encouraging a shift to our low-sulfur coal.

Wyoming's Division of Research and Statistics prepared a report in 1987 for incoming Governor Mike Sullivan. In assessing the reality of Wyoming's population, employment, and personal income growth, the report, concludes:

> The analysis seems to contradict the theory that Wyoming has been a boom-bust economy. Instead, the data suggests that the economy has been one of 'moderate growth' with periods of stagnation until the early 1970s. This state has not experienced a real boom until the energy boom of the 70s.[3]

Between 1970 and 1980 Wyoming's gross state product (GSP) grew by 500%. In millions of then-current dollars, Gross Domestic Product (GDP) was $1.9 billion in 1970 and $10.4 billion in 1980.[4]

The energy boom of the 70s extended barely into the 1980s. 1983 began eight consecutive years of out-migration from Wyoming. Growth returned to anemic levels when the boom ended. Four decades of growth, between 1980 and 2020, have not equaled the population growth during the 1970s energy boom.[5] People express the expectation of—or hope for—another mineral boom. Hope for a 1970s replay is not a strategy for sustained economic growth, nor is it a significant probability.

Climate change is real and so is the continued use of fossil fuels. Oil, coal, natural gas and mineral development will be part of Wyoming for many decades to come. As Mark Twain observed upon reading press accounts of his death, "The reports of my death are greatly exaggerated." So it is with fossil fuels. But the future will not replicate the past.

Russia's invasion of Ukraine and subsequent events have re-ignited a desire for American energy security. Wyoming's energy industry will see a near-term benefit, but it would be a mistake to assume a return to the 1970s or the mid-2000s. Underlying energy markets have changed, energy technologies (including extraction) have changed, and the geographic location of major energy development within the United States has changed.

States, heretofore not seen as oil-producing regions, are now producing significant oil and gas. Historically North Dakota was not viewed as a major oil-producing state. Technology changed that. Snapshot data from the Energy Information Agency demonstrates the degree of change. In January of 2000, North Dakota produced 2,766,000 barrels of oil and Wyoming produced 5,185,000 barrels. January 2020 was an entirely different comparison. North Dakota produced 43,780,000 barrels while Wyoming produced 9,113,000 barrels. [6]

North Dakota is now among the largest producers of oil in America. Wyoming producers face other competition. Pennsylvania and the Permian Basin[7] are now major sources of natural gas and liquids. Geologic formations, weather, and development conditions in Texas and the Southwest simply offer oil and gas producers greater margins than Wyoming production. This echoes the comment made by Representative Barlow in 1984: "Wyoming minerals will not run out. What will run out is society's use for Wyoming minerals."

Low-sulfur coal has been the workhorse of Wyoming's economy for more than five decades. Market forces, federal and state regulatory changes, aging coal-fired plants which are not being replaced, competition from natural gas (including advanced natural gas turbines), and subsidized competition from renewables have devastated thermal coal demand. Renewables have been subsidized since 1992 when George H.W. Bush included the Production Tax Credit (PTC) in his energy bill. The PTC has been extended 13 times under both Democrat and Republican Administrations. Wyoming's coal production peaked in 2008 with 466 million tons. Production in 2020 was 218 million tons.[8] Wyoming faces the same issues faced by the Illinois Basin decades ago when the Clean

Air Act spurred many coal plants to use Wyoming's lower sulfur coal.[9]

Alternative uses of coal and major CO_2 capture, storage, and utilization are well into the future, even as the federal government invests billions of dollars and expanded tax credits in emerging technologies. Wyoming has invested a share of its federal dollars in this area for political and practical reasons. Political because we are a proud coal-producing state and as a practical means to maintain a seat at the table. Wyoming was the first state (2008) to enact comprehensive legislation creating a legal framework for storing carbon underground.[10] Successful developments in these areas are unlikely to return coal production back to 2008 levels.

National administrations can moderate or accelerate trends, but the long-term direction of energy markets is markedly different than in the early 1900s when Wyoming began to earnestly shift the tax burden to minerals, or in 1969 when the first severance tax was passed.

The October 2022 *Wyoming State Revenue Forecast, Fiscal Year 2023-2028* prepared by the Consensus Revenue Estimating Group (CREG) projects literally billions of dollars of increased revenue in the coming years. Combined with unspent federal dollars from various COVID relief programs and the federal infrastructure funding, Wyoming's governmental near-term financial future is quite positive. Public officials are breathing a sigh of relief as they devise ways to spend, save, or hide the anticipated dollars.

While little noted in the press, CREG's report begins with a sober, realistic assessment of Wyoming's fiscal circumstance. In the context of Wyoming's volatile revenue streams, CREG states "In the past three years, Wyoming has experienced two opposite amplitudes of the proverbial revenue pendulum." In FY 2020 severance tax collections were the lowest in 16 years. In FY 2022 severance tax collections were the second highest in the last ten years. None of the eleven factors listed by CREG as contributing to the revenue swings are controlled by Wyoming.

Federal COVID aid is seen as having supported the economy. But CREG's notes of caution conclude on a somber note.

The current forecast relies heavily on the rebound in oil and
natural gas pricing which results in higher tax and royalty
collections. However, volatility in oil and natural gas markets
can reasonably be expected to have an outsized impact on state
revenue collections. CREG forecasts Wyoming coal production
to continue its overall downward trend, despite the recent
rebound in both production and pricing. [11]

Wyoming cannot control events in an ever-changing world. Wyoming *can*
control its response. Wyoming has the time and the financial resources to
recalibrate our approach to the future. Traditional minerals cannot be
expected to single-handedly support us. Nor should we build a foundation premised on periodic federal largesse. We have options and opportunities will emerge.

Rather than perpetually complain about the unpredictable swings in
revenues generated by mineral production and available federal dollars,
we could personally bear more of the cost of public services on a consistent basis. Increasing our personal share of the tax burden is neither
politically nor personally appealing, but it is logical. A 2020 study by
the Wyoming Center for Business and Economic Analysis examined
the consequences of a modest increase in personal taxes.[12] The authors
compared Wyoming's taxation rates, earnings, and cost of living with
surrounding states. They concluded, "If Wyoming were to raise its current sales, property, and fuel tax rates to the median of other states without income taxes, it would generate $2,347,209,186 over the course
of the FY23/FY24 biennium. Adopting rates of either South Dakota or
Nevada, both states without income taxes, but with similar geographic,
demographic, economic and tax environments, would generate nearly
$2.2 billion in additional revenue." When the study was conducted,
Wyoming's Biennial Budget was approximately $4.8 billion. This report
demonstrates that nearly half of state funding could be gathered by simply raising individual taxes in Wyoming.

The authors analyzed whether Wyoming's citizens possessed the
financial capacity to absorb modest tax increases. The data suggests the
answer is "yes."

The median cost of living of these states is three percent higher than the national average, whereas Wyoming's cost of living is nearly five percent lower than the national average. When compared to South Dakota, Wyoming's median household income is $5,740 higher, its median hourly wage $3.31 higher, and its cost of living 1.6% lower. When compared to Nevada, Wyoming's median income is $1,727 higher, its median hourly wage $2.51 higher, and cost of living 13.5% lower.

Modest investments have been made in the travel, recreation, and tourism sector. If we include funds expended to preserve wildlife and open spaces, together these investments have produced significant dividends. Tourism and recreation will, if properly supported, continue the trend of expansion evident over the last few decades. Potential for growth exists in the areas of recreational facilities and outdoor experiences. The opportunity to enjoy scenic beauty, recreate, fish, hunt, and view wildlife gives Wyoming a unique offering. Tourism is Wyoming's second-largest industry. The property tax base in the travel/tourism business is modest. However, sales tax revenues advantage state and local coffers. But this sector alone cannot generate the employment and public revenue levels to which the state has become accustomed.

Agriculture has benefited from preferential tax treatment and investment of tax dollars but climate, water, soil, distance to markets, and aggregation in the red-meat processing marketplace restrict agricultural expansion opportunities. Preservation, not major expansion, has been the goal of the agricultural sector. The tax preference that agriculture receives under the Wyoming Constitution means agricultural expansion would not significantly expand the tax base.[13]

Peaceful use of nuclear energy remains an unfulfilled dream. There is great promise in the new, more limited-scale reactors as a source of electricity that is both reliable and easily integrated into the transmission grid. America's love/hate relationship with nuclear power makes extended, successful development uncertain. Nonetheless, there is a great deal more support for nuclear energy than at any time in the last five decades.

Renewables are a growing source of energy production in Wyoming and their presence is predicted to expand. Electrical power generation by renewable facilities will likely exceed fossil fuel-linked generation in Wyoming. But renewables do not create the employment opportunities or secondary contractor work associated with traditional power plants. Renewable facilities do not need a large parking lot for employees. Likewise, the added tax base is modest compared to a coal-fired generating station. The state has imposed a per megawatt tax on commercial wind generation but rejected imposing the same tax on commercial solar generation (a rejection not on policy grounds but apparently on "no new taxes" sloganeering).

With justifiable pride, Wyoming refers to itself as an "Energy State." But this too, is changing. According to U.S. Energy Information data, Wyoming's estimated primary energy production (including renewables) has declined from a high of 10,879.8 trillion Btu in 2008 to 7,148.3 trillion Btu in 2019.[14]

Wyoming's mineral storehouse referenced in its *Memorial* seeking admission to the Union remains in place. Today, focus has turned to "critical" and "rare earth" minerals. Although commercially viable reserves of such minerals have not been identified in Wyoming,[15] the definition of "commercially viable" is changing. Trona (soda ash) remains an opportunity simply because Wyoming's resource is the single largest source of natural soda ash in the world.

Advanced communications technology such as broadband offers an opportunity for Wyoming to overcome the historically daunting "distance to markets" issue. The Pandemic demonstrated that physical proximity is not a requirement for many types of work. Highways and roads are publicly funded and built, in part, to facilitate commercial activity. High-speed communication is increasingly a requirement for commercial activity. To date, Wyoming has been reluctant to invest in communication networks to facilitate new commercial activity. Investment of federal dollars is the main source of funding this infrastructure.

Discussions of these opportunities usually return to the issue of limited workforce availability and "livable communities." God gave Wyoming a magnificent physical environment. The task of building livable communities is ours.

We know the future will not repeat the past and may only vaguely resemble the present. Resist as we might, Wyoming will change. Rethinking Wyoming's future means those of us enjoying today's low tax/high service reality will need to carry more of our own weight. Only time will tell if the conscience of the present will lead us to pay the price to support the future?

ENDNOTES

Introduction Endnotes

1   David S. Broder, "A State in Trouble," *Washington Post,* October 6, 1999.

2   Bill Sniffin. January 8, 2018. *Tater Heads Outpacing Wyoming?* http://www.billsniffin.com/weblog/default.aspx

3   Wyoming Taxpayers Association. *Direct Tax Collections & Public Service Costs 2020*. Accessed March 10, 2022, http://wyotax.org/wp-content/uploads/2021/11/Cost-of-Services-2020.pdf.

4   Wyoming Legislative Service Office. *Excerpt of Distributional Federal COVID Funding Presentation*. (Cheyenne, April 26, 2021). https://wyoleg.gov/InterimCommittee/2021/02-20211213201-061-LSO-ExcerptofDistributionalFederalCOVIDFundingPresentation.pdf

5   Peter G. Peterson Foundation. 2022. *How Much Coronavirus Funding Has Gone to Your State?* https://www.pgpf.org/understanding-the-coronavirus-crisis/coronavirus-funding-state-by-state

Chapter 1 Endnotes

1   T. A. Larson, *Wyoming: A Bicentennial History* (W.W. Norton & Company, Inc. 1977), p 5.

2   R. Frankson et al., *Wyoming State Climate Summary 2022: State Climate Summaries for the United States*, NOAA Technical Report NESDIS 150. NOAA/NESDIS, Silver Spring, MD: https://statesummaries.ncics.org

3   James J. Jacobs and Donald J. Broz, *Wyoming's Water Resources*, University of Wyoming, Water Resources Data System Library, http://library.wrds.uwyo.edu › wrp

4   Marie H. Erwin, *Wyoming Historical Blue Book, A Legal and Political History of Wyoming 1868-1943* (Bradford Robinson Printing, 1943), p 657.

5   T. A. Larson, *Wyoming* (1977).

6   Wyoming Constitutional Convention. *Journal and debates of the Constitutional Convention of the state of Wyoming: begun at the city of Cheyenne on September 2, 1889 and concluded September 30, 1889*. (Cheyenne, Wyo.: *The Daily Sun*. 1893). University of California Libraries, Internet Archive: http://www.archive.org/details/journaldebatesof00wyomrich

7   Kim Viner. 2015. *Wyoming Lawyer Melville C. Brown: A Man for his Time*. http://wyohistory.org/encyclopedia/

wyoming-lawyer-melville-c-brown-man-his-time

8   Barbara Allen Bogart. 2014. *Clarence D. Clark, Longtime U.S. Senator.* http://wyohistory.org/encyclopedia/clarence-clark

9   "Foundation formed to manage Coffeen history," *Sheridan Press* (August 1, 2014).

10 Wyoming Legislative Service Office. *Management Audit of the Ad Valorem Tax Division of the State Board of Equalization,* (Cheyenne, September 1981), p 57.

11 Wyoming Joint Legislative-Executive Committee. *Wyoming 1988, A Revenue and Expenditure Study,* by David G. Ferrari, Director, with Ruth C. Summers, and Janet Washburn. Volume 1 (Cheyenne 1988), p 18.

Chapter 2 Endnotes

1   Phil Roberts. "A History of the Wyoming Sales Tax and How Lawmakers Chose It from among Severance Taxes, an Income Tax, Gambling, and a Lottery," *Wyoming Law Review,* Vol. 4: No. 1 (2004) Article 4.

2   Wyoming State Board of Equalization. *Biennial Report* (Cheyenne 1926), pp 8 and 9.

3   "Cody's wildcat oil drilling flamed out: Buffalo Bill missed oil 'bonanza' in Oregon Basin," *Cody Enterprise* (April 8, 2015).

4   David W. Miller, "The Historical Development of the Oil and Gas Laws of the United States," *California Law Review,* Vol. 51, No. 3 (August 1963) pp 506, 515.

5   T. A. Larson, *History of Wyoming* (University of Nebraska 1965), p 431.

6   Wyoming State Mine Inspector's Office. *Annual Report of the State Inspector of Mines of Wyoming,* (Cheyenne 2021).

7   Ibid., p 18.

8   Wyoming State Board of Equalization. *Biennial Report,* (Cheyenne 1933-1934) p 4.

9   Ibid., pp 20 and 21.

10 Original mill levy research data provided by Dave Chapman, Wyoming Department of Revenue, provided via email on February 8, 2021.

Chapter 3 Endnotes

1   T. A. Larson, *History of Wyoming,* (University of Nebraska, 1965) p 314.

2   Ibid., p 544.

3   Wyoming History Day. (2022). *Project Wagon Wheel and Nuclear Power.* https://www.wyominghistoryday.org/theme-topics/ project-wagon-wheel-and-nuclear-power

4   Cameron Engineers, "Review and Forecast: Wyoming Mineral Industries," report prepared for the *Wyoming Natural Resource Board* and the *State*

Water Planning Program, (1969) p 118.

5   Ibid., p 18.

6   Thomas Foulke, Roger Coupal, and David Taylor, *Economic Trends in Wyoming's Travel and Tourism Sector*, University of Wyoming Cooperative Extension Service, Bulletin B-1131 (November 2002).

7   Neal R. Pearce, *The Mountain States of America* (W.W. Norton & Company, 1972) p 79.

8   T. A. Larson, *Wyoming: A Bicentennial History* (W.W. Norton & Company, Inc. 1977) p 541.

9   Cliff Hansen, governor of Wyoming, *1965 State Budget*. (Cheyenne 1965) p III.

10 Ibid.

11 Stan Hathaway, governor of Wyoming, *1967 State Budget*. (Cheyenne 1967), pp III and X.

12 Stan Hathaway, governor of Wyoming, *Message to the Legislature*. (Cheyenne 1969).

13 Stan Hathaway, governor of Wyoming, *1969–1971 Biennial Budget*. (Cheyenne 1969) p 3

14 Cameron Engineers, "Review and Forecast."

15 Cameron, p 4.

16 Cameron, pp 5 and 6.

17 Cameron, p 9.

18 Cameron, p 118.

19 Cameron, p 132.

20 Wyoming Joint Legislative-Executive Committee. *Wyoming 1988, A Revenue and Expenditure Study*, by David G. Ferrari, Director, with Ruth C. Summers, and Janet Washburn (Cheyenne 1988).

21 Wyoming State Legislature. *Session Laws*, (1971) Ch. 206

22 Wyoming Department of Economic Planning and Development. *Development of Presently Unused Water Supplies of the Green River Basin in Wyoming*, prepared by Tipton and Kalmbach (Cheyenne, October 1972).

23 Susan LeMaster, "State Sierra Club not against everything but chairman proud of being 'eco-freak'," *Casper Star Tribune* (February 12, 1973).

24 Thomas F. Reese, "The Surface Owner's Estate Becomes Dominant: Wyoming's Surface Owner Consent Statute," *Land and Water Law Review*, Vol. 16: Iss. 2 (1981) pp 541–558.

25 The Land Use Policy Planning Assistance Act § 268 (1973).

26 "Water bill fight erupts," *Casper Star Tribune* (February 3, 1973).

27 "Sweetwater county has 'medical crisis' start," *Casper Star Tribune* (February 19, 1973).

28 "Facility sites set for studies," *Casper Star Tribune* (February 19, 1973).

29 "Plans outlined for giant power plant near Buffalo," *Casper Star Tribune* (March 3, 1973).

30 "Wyoming coal goes at $24 a ton," *Casper Star Tribune* (January 1, 1974).

31 "Teton legislator gets perfect mark," *Casper Star Tribune* (April 1, 1973).

32 "Nothing moved residents like drilling for water," *Casper Star Tribune* (January 11, 1974).

33 Irving Garbutt, "Ecology leader seeks state hike in coal taxes," *Casper Star Tribune* (January 6, 1974).

34 Tom Hough, "Governor says coal bill offers partial solution," *Casper Star Tribune* (January 20, 1974).

35 "Solons favor mineral tax," *Casper Star Tribune* (January 15, 1974).

36 "Boom reaction may plague session," *Casper Star Tribune* (January 22, 1974).

37 Editorial, "Crucial times ahead," *Casper Star Tribune* (January 20, 1974).

38 "Bill asks halting water transfers," *Casper Star Tribune* (January 23, 1974).

39 "Oilman scores tax plan," *Casper Star Tribune* (January 26, 1974).

40 Kathie Magers, "House reaction enthusiastic," *Casper Star Tribune* (January 24, 1974).

41 "Energy Development Information and Siting Act" (House Bill 18)

Chapter 4 Endnotes

1 Dwight D. Eisenhower, Proclamation 3279. "Adjusting Imports of Petroleum and Petroleum Products Into the United States" (March 1959).

2 M. King Hubbert, "Nuclear Energy and the Fossil Fuels," *Drilling and Production Practice* Vol. 95, Shell Oil Company (June 1956). Available at: https://www.resilience.org/stories/2006-03-08/nuclear-energy-and-fossil-fuels/

3 *The Bible*, Matthew 13:31–32 (King James Version, 1900).

4 Richard Nixon, *Annual Message to the Congress: The Economic Report of the President* (January 1972). Available at: https://www.presidency.ucsb.edu/documents/annual-message-the-congress-the-economic-report-the-president-4

5 Charles J. Cicchetti and Willian J. Gillen, "The Mandatory Oil Import Quota Program: A Consideration of Economic Efficiency and Equity," *Natural Resources Journal* Volume 13 No. 3 (1973). Available at: https://digitalre-pository.unm.edu/nrj/vol13/iss3/2

6 According to research documents prepared by the Nixon Foundation: "Elsewhere, President Nixon called for the construction of 1,000 new nuclear plants in the United States, complete with federal funding of new initiatives, public-private partnerships with major energy industries, and regulatory reforms and exemptions to expedite the process of construction." Luke Phillips, *Nixon's Nuclear Energy Vision*. (The Richard Nixon

Foundation, 2016).

7   Richard M. Nixon, *Address to the Nation About Policies To Deal With The Energy Shortages* (November 1973). Available at: https://www.presidency.ucsb.edu/documents/ address-the-nation-about-policies-deal-with-the-energy-shortages

8   Gerald R. Ford, *Address before a Joint Session of the Congress Reporting on the State of the Union* (Ford Library and Museum, January 15, 1975).

9   Ibid.

10 Congressional Budget Office. *President Carter's Energy Proposals: A Perspective* (June 1977).

11 42 U.S.C. 8301 et. Seq.

12 T. A. Larson *Wyoming: A Bicentennial History* (W.W. Norton & Company, Inc. 1977).

13 *Sierra Club and Wyoming Outdoor Coordinating Council v. Morton*, 379 F. Supp. 1254 (D. Colo. 1974).

14 *Sierra a Club v. Morton*, 421 F. Supp. 638, 645, (D. D.C. 1974).

15 *Sierra Club v. Morton*, 514 F.2d 856, 870, (U.S. App. D.C. 1975).

16 *Kleppe v. Sierra Club*, 96 S. Ct. 2718 (U.S. 1976).

Chapter 5 Endnotes

1   "Wilkerson Considers tax plan," *Casper Star Tribune* (February 6, 1974).

2   "Pipeline bill scored," *Casper Star Tribune* (February 10, 1974)

3   "Inaction on siting bill draws council's wrath," *Casper Star Tribune* (February 12, 1974)

4   Phil McAuley, "DEPAD projects growth," *Casper Star Tribune* (March 3, 1974).

5   Wyoming Department of Economic Planning and Development. *Coal and Uranium Development of the Powder River Basin — An Impact Analysis*, Cheyenne 1974.

6   Ibid., p 7.

7   Susan Bangs, "Basin study sees population surge," *Casper Star Tribune* (February 6, 1974).

8   Tom Hough, "Siting comments expected." *Casper Star Tribune* (April 19, 1974).

9   Steve Lobel, "Time is key factor in controversy," *Casper Star Tribune* (April 21, 1974).

10 "Stroock lists plans to preserve the state," *Casper Star Tribune* (April 12, 1974).

11 "Wallop urges action on expansion," *Casper Star Tribune* (April 20, 1974).

12 "Peck announces gubernatorial try," *Casper Star Tribune* (April 18, 1974).

13 "Wallop paints grim industrial picture," *Casper Star Tribune* (March 20, 1974).

14 "Attorney General Files Suit," *Casper Star Tribune* (March 19, 1974).

15 "Wallop announces, relaxes," *Casper Star Tribune* (May 2, 1974).

16 "GOP governor candidates agree the top issue is quality of life," *Casper Star Tribune* (May 13, 1974).

17 *Ibid*

18 Barbara Sonneman, "Candidates lock horns on effects of growth on style," *Casper Star Tribune* (May 25, 1974).

19 "Jones Asks Action on Deep Water," *Casper Star Tribune* (August 5, 1974).

20 "Wallop Plans New Tally," *Casper Star Tribune* (August 27, 1974).

21 "Results 'stun' Wallop," *Casper Star Tribune* (September 7, 1974).

22 Wyoming Intelligencer, *Casper Star Tribune* (April 28, 1974).

23 *Casper Star Tribune* (May 10–13, 1974).

24 "Leimback asks slurry repeal," *Casper Star Tribune* (May 21, 1974).

25 Russ Fawcett, "Father of HB 208 launches campaign throughout state," *Casper Star Tribune* (May 31, 1974).

26 "Winner to 'run scared',"*Casper Star Tribune* (August 22, 1974).

27 Bureau of Land Management, U.S. Forest Service, U.S. Geological Survey, Interstate Commerce Commission. *Draft Environmental Impact Statement on the Development of Coal Resources in the Eastern Powder River Coal Basin of Wyoming* (1974). Available at https://upload.wikimedia.org/wikipedia/commons/2/24/Development_of_coal_resources_in_the_Eastern_Powder_River_Coal_Basin_of_Wyoming_-_draft_environmental_statement_%28IA_developmentofcoa5180unit%29.pdf

28 "Agencies rip environmental study," *Casper Star Tribune* (August 270, 1974).

29 Letter to the editor, "Report defended," *Casper Star Tribune* (September 4, 1974).

30 United States Department of Agriculture. *Final Environmental Impact Statement on the Development of Coal Resources in the Eastern Powder River Coal Basin of Wyoming*, Vol. II, (1974) pp I–460.

31 Phil McAuley, "GOP will 'double team' for General Election votes,"*Casper Star Tribune* (August 29, 1974).

32 *Ibid*.

33 Wyoming Intelligencer, *Casper Star Tribune* (October 3, 1974).

34 Letter to the Editor, "'Speighful' statements," *Casper Star Tribune* (October 12, 1974).

35 "Candidates get funds," *Casper Star Tribune* (October 9, 1974).

36 Joseph Wheelan, "Candidates gird for race," *Casper Star Tribune* (October 13, 1974).

37 Russ Fawcett, "Candidate says most back industry," *Casper Star Tribune*

ENDNOTES

(October 13, 1974).

38 "Herschler wants terms set here," *Casper Star Tribune* (October 16, 1974).

39 Editorial, "Dick Jones for Governor," *Casper Star Tribune* (November 3, 1974).

40 Wyoming Intelligencer, *Casper Star Tribune* (November 3, 1974)

41 Wyoming Department of Economic Planning and Development. *Coal Development Alternatives: An Assessment of Water Use and Economic Implications*, prepared under the direction of the Legislative Special Subcommittee on Consumptive use of Water (Cheyenne 1974).

42 Wyoming Legislative Select Committee on Industrial Development Impact. *Interim Report and Recommendations* (Cheyenne 1974) pp 4–6

43 Ibid., pp 4–6.

44 Ibid., p 9

45 "Legislation would repeal sales, use tax exemptions," *Casper Star Tribune* (November 3, 1974).

46 Joan Wheelan, "Legislators to tour impact areas," *Casper Star Tribune* (March 29, 1974).

47 *Casper Star Tribune* (August 16 and September 12, 1974).

48 *Casper Star Tribune* (September 27–28, 1974).

49 *Casper Star Tribune* (November 4, 16, 23, and 19, 1974).

50 Edgar Herschler, governor of Wyoming, *Message to the Legislature.* (Cheyenne 1975).

51 *Casper Star Tribune* (January 5 and 8, 1975).

52 Wyoming Legislative Service Office. Memorandum addressed to Representative Berger prepared by Nicole Novotny, Associate Research Analyst, *Wyoming Industrial Siting Act: Creation and Exemptions,* (July 30, 2004

53 "Coal policy is endorsed," *Casper Star Tribune* (February 10, 1975).

54 Joan Wheelan, "Governor steps into fray, reminds solons of issues," *Casper Star Tribune* (February 11, 1975).

55 Digest of Legislative Journals of the Wyoming State Legislature (1975).

56 Joan Wheelan, "Emission moratorium squeezes by Senate," *Casper Star Tribune* (February 23, 1975).

57 Wyoming State Legislature. *Session Laws,* (1975) Ch. 131.

58 Wyoming State Legislature. *Session Laws,* (1975) Ch. 120 and 125.

59 "Oil find stirs investors," *Casper Star Tribune* (March 5, 1976).

60 Public Law 94-565, 90 STAT. 2662 (1976). An Act to provide for certain payments to be made to local governments by the Secretary of the Interior based upon the amount of certain public lands within the boundaries of such locality.

61 "Federal tax offset pays 8.5 times Marton Ranch property tax levy," by Angus M. Thermer Jr., *WyoFile* July 6, 2022.

245

https://wyofile.com/
federal-tax-offset-pays-8-5-times-marton-ranch-property-levy/

62 The Mineral Leasing Act of 1920 30 U.S.C. § 181 et seq. is a United States federal law that authorizes and governs leasing of public lands for developing deposits of coal, petroleum, natural gas and other hydrocarbons, in addition to phosphates, sodium, sulfur, and potassium in the United States.

63 Federal Lands Policy Management Act of 1976, Public Law 94-579, 90 Stat. 2743. An Act to provide for the management, protection, and development of the national resource lands, and for other purposes; An Act to establish public land policy; to establish guidelines for its administration; to provide for the management, protection, development, and enhancement of the public lands; and for other purposes.

64 Digest of House Journal Forty-fourth State Legislature of Wyoming, (1977) p 26.

65 Wyoming Legislative Service Office. *Mineral Tax History and Incentives*, (Cheyenne 2021).

66 Editorial, "Leading the nation," *Casper Star Tribune* (February 27, 1978).

67 "High Noon in Cheyenne," *60 Minutes*, Dan Rather, CBS, 1977.

68 Digest of House Journal Forty-fifth State Legislature of Wyoming, (1978) p 7.

69 "Herschler blasts Ostlund," *Casper Star Tribune*, (September 9, 1978).

70 T. R. Reid, "Republican Candidates Thrive in Rich, Uncluttered Wyoming." *The Washington Post* (August 29, 1978).

71 Lou Cannon, "Issues of Scandal, Special Interests Heat up Wyoming Contest." *Washington Post* (October 24, 1978).

72 Digest of House Journal of the Wyoming State Legislature, (1979) p 24

73 Ibid. p 27

74 Editorial Board, *Casper Star Tribune*, (January 12, 1979).

75 Digest of House Journal of the Wyoming State Legislature, (1979) pp 402–404)

76 In 1974, the federal government passed the National Maximum Speed Law, which restricted the maximum permissible vehicle speed limit to 55 miles per hour (mph) on all interstate roads in the United States. The law was a response to the 1973 oil embargo, and it intended to reduce fuel consumption.

77 *Washakie County School District No. One v. Herschler*, 606 P.2d 310 (Wyoming Supreme Court, 1980).

78 Digest of House Journal of the Forty-fifth State Legislature of Wyoming, (1980) p 14.

79 "Morton rips newspapers, TV: House speaker says severance tax coverage is one-sided," *Casper Star Tribune*, (February 23, 1980).

80 Joan Barron, "Severance proposals branded 'greed'," *Casper Star Tribune*, (February 23, 1980).

81 Wyoming Legislative Service Office. *Wyoming Severance Taxes and Federal Mineral Royalties: Updated July 2010*, by Dean Temte, Senior Fiscal Analyst (Cheyenne 2020).

82 Digest of Senate Journal of the Forty-fifth State Legislature of Wyoming, (1979) p 150.

83 Joan Barron, "BLM head says Wyoming will bear burden of energy," *Casper Star Tribune*, (August 1, 1980).

84 Marguerite Herman, "Rep. Cheyey sees state as target for synfuels," *Casper Star Tribune*, October 21, 1980.

85 John Wheaton, "Nearly half of county GOP favors mine tax hike: survey," *Casper Star Tribune*, August 20, 1980.

86 Joan Barron. "Herschler proposes 7% tax on oil, gas," *Casper Star Tribune*, October 25, 1980.

87 Digest of House Journal of the Forty-sixth State Legislature of Wyoming, (1981) pp 22–23.

88 Ibid., pp 22–31.

89 "Republicans won't up severence tax unless additional revenue is needed." *Casper Star Tribune*, January 12, 1981.

90 *Casper Star Tribune*, January–March 1981.

91 Wyoming State Legislature. *Session Laws*, (1981) Ch. 49.

92 Wyoming Legislative Service Office. *2021 Budget Fiscal Data Book*, (Cheyenne 2021) pp 124–128.

93 Wyoming State Legislature. *Session Laws*, (1981) Ch. 134

94 Ibid. Ch. 127

95 Digest of House Journal, (1981) HB. 152A

96 "State jobless total jumps," *Casper Star Tribune*, March 5, 1981.

97 "Tax burden should be on industry," *Casper Star Tribune,* March 12, 1981, and "Audit: Inaction has eroded state's tax base," November 5, 1981.

98 Joan Barron, "Herschler not sure of political future," *Casper Star Tribune*, November 8, 1981.

99 "State population growth isn't record," *Casper Star Tribune*, December 28, 1981.

100 Wyoming Legislative Service Office. *Management Audit of the Ad Valorem Tax Division of the State Board of Equalization*, Cheyenne, 1981.

101 Warren Wilson, "Property tax system faces possible overhaul," *Casper Star Tribune*, February 10, 1982.

102 Digest of House Journal of the Forty-sixth State Legislature of Wyoming, (1982) p 7.

103 Joan Barron, "Sponsor of lamb plant bill admits holding interest in project," *Casper Star Tribune*, February 14, 1982.

104 Shelby Gerking, William Morgan, Mitch Kunce and Joe Kerkvliet. *Mineral Tax Incentives, Mineral Production and the Wyoming Economy*, University of Wyoming (December 1, 2000).

105 Wyoming Legislature. *Wyoming: Legal and Fiscal Frameworks: Best Practices: Analysis and Commentary*, prepared by Daniel Johnston & Co., Inc. (November 2, 2018).

Chapter 6 endnotes

Casper Star Tribune.

1   Digest of House Journal of the Forty-seventh State Legislature of Wyoming, (1983) p 25.

2   Editorial, "State budget really '99 & 44/100% pure': Despite egos, bluster, agreement nearly total," *Casper Star Tribune* (February 16, 1984).

3   Buzzy Hassrick, "Bill would reduce state dependency on minerals: Jones urges wider economic base,"*Casper Star Tribune* (January 5, 1984).

4   P.J. Rose, "Task force study places highest priorities on existing industries" *Casper Star Tribune* (January 10, 1984).

5   Ibid.

6   Anne MacKinnon, "Follow energy market trends, experts tell state: Minerals markets can be influenced by state, UW seminar participants say, *Casper Star Tribune* (January 13, 1984).

7   "Bill would exempt farm land from reassessment," *Casper Star Tribune* (February 22,1984).

8   Digest of House Journal of the Wyoming State Legislature, (1984) p 7.

9   Edgar Herschler, governor of Wyoming. *Governors Message to the Legislature* (Cheyenne 1984).

10   Digest of House Journal of the Wyoming State Legislature, (1984) p15.

11   Wyoming State Legislature. *Session Laws,* (1984) Ch. 43

12   A. Marcos Ortiz, "Industrial bill misses deadline: Donley kills it by not waiving rules," *Casper Star Tribune* (March 7, 1984).

13   Dave Simpson, "Equalizing state school funds working better than expected: System will be updated every year, Sidi says," *Casper Star Tribune* (February 28, 1984).

14   Anne MacKinnon, "Committee learns state permitting drives out some mining companies," *Casper Star Tribune* (January 8, 1985).

15   Digest of House Journal of the Wyoming State Legislature, (1985) pp 18–19.

16   Joan Barron, "State taxes on business rank high," *Casper Star Tribune* (January 10, 1984).

17   Wyoming State Legislature. *Session Laws,* (1985) Ch. 6

18   Ibid., Ch. 190.

19 Ibid., Ch. 235.
20 Wyoming State Legislature. House Bill 433
21 Anne MacKinnon, "Mining aid bill gets committee approval: Senate body reinstates mining industry proposal deleted by the house," *Casper Star Tribune* (February 14, 1985).
22 Digest of House Journal of the Wyoming State Legislature, (1984) pp 19–20.
23 Joan Barron, "State Legislature relied on 'wait-and-see' stance: 48th session controlled by national events, Sidi says," *Casper Star Tribune* (February 25, 1985).
24 Dennis E Curran, "Herschler rates Legislature: Legislators ignored 'some very serious problems,'" *Casper Star Tribune* (March 12, 1985).
25 Joan Barron, "Jones urges development within state: Legislator talks to GOP caucus about business," *Casper Star Tribune* (January 7, 1985).
26 "Assets up in Wyoming banks, examiner says," *Casper Star Tribune*, December 4, 1985.
27 Catherine Warren, "WCDA launches major economic study: 'Positive' effort will address ways to attract venture capital to state," *Casper Star Tribune*, March 23, 1985.
28 "Democrats cautious about governorship," *Casper Star Tribune*, March 31, 1985.
29 Marguerite Herman, "Legislators offer 4 bills that maintain impact aid to cities," *Casper Star Tribune*, January 18, 1985.
30 Erich Kirshner, "Examiner says 3 weak Wyoming banks will probably fail this year," *Casper Star Tribune*, January 8, 1986.
31 "Bank endorses WCDA economic plan," *Casper Star Tribune*, January 18, 1985.
32 Joan Barron, "Property tax ratio still same," *Casper Star Tribune,* January 4, 1986.
33 Digest of House Journal of the Wyoming State Legislature, (1986) p 5.
34 Wyoming State Legislature. *Session Laws*, Proposed Constitutional Amendment No. 2
35 Wyoming State Legislature. Senate File 48
36 "Ag bail-out bill passage unlikely," *Casper Star Tribune* February 26, 1986.
37 Wyoming State Legislature. *Session Laws*, Ch.14.
38 *Session Laws*, Ch. 10
39 *Session Laws*, Ch. 47
40 *Session Laws*, Ch. 40
41 *Session Laws*, House Joint Resolution No. 6
42 Digest of House Journal of the Wyoming State Legislature, HB 204
43 "State to spend 10% more." *Casper Star Tribune*, March 16, 1986.

44 Carol Hegna, "Rig activity drops more sharply in Wyoming than elsewhere," *Casper Star Tribune*, April 20, 1986.

45 Gwen Richards, "Herschler asks Futures Project board to support oil import tax," *Casper Star Tribune*, October 7, 1986.

46 Paul Krza, "Sullivan, Simpson trade jabs in their first debate," *Casper Star Tribune*, October 1, 1986.

47 Andrew Melnykovych, "Wyoming will survive depression, former governor says: Hathaway blames state policy for mineral-industry woes," *Casper Star Tribune*, February 27, 86.

48 Daniel Gearino, "Telling and dispelling Hathaway's myths," *Casper Star Tribune*, March 12, 1986.

49 Kurt J. Repanshek, "Wyoming fared better in Depression than now," *Casper Star Tribune*, October 26, 1986.

50 Phil White, "Experts say Wyoming better off now than in Depression," *Casper Star Tribune*, November 2, 1986.

51 Joan Barron, "Herschler cuts $77.7 million out of budget," May 30, 1986 and "Herschler says agencies fairly treated in cuts, " May 31, 1986.

52 Joan Barron, "State's shortfall to be even more, new figures show," *Casper Star Tribune*, December 17, 1986.

53 Joan Barron, "Shortfall means JAC faces difficult task, Stroock says," *Casper Star Tribune*, December 22, 1986.

54 Ibid.

55 *Rocky Mountain Oil and Gas Association v. State Board of Equalization*, 749 P.2d 221, Wyoming Supreme Court (1987).

Epilogue Endnotes

1 George Will, "The future's only constituency is the conscience of the present," *Washington Post* (August 5, 2018).

2 "The principles of "cowboy ethics" are now part of Wyoming law," *Associated Press* (March 22, 2012). https://cowboyethics.org/cowboy-ethics-become-law/

"Gov. Dave Freudenthal signed legislation adopting an official Wyoming state code. The symbolic measure spells out 10 ethics derived from a "Code of the West" outlined in a book by author and retired Wall Street investor James Owen.

The state code admonishes residents and lawmakers to live courageously, take pride in their work, finish what they start, do what's necessary and be tough but fair. The ethics code carries no criminal penalties and is not meant to replace any civil codes.

It also calls on them to keep promises, ride for the brand, talk less and say more, remember that some things aren't for sale, and know where to draw the line."

3   Wyoming Department of Administration and Fiscal Control. Division of Research and Statistics. *The Wyoming Economy — An Historical Perspective*, (August 1987).

4   Wyoming Department of Administration & Information. Economic Analysis Division, *Income, Employment, and Gross Domestic Product by Industry*, (December 2021). http://eadiv.state.wy.us/pop/BirthDeathMig.htm accessed November 18, 2021.

5   Ibid.

6   U.S. Energy Information Administration. *Wyoming Field Production of Crude Oil,* https://www.eia.gov/dnav/pet/hist/LeafHandler. ashx?n=Pet&s=MCRFPWY1&f=M and *North Dakota Field Production of Crude Oil,* https://www.eia.gov/dnav/pet/hist/LeafHandler. ashx?n=PET&s=MCRFPND1&f=M accessed July 2022.

7   The Permian Basin is a large sedimentary basin in the southwestern part of the United States. The basin contains the Mid-Continent Oil Field province. This sedimentary basin is located in western Texas and southeastern New Mexico.

8   Wyoming State Mine Inspector's Office. *Annual Report of the State Inspector of Mines of Wyoming*, (December 31, 2020) p 20.

9   "The loss of coal jobs in the region began in the 1980s and accelerated in the 1990s, when Clean Air Act amendments spurred many coal plants to turn to the Powder River Basin in Wyoming and Montana for coal with a lower sulfur content … Coal country chases federal aid to prevent 'slow death,*" Energywire*, October 3, 2022. https:subscriber.politicopro.com/ article/eenews/2022/10/03/Illinois-basin-00059802

10 Montana Legislature. *State activities on carbon sequestration*, https:// leg.mt.gov/content/committees.intermim/2007_2008-/energy_telcom/ assigned_studies/co2page/ncslsupplement.pdf, accessed on October 4, 2022

11 Wyoming Consensus Revenue Estimating Group, *Wyoming State Government Revenue Forecast, Fiscal Year 2023-Fiscal Year 2028*, (October 26, 2022).

12 Joe Schaffer and Nick Colsch, *Tax Capacity in Wyoming: a comparison of taxation rates, earnings, and cost of living with surrounding and similar states*, Wyoming Center for Business and Economic Analysis, Laramie County Community College, (December 22, 2020) p ii

13 Legislative action in 1989 set the assessment rate defining the percentage of fair market value subject to taxation. The assessment rate for mineral production is 100%, industrial property is 11.5%, and all other properties are 9.5%. The "all other property" category includes commercial, residential, and agricultural/grazing property. As practical matter agricultural lands are a subclass given the Constitutional language requiring agricultural lands to be valued solely on "the capability of the land to produce

agricultural products under normal conditions." Applicable statutory provisions (W.S. 39-13-103(b)(x)) identify certain land characteristics defining agricultural lands. Such lands can be classified as agricultural so long as the owner derives not less than $500 gross income from unleased lands or no less than $1,000 gross income from leased lands. Fair market value as established by a willing buyer/willing seller has no bearing on the assessed value or taxes established for agricultural land.

This circumstance reflects the political and policy choices of Wyoming. This tax preference was established nearly 50 years ago when agricultural land prices bore a significant relationship to agricultural productivity. At the time agricultural land was most often held by individuals or families working year-round to make a living and to pay for the land.

The link between the sales price of agricultural operations and productivity seems to have at best diverged, or no longer exist. Among the factors breaking the causal link are: (1) a different type of buyer and (2) the arbitrage on federal and state grazing rights attached to the deeded property. A brief review of farm and ranch land real estate listings demonstrates that price is no longer based solely on the income the property can generate. Advertisements emphasize viewsheds, water courses, trees, wildlife presence, hunting, fishing, and the idea of simply owning part of the American West. Sometimes the ads will share the taxes paid on the land or provide a link to the county assessor's website for the potential buyer to illustrate the relatively low tax burden. The ads are not targeting agricultural buyers.

Second is the state and federal grazing leases and permits attached to the deeded property. Federal and state lands are not subject to property tax. Some of this emphasis highlights the amount of acreage the buyer would control but it also helps the buyer calculate the financial arbitrage to be gained by the management or lease of those grazing rights.

The chart below illustrates the advantage of holding federal and state leases. The unit of comparison is referred to as an "animal unit month" (AUM). AUM "means the amount of forage necessary for the sustenance of one cow or its equivalent for a period of 1 month." (43CFR4100.0-5) The rent paid for the agricultural lease is based on the number of AUMs within the leased or permitted tract. Both Wyoming State leases have a surcharge attached to individuals if they sublease the grazing rights to another party. Wyoming leased its agricultural lands in 2022 for $5.24. (https://lands.wyo.gov/trust-land-management/surface-leasing, accessed on October 7, 2022). Wyoming statute 36-5-105(d) requires 50% of the money received by the leaseholder through a sublease be forwarded to the Office of State Lands and Investments. The federal Bureau of Land Management and the Forest Service charge for 2022 was $1.35 per AUM (https://www.fs.usda.gov/news/releases/usda-forest-service-announces-2022-grazing-fees-national-forests-and-grasslands, accessed on October 5, 2022). There is a Wyoming surcharge for subleases of $8.10, roughly 35%

of the private rate. (https://www.blm.gov/policy/im-2022-026, accessed on October 7, 2022).

According to the USDA, an AUM in Wyoming ranged from $18 to $45. (https://www.ams.usda.gov/mnreports/TO_LS150.txt accessed on October 7, 2022) The difference is attributable to location, suitability for a particular buyer, and whether the buyer was responsible for the maintenance of fences, water wells, provision of a mineral block, etc.

Public Land Fees per AUM versus Private Market Value

Assume a hypothetical property with leases and permits providing 1,000 AUMs. The owner of the property pays the government the required fee. The USDA does not provide an average number for private leases. Simply averaging $18 and $45 produces $31.50 per AUM. Anecdotally this number seems high. For purposes of this example, 28 dollars is the assumed average private price per AUM.

In the instance of an agricultural operator who owns and grazes his own livestock:

Cost Per AUM	Cost per 1,000 AUM	Private Lease Cost	Difference
State $5.24	$5,240	@$28 = $28,000	$22,760
BLM $1.35	$1,350	@$28 = $28,000	$26,650

A portion of the benefit is warranted because of the stewardship obligations undertaken by the state and federal leaseholders.

The differential changes if the state and federal policies regarding sublease are followed. In the case of State land grazing subleases, fifty percent of the differential is supposed to return to the State. The differential is reduced to $11,380 ($22,760 X .5). Adding the $8.10 surcharge per AUM on the federal lease, the differential is reduced to $18,550 ($26,650-$8,100).

14 U.S. Energy Information Administration. *State Energy Data 2020: Primary Energy Production Estimates in Trillion Btu, Wyoming, 1960-2020.* http://www.eia.gov/state/seds/sep_prod/pdf/PT2_WY.pdf

15 Nicole Pollack, "Mineral push could help state,"*Casper Star Tribune*, April 4, 2022.

BIBLIOGRAPHY

Additional sources not cited in endnotes

ahcadmin. August 19, 2019. *Back to the Future in Wyoming: Addressing 1980s Energy Impacts in Evanston*, University of Wyoming American Heritage Center. Accessed September 13, 2021. https://ahcwyo.org/2019/08/19/back-to-the-future-in-wyoming-addressing-1980s-energy-boom-impacts-in-evanston/

Albrethsen Jr, Holger and McGinley, Frank E. 1982. *Summary History of Domestic Uranium Procurement Under U.S. Atomic Energy Commission Contracts Final Report*, prepared for the U.S. Department of Energy, Assistant Secretary for Nuclear Energy.

Andersen, Chamois L. and Van Pelt, Lori. November 8, 2014. "Wyoming's Uranium Drama: Risks, Rewards and Remorse," Wyoming Historical Society. https://www.wyohistory.org/encyclopedia/wyomings-uranium-drama-risks-rewards-and-remorse

Bryan, Gene. 2016. From Coloring Books to Twitter, A Personal History of Wyoming Tourism Marketing. N.P.

Burnside and Culbertson. 1979. Trona Deposits in the Green River Basin, Sweetwater, Uinta, and Lincoln Counties, Wyoming, United States Geological Survey, Open File Report 79-737

Casper Star Tribune Archives. https://trib.newspapers.com/

Chapman, Dave. February 8, 2022. *Historical State Mill Levy Data.* Wyoming Department of Revenue.

Environmental Protection Agency, Rocky Mountain-Prairie Region. February 1979. *Existing and Proposed Surface and Underground Coal Mines, Region VIII Summary.*

Gordon, Mark. Governor of Wyoming. *Proposed Wyoming State Budget 2023-2024.* Cheyenne, Wyoming.

Gorin, Sarah. September 1988. *Wyoming's Wealth for Wyoming's People: Ernest Wilkerson and the Severance Tax, A Study in Wyoming Political History. Annals of Wyoming.* Wyoming Historical Society.

Harbour, Jerry L. and Breckenridge, Roy M. August 1980. *Summary of the Overthrust Belt in Parts of Wyoming, Utah, and Idaho.* Idaho Geological Survey Technical Report No. 80-9.

Hathaway, Stan. Governor of Wyoming. *Governor's Message to the Legislature, 1969* and *1974* in the *Digest of Senate and House Journals of the Forty-fourth State Legislature of Wyoming*. Cheyenne, Wyoming.

Hein, Rebecca. November 8, 2014. *Campbell County, Wyoming*. Wyoming State Historical Society. WyoHistory.org

Herschler, Edgar. Governor of Wyoming. *Governor's Message to the Legislature, 1976*, in the *Digest of Senate and House Journals of the Forty-fourth State Legislature of Wyoming*. Cheyenne, Wyoming.

Jack B. Speight, former Chief of Staff for Governor Hathaway and law partner for 40 years, Personal conversations with author.

Johnston v. Herschler, 669 F2d 617, 10th Cir. 1982

Krza, Paul. July 28, 2020. *Ed Cantrell, Rock Springs and Boom-time Crime.* Wyoming State Historical Society. WyoHistory.org

Krza, Paul. July 7, 1997. *While the New West booms, Wyoming mines, drills... and languishes*. High Country News.

Larsen, T. A. 1977. *Wyoming a History*. American Association for State and Local History.

Michael Sullivan, former Governor of Wyoming, Personal conversation with author, August 12, 2022.

Noble, Ann Chambers. 2014. *The Wagon Wheel Project*. Wyoming State Historical Society. WyoHistory.org

Rocky Mountain Oil and Gas v. State Board of Equalization, 749 P.2d 221 (Supreme Court of the State of Wyoming, December 31, 1987).

Steele, Ken, Mark P. Fisher, and Deb D. Steele. W*yoming Uranium Boom and Bust at Gas Hills-Crooks Gap Mining District*. Geology of Wyoming. http://www.wyomingmining.org/wp-content/uploads/2018/01/170626-Wyoming-Uranium-Overview.pdf

U.S. Energy Information Administration. *Petroleum and Other Liquids*. Accessed November 14, 2021. https://www.eia.gov/petroleum/

United States Nuclear Regulatory Commission. *Backgrounder on the Three Mile Island Accident*. Accessed October 8, 2021. https://www.nrc.gov/reading-rm/doc-collections/fact-sheets/3mile-isle.html

Western, Samuel. March 1, 2015. *Leasing Federal Minerals in Wyoming and the West*. Wyoming State Historical Society. WyoHistory.org

Whipple, Dan. November 14, 2014. Coal *Slurry: an Idea that Came and Went*. Wyoming State Historical Society. WyoHistory.org

Wyoming Constitutional Convention 1889, *Journal and Debates of the Constitutional Convention of the State of Wyoming*, (Daily Sun, Book and Job Printing, Cheyenne, Wyoming, 1893). http://www.archive.org/details/journaldebatesof00wyomrich

Wyoming Department of Revenue Annual Reports for 1979, 1980 and 1981.

Wyoming Digest of Senate and House Journals, 1974

Wyoming Digest of Senate and House Journals, 1977

Wyoming Digest of Senate and House Journals, 1979

Wyoming Digest of Senate and House Journals, 1982

Wyoming Digest of Senate and House Journals, 1983.

Wyoming Digest of Senate and House Journals, Budget Session and Special Session, 1978

Wyoming Digest of Senate and House Journals, Budget Session, 1980.

Wyoming Digest of Senate and House Journals, Budget Session, 1986

Wyoming Geological Survey

Wyoming Legislative Service Office. 2001. *Management Audit of the Ad Valorem Tax Division of the State Board of Equalization*. Cheyenne, Wyoming.

Wyoming Legislative Service Office. 2021. *Mineral Tax History and Incentives.*

Wyoming Mining Association. https://www.wyomingmining.org/

Wyoming Mining Association. October 27, 2020. *Wyoming Bentonite Concise Guide*. https://issuu.com/chickencreekcommunications/docs/wyominningasso_bentoniteguide20_web

Wyoming Outdoor Council. March 1974. *Legislative Analysis: Wyoming Legislature 1973 and 1974 Sessions.*

Wyoming Outdoor Council. May 1978. *Legislative Issues: 1977-78 Voting Records*, The Crossroads Monitor, Vo. III, No.3.

Wyoming Secretary of State's Office

Wyoming State Geological Survey. 1998. *Proceedings of the First International Soda Ash Conference. Vol. I*, Public Information Circular No. 39.

Wyoming State Geological Survey. *Wyoming's Oil and Gas Basins—Overthrust*. Accessed on September 13, 2021. https://www.wsgs.wyo.gov/energy/oil-gas-basins.aspx

Wyoming State Legislature. *Session Laws*, 1974

Wyoming State Legislature. *Session Laws*, 1976–1979

Wyoming State Legislature. *Session Laws*, 1980

Wyoming State Legislature. *Session Laws*, 1983

Wyoming State Legislature. *Session Laws*, 1986

INDEX

CPSIA information can be obtained
at www.ICGtesting.com
Printed in the USA
BVHW062057310123
657534BV00017B/623

9 781733 489706